MITCHELL
BEAZLEY
WINE
GUIDES

MICHAEL BROADBENT'S

Wine
Vintages

Michael Broadbent's Wine Vintages

Published in Great Britain in 2003 by Mitchell Beazley,
an imprint of Octopus Publishing Group Ltd,
2–4 Heron Quays, London E14 4JP.

Revised editions 1995, 1998, 2000, 2003

Copyright © Octopus Publishing Group Ltd 1992, 1995, 1998, 2000, 2003

Text copyright © Michael Broadbent 1992, 1995, 1998, 2000, 2003

A CIP catalogue record for this book is available from the British Library.

ISBN 1 84000 853 9

Commissioning Editor: Hilary Lumsden
Executive Art Editor: Yasia Williams
Editor: Juanne Branquinho
Designer: Colin Goody
Production Controller: Alexis Coogan

Typeset in Verailles and Helvetica

Printed and bound by Toppan Printing Company in China.

Contents

Foreword to new edition

Time flies, as do vintages, which in the original publication were recent, and are now part of the recent past. The purpose of this pocketbook is to answer two basic questions: "What is a vintage?" and "Why are vintages important?" and then to rate every significant vintage of all the world's principal wine districts and wine types, assessing quality, advising whether, and for how long, one should keep young wine, and summarizing the maturity and current drinkability of the wines of former vintages.

The main text, arranged by district and type of wine, listing up to a century of vintage years, goes far beyond the familiar vintage charts both in range and scope, explaining briefly the conditions which produced the good, bad, and indifferent vintages and wines. Yet the handy pocketbook format will, I trust, make it both a practical and convenient work of reference.

Michael Broadbent
Christie's, London, 2003

Acknowledgments

Australian Wine Bureau
Bouchard Père et Fils
Bureau Interprofessionnel des
 Vins du Bourgogne
Columbia Winery
Comité Interprofessionnel du
 Vin de Champagne
Comité Interprofessionnel des
 Vins d'AOC Côtes du Rhône et de la
 Vallée du Rhône
Decanter Magazine
Edward Berry (Cape Mentelle)
Eyrie Vineyard
Fladgate Partnership
German Wine Information Service
Grosser Ring VDP
Hamilton Russell Vineyards
Harpers
Italian Trade Centre
James Halliday
John E Fells & Sons Ltd
John Platter
Justerini & Brooks
Laytons
Lindemans Wines Ltd
Lynn Murray (BRL Hardy)
Madeira Wine Co Ltd
Masters of Wine, Institute of
Miguel Torres
Morris and Verdin
New York Grape Foundation

Penfolds Wines Ltd
Pierre André
Port Wine Institute
Quarterly Review of Wines
Rebecca Wasserman
Robert Mondavi Winery
Robert Weil, Dr
Royal Tokaji Wine Co
Spear Communications Ltd
Stephen Tanzer
The Symington Group
Union des Grands Crus
 de Bordeaux
Victoria Morrell
Weingut Max Ferd Richter
Wines from Austria
Wines from Spain
Wine Institute of New Zealand
Wines of Portugal
Wines of South Africa
VDP News
Vintex SA

Introduction

Wine, the oldest, most natural, and healthiest of beverages, is the combined product of nature and man. It is part natural, part man-made. Vines are planted and tended. They produce an annual crop of grapes which, after harvesting, is fermented into wine. Nature produces, man guides.

Unlike most other agricultural products, soft fruits for example, wine is to a certain extent manufactured, its natural fermentation controlled. Its "shelf life" is as varied as its colour, smell, and taste. Grapes for the making of good wine can only be grown in a temperate climate, the basic differences of type being due to the variety of vine cultivated, the soil, subsoil, aspect, and drainage. Once the vineyard is planted these elements are more or less "fixed". Thereafter the hand of man, his skill in tending the vines, and in winemaking, introduces a controllable variable. The other variable, beyond man's control, is the weather. The weather is the key to the vintage.

What is a "vintage"?

The word vintage has two meanings. "The vintage" is the time of grape harvesting; "vintaging", less often used, refers simply to the picking of grapes at harvest time, that short or extended period in the autumn which follows the growing and ripening season, when – all being well – the grapes are at their optimum state of maturity with the desired levels of grape sugar, acidity, and other component parts. The growing and ripening season is annual which means that there is a vintage every year: every wine, strictly speaking, is therefore a vintage wine. Whether it remains so depends on its quality, the best being nursed and nurtured to retain its individuality. In practice a high proportion of the world's annual production of wine loses its vintage identity shortly after it is made because it is blended either with other wine made in the same year or with vatted wines of previous vintages. Examples of the latter are sherry and "wood port".

In the broader context, however, the term "vintage" in relation to wine has an implied quality connotation, not necessarily good, but sometimes most specifically so, as in the case of vintage port and vintage Champagne.

Why are vintages important?

The producers of fine wine, the importers, merchants, investors, and consumers are acutely conscious of vintages. They have a direct bearing on the value of the wine, whether youthful and immature or old and mature. For the connoisseur vintages provide an endless fascination – nuances noted, understood, and appreciated.

The value of a vintage wine is directly proportional to its perceived quality, though the price demanded at source, or paid on the open market, is greatly enhanced by its scarcity value – where production is small (for example Château Pétrus, a small vineyard compared to the first-growths of the Médoc; also the world demand for the minute supply of Romanée-Conti and Le Montrachet) or where availability of a great, mature, and by now mostly consumed vintage is limited (for example Château Mouton-Rothschild 1945 or Château d'Yquem 1921).

That poorer vintages of the wine of great estates command lower prices than those of the best vintages is amply borne out by prices in the London salesrooms. For example the 1968 vintage of Château Lafite sells for roughly one-eighth the price of the 1959, the 1963 one-sixteenth that of the 1961. Quite apart from price, there is the important matter of how good the wine is as a drink: its character, its balance, weight, acidity, and so forth; all are functions of vintage. In short, vintages vary, and a knowledge and understanding of this is an important part of wine appreciation.

What makes a good or bad vintage?

Given the fixed elements of temperate climate, soils, vine stocks, and winemaking traditions and techniques, the joker in the pack is the weather. No matter where in the world vines are grown, all are subject to variations of weather conditions during the grape growing and ripening season which vary from minor and subtle to dramatic and highly significant. Growers can do little except take evasive action, by no means always effective.

The timing and permutations of cold, heat, dryness, rain, sunshine, lack of sun, and humidity have a direct bearing on the eventual quality of grapes and of the style and quality of the wine made. Rather like the human face, none is identical despite the commonality of eyes, nose, mouth, hair etc.; the vine's growing season has bud-break, flowering, grape set, ripening – yet no one year is like another. Whether the vineyard is a small holding managed by a part-time farmer who has a job in town, a major full-time family operation, a managed estate, or vast rolling acres of vines owned by a multinational company, the basic elements of vine husbandry are the same. The vine management season begins soon after the annual grape harvest.

Late autumn/winter After the harvest, long shoots are removed, and ploughing between rows is carried out to cover the base of the vinestocks as a protection against severe chill and frosts. Pruning can start from mid-December (for simplicity I am assuming that the vineyard is in the northern hemisphere). A cold winter is good for the vines. They are dormant, resting after the exertions of the previous season and harvest. The bigger and better the crop, the greater need for rest.

New year and spring Pruning continues until early March when the sap starts to rise. The winter covering of the vines is reversed, the soil being removed from their base. This period can be one of happy anticipation or worry. If too mild, the vegetation is advanced, and the likelihood of frost-damage far increased. Just one frost in April or early May can wreak havoc, critically reducing the potential crop (as was the case in 1991, the new shoots being literally nipped in the bud) or, if severe, can even destroy the vines.

Action can be taken as a precaution against frosts – "smudge pots", stoves in the vineyard, wind machines – but can be expensive and often ineffective. A severe frost will be crippling, but it can also have a beneficial outcome, for what is in effect a drastic pruning results in a small crop which, if the summer is hot and dry, can lead to concentrated, high quality grapes – as was the case in 1945 and 1961 in Bordeaux.

Late spring, early summer Let us assume that there has been no crippling frost. Weeds are cleared and vines are sprayed with fungicides to prevent two potentially leaf damaging diseases, *oidium* and mildew. The next period is also crucial: the flowering of the vine.

Ideal conditions are warm and dry so that the flowering takes place early and over a short period. The earlier the flowering the sooner the harvest. Cold and wet weather causes delayed and prolonged flowering, resulting in failure to pollinate (*coulure*): the embryo grapes do not develop, and eventually fall off. Another problem is partial pollination (*millerandage*) resulting in tiny seedless berries which, though usually very sweet, reduce the volume of grape juice. Shoots are thinned. More spraying is carried out if necessary.

As a rule of thumb the vines need one hundred days of sun between flowering and picking. The later the flowering the later – and generally the more risky – the vintage.

Mid- to late summer Ideally, what is needed is a judicious mixture of warm sunshine and light rain, the one to bring on the ripening, the other to swell the berries. August can be uneventful. There is more thinning and weeding as the grapes change colour (*véraison*). In particularly good years with potentially bountiful crops, some growers in the best vineyards "green prune", cutting off whole bunches to reduce quantities. Nourishment from the soil is then concentrated in fewer grapes. This is an expensive process and only justified if the increase of quality is matched by a satisfactory price for the wine.

Early autumn If the spring and early summer – bud formation and flowering – are responsible for the potential size of the crop and earliest possible date of picking, the very late summer and early autumn ripening period is responsible for the creation of adequate sugar content and richness of component parts. The balance of acidity and sugar is important. The riper the grapes, the higher the sugar content and the stronger the alcohol after fermentation. But as grapes ripen beyond a certain stage the level of acidity is reduced.

Acidity is vital for the life, vigour, refreshing quality, and longevity of the wine. I personally think of acidity – tartaric, the grape acid – as the nervous system of the wine. Conversely, unripe grapes have too little natural sugar and an insufficiency of potential alcohol, a situation which can be remedied, if officially sanctioned, by the addition of cane sugar to the grape juice or "must" prior to fermentation. In unripe grapes, acidity tends to be high and of the wrong sort: malic acid, which is tart, like cooking apples.

The harvest – "the vintage" – itself takes place when the grapes have achieved optimum ripeness and before the cold weather sets in. In Bordeaux mid-September is considered early, the end of September usually satisfactory, early October not abnormal, but later is risky. After exceptionally hot summers the picking of white grapes for dry wine can start in August, though this very rarely happens for reds. The grapes for naturally sweet wines made in classic districts like Sauternes and in Germany will generally be picked later than those for the dry whites and reds to obtain the extra ripeness.

Destalking and fermentation – in short winemaking – are man-controlled operations, and depend on the experience and expertise of the owner, manager, or oenologist, upon local practices, and on the style and quality of wine aimed for. The differences are important but are either predictable, because the methods are well tried, or manageable.

The only unpredictable variable is the weather. This, I stress again, is what makes vintages important.

Postscript

It is often said that good wines can be made in bad vintages just as bad wines can be made in good vintages. This is a half-truism. Mistakes, carelessness, sheer ineptness can spoil a potentially good wine. Conversely, a skilled and conscientious vine-grower and winemaker can mollify disasters, making the best wine that inclement weather will allow. But in the final analysis, good wine can only be made from good grapes, and good grapes can only be grown in suitable conditions.

Star rating

★★★★★	Outstanding (vintage or wine)
★★★★	Very good
★★★	Good
★★	Moderately good
★	Not very good, but not bad
~	Poor

French Classics

Bordeaux

Bordeaux, one of the oldest, largest, and most famous classic wine regions of the world, is situated in the southwest of France. The various districts which radiate from its hub, the surprisingly big and now sprawling city and port, produce a vast quantity of red wine ranging in quality from everyday to the finest, a substantial volume of dry white, some of the highest quality, and sweet white wine from the merely pleasant to the sublime.

Bordeaux has a maritime climate, temperate and perfect for vine growing. However, rather like an island, the weather throughout the growing season is subject to manifold changes, some minor and subtle, others major and crucial: conditions that affect the timing and success of the budding of the vine, its flowering, ripening, and harvest. In short, each season has its variations, resulting in wines of different style, weight, and quality. Here, as elsewhere, the vineyard manager must tend his vines, cope with the exigencies of weather, and take evasive action against pests and diseases; the *maître de chai* and oenologist must make the best of the grapes harvested. The wines of Bordeaux are an infinite challenge for producer, broker, négociant, importer, merchant, and finally, most important of all, the consumer.

RED BORDEAUX

One of the most important and significant differences between red Bordeaux, known by the British as "claret", and red wine of many other classic districts is that it is made not from just one major vine variety, but several, each with different characteristics; the choice between them being dictated by the soil type which, again, varies throughout the region, and the style of wine aimed for. Moreover, each grape variety has, in effect, its own life style: Merlot, for example, is an early ripener, susceptible to rot, and the small-berried Cabernet Sauvignon is firmer and ripens later. The latter grape has the strongest association with Bordeaux, the proportion cultivated usually being by far the highest, certainly the most dominant, in the Médoc and Graves, yet rarely planted in the Pomerol and St-Emilion districts where Merlot is favoured. Cabernet Franc is a major partner to the Merlot in these hillier districts to the north and east of Bordeaux, but is just one of the supporting cast of grapes in the Médoc. Other varieties, notably Petit Verdot, are grown but only as a small proportion, two to five per cent, of the varietal or *cépage* mix, if at all.

The importance of these different grape varieties is that in juxtaposition they provide the correct balance of component parts to create red Bordeaux. To a lesser extent they are a sort of insurance: if the Merlot fails the Cabernet Sauvignon and Franc might well survive for the winemaker to use; if the Merlot is ripe but the weather deteriorates and the Cabernets fail to ripen, a Merlot-dominated wine will be made.

It is these infinite variations, of *cépage* mix, of age and maturity, of soils and subsoils, of literally thousands of individual vineyards and wine makers, of weather throughout the growing season, and of the subtle manifestations of change as the wine matures, first in cask then in bottle, that make red Bordeaux – claret – so endlessly fascinating. A kaleidoscope, warranting a life-time's study; an endless challenge, affording endless enjoyment.

A word of warning: it is not possible in a paragraph to sum up the characteristics of the wines of every district, let alone of individual châteaux. Though the overall weather pattern in a given year is common to all, microclimates (or, more correctly, mesoclimates) do exist, and vine growers and winemakers are only human.

Lastly, a word about longevity. Only major châteaux, the classed growths and their equivalents, with vines on prime sites, are capable of producing true *vin de garde* wines which will not only keep but improve with bottle-age. Minor wines from less favoured vineyard sites and districts will, in a good vintage, keep but they will not necessarily improve: softening a little perhaps, but not developing the richness of bouquet, the extra dimensions of flavour and refinement of the great growths. *Bourgeois* claret is best drunk between three and eight years of age, depending on the vintage, whereas classed growths need, in a good vintage, from six to fifteen years, great wines in great vintages keeping and improving for over twenty years.

2002★★★ variable

Vintage variations are of endless fascination for wine buffs but problematic for wine growers, particularly in Bordeaux, with its ever changing maritime climate; indeed, no one set of growing conditions is quite like another. Meeting the challenge is more than a game, it has quality and commercial repercussions.

The growing season in this vintage is a case in point. The post 2001 period from October 1 to March 31 was unusually dry, well below the average of the past twenty years. Winter was also very cold, not that this is a worry when the vines are dormant. However, the spring and early summer were mild.

Bud-break was normal but the vital flowering period, though fairly early, was troubled with cold and damp weather, which caused heavy losses due to *coulure* and *millerandage* affecting, in particular, the Merlot. A small and early harvest was therefore predicted.

July and August were cool, the latter month being damp though *véraison* occurred at a normal time. The maturation process was slowed down during the whole of August and, by the end of that month, hopes were not high. The dramatic change for the better, not unlike 1978, occurred in September, the sunniest September for twelve years and unusually dry.

On the right bank, 2002 produced the smallest crop since 1991 though the reduced harvest of Merlot was of high qualtiy and the Cabernet Franc excellent. On the left bank, in particular the Médoc, the harvest was late, the Merlots being brought in first, then the very ripe Cabernet Francs, and, lastly, the Cabernet Sauvignons.

Frankly, results are – not unusually – mixed, but on the whole better than expected. The wines are very tannic and will need a fair amount of bottle-ageing. At the time of writing (the spring of 2003), the main concern was the market: it is clearly not destined for a major en primeur campaign but the wines should prove very useful, commercially, in due course.

2001 at best★★★★

Another very uneven vintage, partly – as always – due to unpredictable weather conditions but, as far as quality is concerned, much to do with work in the vineyards: crop thinning, de-leafing, and, finally, strict selection.

Between the end of the 2000 harvest and early spring the rainfall was heavy and fairly incessant, over twice the average precipitation (and three times higher

than in 2002). It filled the water tables but this, and a wet July, clogged and
retarded vines on clay soils.

Bud-burst was early but a cool April slowed growth. Flowering in
June was early and quick with an accelerated harvest predicted at this
stage. However, July was cold and wet, August alternating between cool
and extremely hot (up to 35°C/95°F) delaying *véraison* which pushed back
the harvest date to September 24 for the Merlot, on both left and right banks.
The late-picked Cabernet Sauvignons were satisfactory; though the grapes
were small, with more skin and pulp than juice, they had excellent phenolic
maturity. Cabernet Franc and Petit Verdot (on the left bank) were of high quality.
*Certainly there are wines with finesse and elegance, and the ripe Cabernets
are delightfully aromatic. A useful vintage with some really appealing wines for
mid-term drinking.*

2000★★★▷★★★★★

The millennium vintage largely lived up to expectations, the best for reds
since 1990.

The winter was mild and wet, with persistent drizzle during December
(1999) and February. Eighteen days of frost in mid-January was followed
by three short cold spells, which inhibited sap rise and dispelled fears of
premature budding. The second week of March was warm, Merlot budding
around March 10. However, the mild wet winter and damp April was follwed
by a heat-wave from April 18 to May 4, providing perfect conditions for the
rapid development of mildew and catching out ill-prepared growers who
had not anticipated the need for preventative spraying.

The first half of May was hot; storms followed, one of which resulted in
severe hail damage in parts of the norhern Médoc. Damp, warm, and windless
days in late May, a downpour (June 3–4), and a heat-wave (June 13–20) caused
considerable problems for growers. At best, the loss of bunches acted as a sort
of *vendange verte*, at worst severely reduced yields.

From July 29 there was an abrupt change. A high-pressure system
brought stable, hot, and dry conditions, eleven days in August being
excessively hot, alternating with cool, dry, and overcast conditions, which
put a brake on mildew development and vegetation, concentrating the berries,
and re-invigorating the vines. September brought almost unbroken sunshine,
resulting in fine ripening conditions, perfect for Merlot, for which the harvest
was brought forward to mid-month, for Cabernet Franc in early October, and,
for those who waited, ripe and healthy Cabernet Sauvignon.
*The wines are developing well and their original promise amply justified. Lesser red
Graves and St-Emilions are well underway for enjoyable early drinking and the more
serious right and left bank wines clearly in for a long, satisfactory life. A highly
recommended vintage.*

1999★★▷★★★★ variable

One of the most difficult years in vine growers' memory necessitating
unremitting care, toil, and expense. Unlike many years, when the right bank is
more successful than the Médoc, both are on a par – and both, unusually, were
harvested at the same time. The successes are not by district but estate by estate,
grower by grower. Happily, there have been many successes.

The wet autumn and winter of 1998 topped up the water tables. January and
February were cool and dry (thirty per cent of normal rain). Bud-burst came at

the end of March, with temperatures soaring to 22/23°C (71/72°F), threatening potential overproduction. April and May were very hot (4°C/39°F over the seasonal average), but humidity necessitated early spraying; the last ten days of May saw temperatures up to 31°C/87°F, resulting in early flowering. June 4–8 were stormy, with some *coulure*; it was then very hot and dry through to the end of July. Early August was variable: hot and slightly humid with some heavy showers delaying *véraison*. The end of the month and early September were dry and very sunny. Three ideal weeks were interrupted on September 5 when a severe thunderstorm hit the region, a swathe of hailstones shredding vines in a line from Libourne to St-Emilion with variable damage to some fifty châteaux necessitating some emergency picking. The right bank started picking on September 13 following two days of heavy rain, and the Médoc began on September 22, both ending early October. Merlots seemed perfect in Pomerol. Predominance of Cabernets and very good Petit Verdot in Médoc.

Apart from judicious spraying, the most prudent growers had a "green harvest" at the end of June, thinning out leaves on one side in early July, the other side in August. At the same time bunches were thinned and grapes removed. In short, selection, selection, selection in the vineyards and *les tables de tries* (sorting tables). An expensive business. The best wines are deep coloured with supple tannins.

Upstaged by the much-awaited Millennium Vintage the 1999s are underrated. Though variable there are many quite attractive wines for medium-term drinking.

1998 ★ ★ ▷ ★ ★ ★

A potentially excellent vintage, this time inhibited by a baking August and then by much rain at vintage time. However, some good wines were made and, in Pomerol, some claims to greatness.

After a mild rainy winter 1998 got off to a good start with dry, warm sunny weather and early bud-break in March. April was wet and cold, but happily with no frosts. From May 7 fine, dry and sunny weather speeded up growth leading to a quick, even flowering at the end of the month, from May 24 to June 8 in the Médoc, a week earlier than any other this decade. June was normal, July erratic with some green harvesting towards the latter half. August, however, "the month that makes the must", was sunny, too dry, and far too hot. On August 9–10, literally scorching the vines, temperatures rose up to 39°C (102°F) shrivelling leaves, grilling the grapes, and inhibiting sap, particularly in the Médoc. September was cooler, the first ten days fine, followed by three days of storms, then sun from the 16th to the 23rd, and then heavy rain from the beginning of October.

Growers in Pomerol and St-Emilion were able to pick the early ripening Merlot around September 20–26 before the serious rains set in and some of the top châteaux in Pomerol reported wines of outstanding quality. In the Médoc the Cabernets struggled to mature and were generally picked from about September 22 to October 5, worryingly between showers.
Overall a very big harvest, the second largest this century. Early pickers benefited, Merlots particularly. Cabernet Sauvignon tannin levels are high. Médocs are uneven though the best have good colour and fruit.

Clearly a vintage of winners and losers demanding great care in selection. The Médocs are somewhat unyielding and tannic and need bottle-ageing; the Pomerols and St-Emilions more amenable.

1997 ★★▷★★★★

A difficult year. Producers had to react quickly to whatever mother nature decided to throw next. Skill, and luck, had a bearing, making it particularly difficult to generalize. The market was equally chaotic, the trade reacting strongly to what were considered over-optimistic and unrealistic prices.

Winter was short with snow in early January allowing the vines to rest. February then became unusually warm and the conditions stayed this way until June (recorded as the warmest spring in fifty years). Consequently bud-break was two weeks premature and long, causing uneven development. Flowering was three weeks early and also very long. Unfortunately, due to May being cool and wet, *coulure* and *millerandage* resulted in poor berry set. At this point most producers green pruned to even out development. Rain again in late June and August made *véraison* slow and some rot was evident, requiring more pruning. It was also obvious just how much energy the vines were putting into foliage growth. Late August saw the first real sun and this fortunately continued throughout the harvest.

Harvesting commenced on September 8 and took longer than usual: fifty to sixty days altogether. The weather was warm, clear, and sunny (similar to 1990), while cooler nights ensured potential quality. Differences in style occurred here as some opted to pick early, giving good acidity and aroma to a lighter-weight wine. Others waited, leaving grapes on the vine up to 140 days, giving phenolic ripeness and a fuller, deeper wine. One generalization could be made – Cabernet Sauvignon benefited from its later ripening, fortunate for the left-bank (Médoc) producers. The right bank (Pomerol and St-Emilion) made some good, supple Merlot but were caught by rain in early September. Blends of the two varieties made very successful wines. This was definitely a year for the extra diligent producer.

Until recently, largely underrated but some surprisingly attractive wines: top-growth Médocs with good fruit and soft tannins for mid-term drinking, say 2005 to 2010. Pomerols rich, soft, and silky, St-Emilion easy and approachable, and minor Médocs delicious now.

1996 ★★★▷★★★★

A vintage definitely not to be ignored. Underestimated at first, due to the market's continuing obsession with the previous vintage. After a very unsettled growing season the results are exceptional, one of the best vintages of the 1990s, particularly in the Médoc.

Frost prevailed in February and March with a slightly delayed budding starting in mid-April. Flowering was quick, even, and completed by June 20. This was due to very hot temperatures in June, resulting in an explosion of growth and a general feel of well-being about the vineyards. As this weather continued, there were some problems of *millerandage*, particularly for Merlot.

August temperatures were very cool early in the month, but by the end, sunny days and cool evenings were welcomed and the danger of rot did not materialize. Rain dampened high spirits pre-harvest and then again towards the end of September. As a result Pomerol and St-Emilion suffered reduced crops and dilution in the grapes, especially Merlot, whereas in the Médoc rainfall was far less – about half that of the right bank – with hardly any in the very north of this region.

Later picking dates made it a year for Cabernet Sauvignon. The vintage started on September 12, and those grapes harvested between September

30 and October 12 were to produce the finest wines: strong, rich, and concentrated, resulting from skins toughened by changing conditions throughout autumn. In the Médoc, some compare the wines to those of 1986, but with more balanced tannic structure. A "classic" claret style, potentially wines for ageing. Unfortunately, the right-bank producers suffered large losses and not such high quality, largely due to the rain.

This is definitely a Médoc vintage, particularly in the northern half, where even the petits châteaux of the Bas-Médoc made exceptional wines. Top châteaux 2005 to 2015, bourgeois growths now to 2006. Most right-bank wines are for early to mid-term drinking.

1995★★★

This vintage was hailed a success after the previous four rain-plagued years. The wines show excellent ripeness, the result of the high sugar to acid ratio found at the time of picking. Concentration, balance, and aroma are all reflective of the wine style, with supple, balancing tannins to support mid-term ageing.

Winter was one of the mildest of the 1990s. Substantial rainfall also raised the water-table, equipping the vines for a long, hot summer. As a result the growing season was early and consistent. Bud-break was regular with rapid flowering before the end of May, and the vines were in good health. The driest summer in twenty years raised fears of a drought as temperatures soared to 30°C (86°F) – with the average usually 22°C (72°F). Happily winter rain had boosted the water tables and *véraison* was ten days early.

The vintage started one week early on September 11, and potentially disastrous rain threatened soon after, persisting lightly and sporadically until September 20. Most producers picked after this time, when temperatures rose again and October basked in an Indian summer. Cabernet Sauvignon was picked last with sugar levels almost unheard of for Bordeaux. Some Merlot was caught by the early rain, but Cabernet Franc achieved success, producing aromatic and supple wines.

The result: ripe wines backed by a firm structure, deemed tender and charming. The yields this vintage were up by fourteen per cent compared with that of 1994, yet keeping good concentration. Most areas did well, with the Cabernets performing outstandingly.

Definitely a vin de garde, *though the minor reds are pleasant now. The best growths to 2010 and beyond.*

1994★★★

A difficult year, but some good wines were produced with deep colour, high tannins, and varying ageing potential.

The winter of 1993 was one of the warmest on record, rainy with mild temperatures and a lack of sunshine, and budding took place at the end of March. Once into April, temperatures began to drop and heavy rain fell during the first ten days. By April 15 the entire region had been hit by frost. Generally the damage amounted to fifty per cent but was as much as seventy to one hundred per cent in some plots. Warm weather picked up again – temperatures in the high 20s°C (70s°F) and continued well into May. Quick re-budding of the frost-affected vines was facilitated and although the weather became more unsettled with storms and even some hail, the vegetation was not harmed. June and, particularly, July were hot and these heat-wave conditions consolidated a rapid flowering and the grapes continued to ripen in perfect conditions. By the end of August the region was on course for a great vintage and the grapes were in a strong, healthy condition – physiologically more advanced than 1993 by about a month.

September 9 was set for the *ban de vendange*, the opening of the harvest, and many châteaux started picking the following day. However from September 7 heavy rains hit the region. Picking resumed or started on September 19 and was completed by September 29. As usual, Merlot and Cabernet Franc were picked ahead of the later ripening Cabernet Sauvignon, most of which was harvested on September 24/25 before heavy showers fell again during the following two days. Some properties chose to wait until fine weather returned on September 28 and brought in their final Cabernet Sauvignon by October 7.

The initial response to the vintage was favourable. Yields were small and the quality of Merlot and Cabernet Franc was good as maturity had been reached before the rains. Cabernet Sauvignon was variable, but with a greater level of ripeness than in 1993. Careful selection produced the best wines.

Quite apart form being upstaged by the deservedly popular 1995, this vintage has lost its attractions. Minor wines for drinking now, top châteaux from the Médoc probably best mid-term, say now to 2010, the more successful right-bank wines are drinking reasonably well now.

1993★★▷★★★

This will never be perceived as a great vintage, but the wines do have good colour and where careful selection took place, they have substantial body and character. Unfortunately, the overriding climatic feature was rain that occurred on 160 days out of 365. The first three months of the growing season were unusually, almost worryingly, dry and by contrast the final four months were wet to the same dramatic extent. Unfortunately, the wettest month of all was September. Despite damp conditions the vines were generally in favourable shape. Merlot-based wines are potentially the most successful as by mid-September these grapes were extremely close to perfect ripeness. The risk of dilution was greater for the slower ripening Cabernet Sauvignon. The harvest began and in most cases was completed in the rain.

Nevertheless, overall, the results were better than expected and some properties produced fairly impressive wines thanks to extremely careful selection and advanced technology in the winery. St-Emilion and Pomerol produced wines with good colour and fruit density. The Cabernets have a lighter style with marked differences between the Médoc communes.

Frankly variable, the Médocs and Graves depending on the quality of wine making and selection, the most successful quite clearly being the right bank – Pomerol and St-Emilion. The top growths are, frankly, not up to standard and most 1993s are best drunk soon.

1992★

In the past, a sodden year such as this would have been a complete disaster. Technological advances and the rejection of as much as half the crop by those who could afford to, enhanced the potential of the vintage. The wines are extremely varied and too many are simply mean and dilute.

The problem with 1992 was that the growing and harvesting conditions were execrable. The summer was the wettest for over half a century and sunshine hours were the fewest since 1980. The spring was warm and humid and during June heavy rains delayed and extended flowering, causing uneven ripening. Rot had set in by this point, only progressively to worsen as rains continued through the summer. August was particularly torrential and some localized hailstorms occurred, most notably in Cantenac on August 8. The better properties removed many bunches of grapes that realistically had no chance of ripening. The harvest for this unprecedentedly large crop was extremely wet and prolonged.

Fortunately, most of the Merlot crop was brought in during three dry days, September 29 to October 1, and did not suffer as much dilution as Cabernet Sauvignon which was harvested during the heaviest downpour (October 2 to 6). Pomerol was most successful due to the high proportion of Merlot. Bordeaux's better wines from this poor year are generally soft and fruity with low acidity and moderate tannins and concentration.

Frankly, disappointing wines, the least satisfactory of the decade though no fault of the growers and winemakers. Rather thin and uninteresting. Drink up or avoid.

1991 ★▷★★

An uneven year. Small production due to severe spring frosts. A vintage that veered from the verge of great success to, literally, a wash-out.

The winter of 1990 was very wet; December was cold but ended with a record 19.5°C (67°F) on December 29. January was very dry, with eight days of frost and two of snow; February was also very dry, with five days of snow, during which time the vines were dormant. March was dry and mild; April, until April 17, was also mild with average rainfall, vegetation advancing satisfactorily. On the night of April 21/22 the temperature plummeted to as low as -8°C (18°F). Vines were frozen, new shoots destroyed overnight, and the potential crop severely reduced. Cold weather continued, warming up as May progressed, with average rainfall. June was unsettled; first ten days wet; last ten days dry. Flowering, from around June 15 to early July, was late, prolonged, and uneven. July was hot, with above average rainfall which caused more worries about rot. August was dry and hot, in fact the hottest August since 1926. Above-average temperatures continued into September, advancing ripening and encouraging some growers, particularly in the Médoc, to anticipate another high quality, small, concentrated crop like 1961. However, the riper the grapes the greater the rot problems. The *coup de grâce* came towards the end of the month, with eight days of rain prior to harvesting. Those whose vines had survived the big frost had now to sort out the ripe from rotten grapes, this separation being crucial for quality. Despite these vicissitudes some good wines were made, particularly in the more favoured areas of the Médoc. The surviving grapes were fully ripe, had excellent acidity, and good soft tannins, the Merlot had the best sugar levels. But throughout the region the crop was small, the worst off being St-Emilion, the production of some châteaux being down to ten per cent of normal.

Drink up. The better châteaux' wines have turned out reasonably well, though not for long keeping.

1990 ★★★★

A large and successful vintage. It is very rare, and indeed unprecedented, to have three successive vintages of the quality of 1988, 1989, and 1990.

January to March was unusually warm, resulting in an early budding, but progress slowed during a cold, frosty patch in late March and early April. Beneficial rain in April was followed by a very hot, dry, sunny May. A second spurt of growth resulted in unevenness in the vines in parts of Bordeaux. In particular there were variations between Merlot and Cabernet Sauvignon.

Hot, sunny weather lasted until the end of August but, despite the heat and drought, ripening was excellent. Happily, gentle rainfall saved the day, swelling the grapes. Picking only became general in mid-September. The best grapes came from estates where the bunches had been carefully thinned. The Merlot grapes were in excellent condition with some of the highest sugar levels ever recorded. The Cabernet Sauvignon grapes tended to be small and thick, due to their difficult, prolonged flowering, prompting fears that wines from the Médoc would be inferior to those from St-Emilion and Pomerol where Merlot dominates.

This was an abundant, exciting vintage, particularly for the Merlots which have enormous amounts of tannin. The best Cabernet Sauvignons were made by growers who held out before picking, giving enough acidity to balance the slightly lacking Merlot. Overall, well-constituted, fairly substantial wines.

Many minor wines from lesser districts are delicious now, some crus bourgeois best ever; good quality St-Emilion and Pomerol from now to 2010. Though the classed-growth Médocs will continue to develop well into the present century, some are more advanced than their unidentical "twins", the 89s.

1989 ★ ★ ★ ★ ★

An extremely attractive vintage following an exceptionally hot summer – the hottest since 1949 – which produced wines of real promise, though not without a few problems along the way.

By May, growth was already three weeks ahead of normal. Early flowering in excellent conditions ensured a substantially sized crop. The hot weather continued through to September with uneven, but surprisingly good, levels of rainfall. Picking began on August 28 – the earliest harvest since 1893. Growers in the Merlot-dominated vineyards of the right bank found that the grapes, though technically ripe, did not have ripe tannins; where tannins were allowed to ripen, the acidity level dropped. Problems were further compounded throughout Bordeaux by the high sugar levels, which contributed to fermentation difficulties.

Despite the problems, these are rich, ripe wines with excellent fruit and very good tannin levels.

Full of tantalizingly appealing "puppy fat" when young these wines now show more masculinity yet combine wonderful fruit with life-enhancing tannin. Classed-growth Médocs have a great future, say 2010 to 2025, the lesser growths very drinkable now as are most of the right bank wines.

1988 ★ ★ ★ ★

Undoubtedly a very good vintage – particularly from those estates where the growers nervously sat out the late September storms and harvested in an exceptionally warm, sunny October.

A mild, wet winter and spring necessitated widespread spraying and resulted in an uneven flowering. This was followed by a hot, dry summer which lasted right through from July until September. This produced wines with great depth of colour and high levels of tannin, especially in the Merlot-dominated vineyards of the right bank. Where the grapes were picked late, the tannin was complemented by good levels of fruit. Firm, well-structured wines, not as appealing as the 1989 and 1990 but capable of long life.

Classed-growth Médocs are still immature and their promise uncertain. Not in the same class as the two succeeding vintages but undervalued and worth cellaring. The best Graves, Pomerols, and St-Emilions drinkable from now to around 2010.

1987 ★ ★

This year suffers from comparison with the two good vintages it followed and the three it preceded. However, these were, on balance, light, attractive wines, suitable for early drinking.

A long, cold winter and spring followed by a cool, humid June, resulted in prolonged and uneven flowering. July and August were relatively cool and dull. Thereafter, apart from some rain in early September, the weather was generally fine, hot sun being succeeded by an unsettled October, the grapes being harvested in dull and rainy conditions. This year yielded an average sized crop of sound wines.

I have upgraded this vintage, the wines are undoubtedly attractive, easy to drink, and undervalued. Not for long keeping.

1986 ★ ★ ★

The biggest crop since World War II: fifteen per cent larger than that of the 1985 vintage. A cool, damp spring delayed bud-break, but the weather improved during May and June. After a successful flowering, the summer was hot and dry until the harvest, which began during the last week in September. The size of the crop provoked some worries about its quality. These are, however, intense, powerful, tannic wines and those with sufficient extract and flesh will last well.

This vintage has also gone up in my estimation. One or two great wines, the top growths, say 2008 to 2020; most of the rest – all districts – drinking pretty well now.

1985 ★ ★ ★ ★

Very appealing wines after a growing season veering from one extreme to the other. Winter was one of the coldest on record, causing considerable frost damage in some areas. A very early, successful flowering took place at the start of a long, extremely hot summer. This continued until the harvest, which took place in ideal conditions in late September/early October.

The 1985s, unusually, combine high quantity with high quality. The best are ripe, almost opulent and luscious with soft fruit. Some lesser areas showed a tendency to overproduce, resulting in slightly diluted wines. Overall, however, beautifully balanced wines.

My favourite claret vintage of the decade. They are most attractive to drink now, yet the best can be kept and will continue to evolve to 2010 and beyond. The lesser wines might as well be drunk whilst the going is good.

1984 ★

Difficult weather conditions, including the arrival of hurricane Hortense on October 5, resulted in variable wines. After a cold February and March, conditions improved with a warm April. The cold weather returned in May and an incomplete flowering took place during an excessively hot, dry June.

The summer was fair, followed by a humid September and wet October. Picking began in late September/early October and was interrupted by the hurricane. Merlot vines suffered from *coulure*, reducing crops drastically: the result was that few quality wines were made on the right bank. In the Médoc wines were virtually dominated by the Cabernets.

The 1984 vintage does not compare well with so many other remarkably good vintages of the decade: they are lean, hard, somewhat ungracious wines which, illogically, also suffered from over-pricing. This made them, in some instances, more expensive than the superior 1983s and 1982s. Not now. *My advice: drink up or avoid. The best will not improve much, nor will the minor wines soften.*

1983★★★

A large crop of good quality grapes, which produced some very appealing wines, initially more typical of Bordeaux than the 1982s.

After a poor start to the year conditions improved for flowering and the summer was hot and dry. Graves experienced hail during early July and other areas suffered disease due to excessive humidity. The harvest, which began September 26, took place in ideal conditions. Margaux was the most favoured district. Wines from the right bank were generally less fine. Despite good structure, with adequate tannin, fruit, and acidity, the 1983s lack the power and substance of the 1982s and are not as beautifully balanced as the 1985s.

Apart from the top-class Margaux, my recommendation is to drink the 1983s soon, as many classed-growth Médocs are on the decline.

1982★★★★★

An exceptional vintage throughout Bordeaux – the 1982s were immediately perceived as a potential "vintage of the decade". Not, however, typical Bordeaux: described by some as more like California Cabernet than claret.

Flowering was early and even. The climate provided ideal growing conditions for the vines. Consistently hot, dry weather held throughout the summer, though some areas in the Médoc and Graves experienced a hot, stormy July. The harvest started on September 14 in perfect conditions. A substantial crop of exceptionally ripe grapes was gathered, causing some concern that the wines would not, as a result, have the necessary structure to mature into good claret. The results, however, are huge, opulent, luscious wines with high extract masking considerable tannin content, which will take some time to mature.

The top wines of the Médoc have been going through an extended period of seemingly little development but are proving magnificently rich and deliciously drinkable. Lesser Médocs are beginning to dry out. Most Pomerols, St-Emilions, and red Graves are drinking well now. Minor wines should have been consumed.

1981★★▷★★★

A small crop of good quality wines. This vintage was overshadowed by the immensely impressive 1982s and by some of the other successful vintages of the 1980s.

Flowering took place early in hot, dry weather which held throughout the summer. September saw some gentle rain which cleared up in time for the harvest, which began on October 1.

More of a claret man's claret than the 1982. The top growths are holding better than the 1983s though most are on the lean side. Some particularly good Pomerols. Drink soon.

1980★

With the odd exception, this was an average vintage which, like 1981, suffered in comparison to the high quality of most of the other vintages of the decade.

A cool spring resulted in a late and uneven flowering; June was consistently cold and wet, followed by a moderate summer. Grapes ripened very slowly, delaying the harvest. Picking started as late as October 20 in some areas. These were "lunchtime" clarets, ideal for early drinking.
Few to be seen. Drink up.

1979★★

The biggest harvest since 1934. Initially unwanted by the trade which had bought heavily of the 1978, 1976, and 1975 post-recession vintage. Upstaged by the 1978s, the 1979s began to be appreciated in the mid- to late 1980s, but have long since lost whatever appeal they had. A cold, wet spring, which followed a hard winter, delayed bud-break until mid-April, but the summer was fine apart from a cold spell in August. Good conditions mid-October for harvest: a very large crop of small, thick-skinned grapes, lacking full ripeness, and resulting in deep-coloured, tannic wines. The right-bank vineyards had a very successful year, with a fine, ripe crop adding a more luscious note to the vintage.
The best right-bank wines – fully mature – are drinking quite well, but the more tannic Médocs are tannic, drying out, lacking sufficient fruit. The latter should be consumed or avoided.

1978★★★

The year described by the late Harry Waugh, then director of Château Latour, as "the year of the miracle": appalling growing conditions saved by perfect early autumn weather. The spring was late, with bud-break and harvest delayed a little. But after the late grape set in mid-August conditions improved, ripening taking place in unbroken sunshine until the start of the harvest on October 9. At some properties picking continued into late October. The vintage was well received for several reasons: it turned out far better than originally feared; the 1977s were poor; the market was right.
This vintage has been overrated and is on the decline. Some drinking quite well; I doubt if many will improve. Drink soon.

1977

A poor vintage, the worst of an uneven decade. An early bud-break was damaged by spring frosts, then rain throughout the summer was followed by the driest September since 1851, which saved the crop from complete disaster. Generally unexciting; colour was sometimes good but most wines lacked length and depth. The best showed a specious chaptalized fruitiness which soon wore off.
Avoid.

1976★★▷★★★

On release a deservedly popular vintage. A year of severe heat in northwest Europe, Bordeaux included, with a summer-long drought that broke during the harvest. Bud-break occurred at the normal time, during late March. Flowering, grape set, and vintage were all early as the great heat carried out its work. The harvest started on September 15, the earliest of the decade. The wines were easy and agreeable, but many, from high class to low, lacked flesh; more lean and

supple than pleasantly fresh, some of the first growths combined substance
and elegance. Never a classic claret vintage, though many were beguiled by
its youthful appeal, attractive colour, and initial fruit.

*Some continue to charm and delight. Many are flavoury, most are fading. One or two
top growths have time in hand, despite being well past their prime. Drink up.*

1975★▷★★★

Unhesitatingly pronounced a *vin de garde* by the Bordelais following three
mediocre, graceless vintages. But, the wines are variable, unbalanced, all
tannic, some lacking extract. A mild, wet winter, followed by a mild spring
with occasional frosts, provided favourable conditions for flowering. The
summer was hot and dry with some gentle, welcome rain before the harvest
(beginning on September 26), which was generally dry except for a few
hailstorms. Fruity wines with a dark colour resulting from a deep pigment
in the grape skins, plus a high sugar content assuring a satisfactory alcohol
level. However, despite some good fruit and high extract, the tannins were
excessive: many soon developed a "rusty" orange tinge, misleadingly mature-
looking but packing a swingeingly dry and tannic finish.

*This has been one of the most difficult vintages to assess. The Médocs fall into two
camps, depending on the skill and conscientiousness of the producer. The best, with
good, rich fruit and extract to balance the tannin are still drinking well, the rest are
pinched, mean, and drying out. On the whole: drink up.*

1974

A very large, unwelcome vintage at a time of slump in Bordeaux. As there was
no market, the beleagured châteaux proprietors had no incentive to prune hard
or make selections. Good flowering; hot summer; then a wet and increasingly
cold autumn. Picking began on October 3.

Raw, ungracious wines. Few remain. Drink up or avoid.

1973 at best★★

A prolific vintage of light, at best modestly attractive wines, which coincided
with the severe recession in the Bordeaux market.

Fine weather all summer except for a very wet July. The vintage started on
October 1 under satisfactory conditions, yielding a huge crop. The majority of
wines lacked colour and substance. Had the market been more propitious it
might have paid the growers to prune harder and be more selective. Better
wines would have resulted.

Drink up, though some can surprise.

1972

One of the latest vintages since records began. Overpricing of these poor wines
triggered the collapse of the Bordeaux market. A fairly large crop of immature,
uneven quality grapes. Dismal but not totally undrinkable wines.

Drink up. Better still avoid.

1971★★★▷★★★★

A good vintage with some elegant wines, though yields were much lower
than in previous years. A cold, wet spring and early summer, followed by
warm and sunny weather with light rain – an ideal combination. Picking
started on October 4. Pomerols were outstanding and some Médocs excellent.

Many pleasant surprises though some of the top Médocs are lean, some even feeble. Many red Graves, Pomerols, and St-Emilions are still delicious.

1970★★★★

An imposing vintage, combining quantity with high quality, though, in my opinion, not as uniformly excellent as 1966. Spring was late but the vines blossomed in good conditions. July's great heat and drought was followed by a rainy, cool August with hot intervals. September was stormy and cold, but soon gave way to a long run of hot sunshine throughout the vintage which started on October 4. These weather conditions permitted all the main grape varieties to ripen fully simultaneously. Some disappointments, particularly in the Médoc.
Now very variable. Many of the top Pomerols and St-Emilions are still delicious. The originally well-constituted wines of the Médoc went through a rather long drawn-out, unyielding period. Generally far less exciting now than their original promise implied, yet some are at a peak of perfection, one or two with another decade or so in hand.

1969★

Lean, acidic yet flavoury, they soon lost their youth and appeal.
Avoid.

1968

Arguably the worst vintage since 1951; thin and acidic wines.
Avoid.

1967★

Quite attractive when young. Flowering late, July/August hot and dry followed by generally cold weather with the odd fine period. Chaptalization enabled some attractive wines to be made. They peaked in the mid-1970s but most were cracking up by the 1980s.
Now well past their best. Avoid.

1966★★★★

An excellent long-haul vintage. Lean rather than plump, though with good firm flesh. Flowering was early after a mild winter and early spring. The cool and fairly dry summer was counter-balanced by a very hot, sunny September. The grapes were harvested in perfect conditions on October 6.
    This was a vintage of real quality and great style; Bordeaux at its most uncompromising, yet elegant. The first growths all warranted five stars.
The top-class Médocs, if well kept, are still delicious: what good claret is all about. Minor wines, lacking flesh, are drying out and well past best.

1965

One of the worst post-war vintages. The result of a wet summer which delayed ripening. Thin, short, acidic wines.
A pity to tip down the sink. Skinny but flavoursome first growths; do not hesitate with the rest, or keep for salad dressings.

1964★★▷★★★★

On the whole a very good and abundant vintage, one of the biggest since the war. Now, like the wines of 1962, undeservedly forgotten. A mild, wet winter and rather warm spring provided very good flowering conditions. The hot, dry summer resulted in a sound, healthy, ripe crop by mid-September, though the second half of the harvest was seriously affected by two weeks of continual rain, particularly in parts of the Médoc.

Château Latour picked early and made a magnificently beefy wine; Châteaux Lafite and Mouton picked late and the wines have the thinness and piquancy of a lighter vintage. At best, however, many of the wines are still very agreeable, especially those of Graves and St-Emilion. Worth looking out for.
All fully mature but capable of giving great pleasure.

1963

A poor vintage. Cold summer caused rot. Light, acidic wines.
Some thin yet modestly flavoury first growths; otherwise avoid.

1962★★★★

A vintage overshadowed by the incomparable 1961. Abundant crop, *une très bonne année*. Cold and rainy conditions to the end of May; flowering in mid-June in good weather; very hot summer tempered by welcome showers in September which swelled the berries; and a late harvest, beginning October 9.

Firm, well-coloured wines, with some of the leanness of the 1966s. Never fully appreciated. Pleasant Pauillacs: excellent flavour and balance; hard, dry tannic finish. Fine classic wines.
If well kept many still drinking well. Worth looking out for.

1961★★★★★

One of the greatest post-war vintages to date and one of the best of the twentieth century. The top 1961s became the gold dust of the wine world. As with the 1945 vintage, quality was due more to luck than management. Vegetation was advanced despite March frosts; cold weather during flowering, rain washed away pollen with the direct result of reducing the crop size. Persistent rain in July, drought in August, and a very sunny September left small, concentrated, and well-nourished grapes. The pre-harvest sun brought them to full maturity, thickening the skins to a good depth of colour. The harvest began at the end of September.

The hallmarks of the 1961s are intensity of colour, concentrated bouquet, sweetness, high extract, flesh, and tannin, acidity levels enabling long keeping, and great length.
Some, Château Latour for example, could benefit from a further ten years in bottle. Others, however, are drying out. Many are still delicious; a privilege to drink a vintage of this rare stature. Storage and provenance, however, are crucial. Some corks are deteriorating. Bottles stored unmoved in a cold, slightly damp cellar are best.

1960★

Some light and flavoury wines made. Perfect flowering weather around May 25 despite a cold January and late frosts. A good June but a cold summer followed. Some more than adequate wines made, but unfortunately hemmed in by the 1959 and 1961.
Few seen. Drink up.

1959★★★★★

The press deemed this at the time "the vintage of the century". Hugely popular with the English trade and certainly one of the most massively constituted wines of the post-war era. February and March were the finest in living memory: frost at night, early morning mists, and hot sun. A cold April followed and a fine summer thereafter, with much rain falling from September 13, but clearing up in time for the harvest which began on the 23rd of the month. A crop of average quantity was bought in, the results of which were rated *très grands vins*. At best opulent and magnificent.

Despite some talk of "lacking acidity" many 1959s are still marvellous to drink, the best having the inner richness for an almost indefinite life. For once the press was more or less right. Great wines and less expensive than the renowned 1961s.

1958★★

An attractive vintage immediately appreciated by English claret connoisseurs but bypassed by the English trade which had bought 1957s and then invested heavily in 1959s. Spring was cold, but a good flowering took place in June. Towards the end of summer the weather improved, resulting in a late harvest. Easy, attractive wines – for about a decade.

Now mainly well past their best. Drink up.

1957★

Uneven, aggressive vintage. Perverse weather conditions: hot March, April frosts, poor flowering, the coldest August recorded. Unripe grapes picked in an early October heat-wave. Despite this, popular with the trade at the time it came on the market.

Mainly raw, ungracious wines, most long past their best. Some surprises though. My advice, drink up.

1956

One of the most dismal post-war vintages. Most severe winter since 1709. Summer cold and wet.

Avoid.

1955★★★★

A very good but always somewhat under-appreciated vintage. Alternating weather patterns early in the year; a fine summer with a perfect July and welcome rains in September; fine conditions for harvest on September 22. Optimistic reports at the time but not as attractive as the heavily bought 1953s. The best, and best kept, however, are still lovely – undervalued, some even warranting five stars.

Top growths, particularly of the Médoc and Graves, can still be delightful, assuming good storage; all others, drink soon.

1954★

Despite one of the worst summers on record some quite nice wines made.

Rarely seen. Drink up.

1953★★★★★

A really beautiful vintage: the personification of claret at its most charming and elegant best. An early, dry spring with insignificant frost; flowering started well but cold and rain caused some *coulure*; fine summer with perfect August; excessive rain in mid-September delayed the harvest which eventually started on October 2 in perfect weather. An average and ample yield. A vintage that never went through a hard or dull period. Attractive in cask; an appealing youth; perfect maturity.

The finest still lovely despite being past their best. Some delightful, if faded old ladies. Drink soon before they slip away.

1952★★▷★★★★

Considered a *bonne année* at the time, now largely forgotten. A warm spring and hot June (flowering under exceptionally good conditions); July and August were hot; September was cold; picking took place in poor weather. Below average quantity. Pomerol and St-Emilion excelled, Graves were good, Médocs hard and though good, firm, and long-lasting, lacked plump flesh.

Difficult to generalize, even top growths were variable. The right bank wines can still be delicious, also the top red Graves, but Médocs are rather stern, even harsh. Drink up.

1951

One of the worst vintages since the early 1930s – thin, acid, decayed.
Avoid.

1950★★

An abundant vintage, nearly double that of 1949, but of uneven quality, which helped fill war-depleted cellars. Good flowering, but harvested in changeable weather. Middleweight, lacking the style, charm, and balance of 1949, but sometimes surprisingly nice. Rarely seen. Some good Pomerols, but most successful in Margaux and Graves.
Drink up.

1949★★★★★

A great vintage following extraordinary weather conditions. After the driest January and February on record, flowering during cold and rain resulted in the worst *coulure* ever remembered; increasingly hot weather followed, with an almost unprecedented heat-wave: 63°C (145°F) recorded in Médoc on July 11; storms thereafter in early September, fine harvest weather on the 27th, with a little beneficial rain.

A small quantity of supple, beautifully balanced wines. More finesse and elegance, and firmer than the 1947s; less intense and concentrated than the 1945s. Claret at its middle-weight, fragrant, superfine best.

Many, if of impeccable provenance, are still perfect to drink, certainly all the top St-Emilions, Pomerols, Graves, and Médocs – notably Margaux and Pauillac.

1948★★★

A rough diamond, lacking polish and charm; sandwiched between two more attractive vintages and consequently neglected. This year was characterized by perverse weather conditions: an exceptionally good spring then a cold summer which suffered much *coulure*; the critical month of September, however, provided good picking weather. The crop was three-quarters the size of 1947. Quality was good, but 1947 and 1949 were, rightly, preferred.

Can afford some pleasant surprises. Drink now.

1947★★★★★

Another post-war milestone, the "Edwardian" summer produced wines of an entirely different character to the 1945s: big, warm, fleshy, and generous.

A late spring and fine, increasingly hot summer. Picking in almost tropical conditions began on September 19. A problematic fermentation caused by the heat resulted, for some winemakers, in "pricking" and acidity. But, there are some rich, ripe, exciting wines. Pomerols superb.

Drink now, at their opulent best.

1946★★

An odd rather than "off" vintage which suffered an invasion of locusts. Rarely seen. Some, tasted fairly recently, were surprisingly good.

Drink now – if you can find any.

1945★★★★★

A year which heralded a string of vintages to match, if not exceed, the quality of the 1920s. Welcome after the misery of the war; 1945 is one of the top three vintages of the century and, in my opinion, greater than even the great 1961. The crop was severely reduced by late frosts, hail, disease, and exceptional drought which lasted until early into the harvest.

The wines are very concentrated and, having drawn the nutrients from the soil which would normally have fed a larger crop, are still packed with flavour. *Though some are drying out, top Pomerols and top-growth Médocs are virtually unmatched for depth of colour, richness, and concentration.*

1944★★

A slightly larger than average crop. Rain towards the end of the harvest resulted in wines of irregular quality: lightish, short, and at best charming, spicy, and flavoursome. But better than expected.

Scarce. Drink now, before they fade away.

1943★★★▷★★★★

The best of the wartime vintages. An average sized crop after good weather conditions. Overall richness and fruit, pleasant but lacking persistence.

Drink now.

1942★★

After a very cold winter, a small crop of light, pleasant, and useful wines.

Now variable, and risky.

1941★★

A small crop; vines suffered neglect and disease. Interesting.

Drink up.

1940★★

Vines suffered wartime neglect. An average crop of uneven wines.

Some still very attractive but drink up.

1930s

1939★ A very late vintage of light, though fragrant wines.

1938★ Bottled at the start of the war. A below average vintage.

1937★★★ An important, and originally highly regarded, vintage. A dry but cool summer produced wines high in tannin and acidity. Now austere, many distinctly raw and unpleasant. Margaux the best.

1936★ Bottled in 1938. Rare, though some pleasant surprises.

1935★ An abundant vintage of irregular quality. Rarely seen.

1934★★★★ The best vintage of the decade. The grapes were saved from a two-month drought by September rain, producing a good quality, abundant harvest. Rich, now overmature, but some exciting and attractive wines.

1933★★★ Light, charming wines, upstaged by 1934. Some still delicious.

1932 The latest harvest on record (completed December 1). Avoid.

1931 Very poor wines, rarely seen but some just drinkable.

1930 Bad weather, bad times, bad wines.

1920s

1929★★★★★ Considered the best vintage since 1900. A good summer followed difficult flowering and an average sized crop was harvested. The results were wines of charm and delicate balance, some distinctly opulent. The top wines can still be lovely despite being well past their best.

1928★★★★★ A monumental year: an extremely hot summer with some much-needed rain produced a promising harvest. This is the longest-lived vintage of the decade. Initially overpoweringly hard and tannic, some of the top wines, Château Latour in particular, took fifty years to become drinkable. Others have mellowed and can still be superb.

1927 A poor year. Rarely seen.

1926★★★★★ A very good year. A hard winter, cold spring, and small flowering, followed by long, hot summer. The small size of the crop coincided with the 1920s boom period and resulted in prohibitively high prices. Top wines, if in perfect condition, can still be incredibly rich.

1925 A sunless year, producing weak and watery wine.

1924★★★ Not unlike 1978, saved by three beautiful weeks in September following a cold spring and wet summer. Wines of considerable charm, rich but delicate, a few still drinking beautifully.

1923★★ Moderate vintage; some initial charm, few wines of interest.

1922★ Enormous crop of uneven quality. Few have survived.

1921★★★★ A year of exceptional heat and consequent problems with vinification. Good winemakers were rewarded with wines full of fruit, alcohol, and tannin. The vintage that made Château Cheval Blanc's reputation. Some still impressively good, but risky.

1920★★★★★ The first unquestionably *grande année* after 1900. A mild winter; excellent spring; perfect flowering and an exceptionally cold summer. *Oidium* and black rot severely reduced the size of the crop to a third that of 1919. The best-kept have survived.

1910s

1919★★★ Began well with a good flowering, the grapes then suffered *oidium* and mildew during a damp July, and were then scorched by ensuing heat. Château Lafite enjoyed abundance whilst others were reduced by the excessive August temperatures. Moderately good wines, though light and somewhat overtaken by acidity.

1918★★★ A good summer with no temperature extremes. A slightly larger crop than 1917's: good colour and sound, reasonable body; can still be quite attractive, but risky.

1917★★ Was a pleasant vintage, though the quantity suffered due to a shortage of labour; now scarce, variable, and risky.

1916★★ Produced good if somewhat hard wines, lacking charm.

1915~ A poor summer, the vines suffered mildew, pests, lack of treatment, and shortage of labour. Few made, never tasted.

1914★★ Was generally disappointing after a bright start, but some excellent wines were made: few have survived.

1913~ Pests and miserable weather brought this year close to disaster. Now dried-out and tart.

1912★★ Unsettled weather; an abundance of light, fairly satisfactory wines; surprisingly some have survived.

1911★★★★ A small yield of good quality wines: now variable, some still impressive, though faded.

1910~ Mildew, late harvest. Thin, tart wines.

1900s

1909★ Produced an average crop of light wines; distinctly *passé*.

1908★★ Was an average year, but now risky. Tannins helping some wines to cling precariously to life.

1907★★ Produced an abundant crop of appealing wines, but they lacked staying power: now well past best.

1906★★★ An unusually good start to the year was followed by excessive heat and drought in August. This reduced the yield and produced wines of robust, high quality: now faded yet still some remarkable survivors.

1905★★★ A large crop of light, moderately elegant wines; now variable, faded but flavoury.

1904★★★★ Excellent overall climatic conditions produced an abundant crop. Some lovely wines. Amongst the great survivors.

1903~ A freezing April and sunless summer: poor wines.

1902★ A moderately large crop: light, ordinary wines.

1901★ A big harvest of very uneven quality.

1900★★★★★ Heralded the start of the twentieth century, with one of the finest vintages ever: excellent weather throughout the year led to a superabundant harvest; the finest, if of immaculate provenance, are still beautiful to drink, though most, of course, past their best.

Pre-1900

1899★★★★★ Was to be the first of the great *fin de siècle* twins: outstanding and of exquisite flavour and delicacy; the best, most well-stored, still beautiful.

1898★★▷★★★ Produced uneven and tannic wines, which generally took time to soften; some have survived.

1897★ Was the smallest crop between 1863 and 1910 due to unusual salt winds blowing in off the sea.

1896★★★★ Favourable weather conditions produced an abundant crop of good wines: fine, delicate, and distinguished; now faded.

1895 at best★★★★ Uneven weather conditions and picking in an exceptional heat made winemaking very difficult: those who sought scientific advice made very good wine.

1894★ Produced a small crop of thin, uneven wines; now faded.

1893★★★★ After fifteen dismal years, the weather was exceptionally good, no frosts, diseases, or pests. The harvest was the earliest on record (August 15), yielding the biggest crop in eighteen years of good quality grapes. Some wines still superb, but risky.

1892★▷★★★ A small crop of weather-ravaged grapes: irregular in quality; one or two survivors.

1891★ Green, mediocre wines; yields severely cut by *cochylis*.

1890★★ Colour and body at the expense of quantity – average.

The great pre-phylloxera years
1878, 1875, 1874, 1870, 1869, 1865, 1864, 1858, 1848, 1846, 1844.

WHITE BORDEAUX

A great deal of white wine is made in the Gironde department. Most is dry and of an everyday standard, some is of superior quality; there are also fairly sweet wines of modest pretensions and, arguably, the greatest sweet white wines of the world. Although the climate is common to all Bordeaux districts, the weather conditions in the late autumn, after the grapes for the dry wines have been picked, are crucial for the sweet wines, and can vary significantly. Moreover, the methods of making the classic sweet wines are so different that they warrant separate descriptions.

Dry white Bordeaux Though a quantity of fair to middle quality wine is made in the Entre-Deux-Mers, to the southeast of Bordeaux, the finest dry whites are made from grapes – almost exclusively Sémillon and Sauvignon Blanc – grown in the vineyards scattered throughout the extensive Graves district south of the city of Bordeaux; the two finest, Château Haut-Brion *blanc* and Laville-Haut-Brion, are actually situated in the suburbs due west of the city centre.

No white wines are made in Pomerol and none to speak of in St-Emilion and its hinterlands. In the Médoc, the classic claret district, very few white wines of note are made, notably Pavillon Blanc de Château Margaux, Blanc de Lynch-Bages, and Talbot.

The white wines of the Graves share an identical climate and enjoy – or otherwise – similar variations of weather during the growing season, as do the reds. For this reason, the notes on the white wine vintages will not restate in full those that appear in the preceding red Bordeaux section unless there has been some significant aberration. Differences that arise are due also to the grape varieties, their ripening dates and their specific characteristics. Generally, but not always, Sémillon and Sauvignon Blanc are picked before the red grapes, principally to capture the fresh acidity that is so essentially a feature of all dry white wines.

Importantly, most dry white Bordeaux is meant to be drunk young and fresh, those made predominantly, sometimes exclusively, from Sauvignon Blanc, within a year or so of the vintage. Only the relatively few whites made at classed-growth châteaux, and mainly within the Pessac-Léognan appellation, will benefit from bottle-age, whereas the others, even if made classically from Sémillon and Sauvignon Blanc, should be consumed within three to five years. There are exceptions, depending on the vintage. The two great odd-men-out have already been mentioned. Both Châteaux Haut-Brion *blanc* and Laville-Haut-Brion mature well in bottle. In a top vintage these wines are too powerful to be drunk young and are both best somewhere between five and ten years after the vintage: both capable of lasting, and drinking well, for more than twenty, even on occasions up to fifty years.

Sauternes A relatively small rural district of rolling hills and hamlets at the most southerly end of the Bordeaux wine region, with a fair concentration of vineyards, and "châteaux" ranging from modest farm house to medieval castle and grand mansion.

The four communes, or parishes, plus the neighbouring lower-lying Barsac, specialize in sweet white wine. They grow the same grapes as in the Graves: Sémillon and Sauvignon Blanc, with a *soupçon* (as little as one per cent) of Muscadelle occasionally added at the discretion of the proprietor.

The essential difference between these and the dry whites is that the grapes are left longer on the vines and allowed to develop a beneficial mould, *Botrytis cinerea* or *pourriture noble* (noble rot), the effect of which is to reduce the water content, increase the concentration of flesh, and augment the sugar. Botrytis also adds a distinctive and highly desirable scent and flavour.

But it is a risky business. The crucial autumn weather can change for the worse or, less disastrously, lack of early morning mists will prevent or slow the formation of botrytis. It is also expensive: labour costs are high as the vineyard must be combed several times to select only those grapes at an optimum state of development; and the juice, reduced and concentrated, produces very little wine per vine.

The vintage notes that follow concern principally the classic sweet wines of Sauternes and Barsac, though the same conditions apply to the lesser but similar style sweet wines of Loupiac and Ste-Croix-du-Mont across the river Garonne to the east.

Top quality Sauternes, particularly from good vintages, not only keep well but need bottle-age to arrive at their peak of perfection. The quality, state of development and anticipated best drinking dates are summarized below.

2002

Dry White★★★★ Sauternes★★★★ Weather patterns from the winter and through the growing and ripening season matched those affecting red Bordeaux. The main situation in common was widespread *coulure* reducing volume and causing uneven ripeness, the Sauvignon Blanc in particular being prone to bursting, causing rot in many parcels. Sémillon fared better. Hot September weather helped the grapes to catch up, the best producing wines with crisp fruitiness and brisk acidity. In Sauternes the early spread of botrytis necessitated up to four *tries*, the Sémillon starting September 20. The Sauvignon Blanc showed potential alcohol, the Muscadelle being very aromatic. *At the time of writing, and soon after the first tastings in April (2003), many of the whites, both dry and sweet, ranged from hazy to cloudy, though behind that state of unreadiness the potential could be judged. My assessment for both the dry whites and Sauternes is optimistic. The former will make attractive, refreshing, early drinking, and whilst the Sauternes do not reach the levels of brilliance of the 2001s, they are certainly good, the best due to provide satisfactory mid-term development.*

2001

Dry White★★ Sauternes★★★★★ The wet winter and early spring, the cold and wet July and extremes of August did not bode well for the freshness and acidity of the dry white Bordeaux; the change to hot and sunny weather came far too late. Barsac and Sauternes, on the other hand, enjoyed ideal weather conditions with rain and unseasonably high temperatures at the end of September which provoked a uniform onset of noble rot. The favourable east wind dried out the grapes from the morning dew and dispersed the mist enabling picking to proceed in perfect conditions in early October.

Dry whites, drink up, Sauternes buy, keep, and savour – unquestionably a great vintage, in a similar league to 1971. The leading châteaux of Barsac and Sauternes will be at their best between fifteen and twenty-five years of age and many will continue to develop a golden hue, exquisite bouquet, and exquisite honeyed flavour.

2000

Dry White★★★★ Sauternes★▷★★★ A distinctly better vintage for reds and dry white, much less successful for sweet white Bordeaux. As always, the joint benefactor and culprit was the unpredictable weather.

April was dry with frost wreaking havoc though damage was not widespread. Hot and sunny weather in May and June reduced the risk of mildew and encouraged even flowering and fruit set, while cool nights and warm days in August brought the grapes to full maturity. Weather conditions for the Sémillon and Sauvignon Blanc harvest were good. But the rains which had held off for the dry white harvest came down in October, ruining for Sauternes and Barsac what had started out as a potentially fine growing season. Many châteaux still thought that the vintage would be exceptional, harvesting roughly a third of their crop in excellent conditions. When, on October 10, the rains came, some growers had a small quantity of fine wine, the rest virtually a washout.

Dry whites, the ever-improving Graves, and those from the more and more appreciated Entre-Deux-Mers, are drinking well now. The best of the early picked Sauternes are very attractive albeit available in relatively small quantities. Not a classic sweet wine year but agreeable for early drinking.

1999

Dry White★★★ Sauternes★★★★ A far more satisfactory and uniform year for the whites, both dry and sweet, the latter, thanks to an Indian Summer with excellent botrytis, enjoying the fifth excellent year in a row. From early January through spring and summer, weather conditions were as described in the red Bordeaux chapter.

The dry white vintage began in Pessac on August 30 in baking heat, Sauvignon Blanc first, Sémillon later. Unusually, and contrarily, the Sauvignon Blanc provides the power and the later-picked Sémillon the fruit, both attaining alcohol levels over twelve degrees.

In Sauternes, there had been earlier botrytis but on October 5 a high pressure system moved in, with cooler, fine days and perfect conditions for "noble rot": river mist and fog in the mornings and warm, drying sunshine in the afternoons. The growers had the benefit of excellent early maturation of Sauvignon Blanc and the later Sémillon and Muscadelle picked selectively in *tries*. A small harvest of sweet wines of high quality.

Lesser dry whites should have been drunk; finer Pessac-Léognan growths from now. The quality of Sauternes is somewhat variable but the best, and best-known, produced very good wines to be drunk between 2005 and 2015.

1998

Dry White★★★ Sauternes★★★★ Because of the excessive heat in August the Sauvignon Blancs were picked early, either side of the beginning of September, the Sémillons a fraction later. The top Pessac-Léognan estates made whites perhaps lacking in acidity. Sauternes is always at the other end of the spectrum, never more so than in 1998. For the third year in succession some top-class wines were made, the best from early picked first *tries*: very ripe, botrytis affected vines between September 16–29 and again, well after the worst of the rains, from October 10–22.

Dry whites: drink soon. Sweet white: from 2005 to 2015 depending on quality.

1997

Dry White★★ Sauternes★★★★ A roller-coaster year for the vines, as in the rest of Bordeaux, made very variable results here also. One major problem was the incidence of both grey and sour rot. The latter occurred due to the changing conditions in June causing berries to split, attracting the attention of insects. This then caused vinegar to be produced in the grapes, affecting Sauvignon Blanc in particular.

The vintage started very early, on August 18, in the region of Pessac-Léognan. The Sauvignon Blanc grapes showed high sugar content, but below average acidity due to low malic acid levels. The later ripening grapes surviving into September, especially Sémillon, achieved good levels of ripeness. Sauvignon Blanc was elegant and fragrant, but not as concentrated as 1996; consequently it was used less in the blends. Sémillon gave broader wines, with a good depth of fruit.

Frost affected Sauternes in April, as did the aforementioned rots. A rigorous *trie* system helped raise quality by weeding out the unsalvageable grapes. These were in small lots as pickers had to frequently move around the vineyard to find suitably ripened bunches. The *tries* taken mid-season around October 17 produced the finest results. Yields were especially low, but of great power and concentration with lip licking acidity.

Dry whites for drinking now, the exception being châteaux of the eminence of Haut-Brion. Sauternes for mid-term drinking, now to 2012.

1996

Dry White★★★★ Sauternes★★★★★ A very favourable crop and larger than usual. In fact, this vintage was possibly even more successful for the whites than for the reds. A long and slow ripening occurred as a result of fluctuating weather patterns during the growing season. This produced wines with wonderful aromas and fine structure.

The dry whites marked the onset of vintage, starting with Sauvignon Blanc on September 12. Luckily most had picked before the rains, but the harvest was still difficult. The majority had to be hand-harvested, with much sorting required. Sémillon had a less consistent vintage, with very powerful wines made in the north and softer styles in the south. The result, when blended with the austere and highly aromatic Sauvignon Blanc, are wines of great finesse and longevity.

In Sauternes botrytis was slow to start on the sugar-rich grapes. It first appeared towards the end of August on Sauvignon Blanc which necessitated some thinning as some grapes shrivelled to dryness before harvesting began. The first two *tries* were difficult due to the September rain. However, the third *trie* on October 4 (Château d'Yquem's first) and fourth *trie*, after a final burst of botrytis on October 17, were picked in perfect conditions. These are the most concentrated and pure wines of the past six years for the majority of Bordeaux's sweet wine producers.

The best white Graves from the Pessac-Léognan appellation are still drinking well. The Sauternes are richly constituted, the top châteaux probably reaching their fullest expression between 2010 to 2020.

1995

Dry white★★★★ Sauternes★★★★ The growing conditions throughout the
year benefited both dry and sweet wines, with yields increased by twenty-two
per cent over 1994. Vintage started early on August 28 and the dry wines were
mostly harvested by September 4 before the onset of rain in the second week.
Excellent wines were made with aromatic Sauvignon Blanc and full, ripe
Sémillon. This resulted in robust, perfumed styles with great structure and
more balanced acidity than the 1994s.

The sweet wines were blessed with an Indian summer, the rain in early
September being followed by warm weather well into October. Some châteaux
proprietors took small first *tries* between September 6 and 13 before the rain
started. By September 20 the rains had well and truly ceased; three quarters of
the crop remained on the vine and botrytis spread rapidly. The grapes ripened
quickly and there was an urgency to start picking. Harvest finished in record
time by the second week of October. The resulting wines were fat, yet soft and
clean, with heavy floral aromas and the honeyed overtones of botrytis.

*All the dry whites should have been consumed by now except for top châteaux like
Haut-Brion blanc and Laville Haut-Brion. Sauternes, despite being temptingly
delicious when first tasted are of four rather than five-star quality, though the best will
benefit from further bottle-age.*

1994

Dry white★★★★ Sauternes★★ Despite April frosts, the conditions during
the growing season in Bordeaux were highly favourable for the dry whites
as most of the grapes were harvested before the rains hit the region mid-
September. The must from fat, aromatic Sauvignon Blanc and Muscadelle
grapes was of very high quality. Sémillon vines had much larger bunches
and took distinctly longer to ripen. Good, yet soft wine was the result, perfect
for blending with the more assertive Sauvignon Blanc.

Unfortunately the sweet wines from Sauternes and Barsac were affected
by wet weather conditions. Their hazardous and prolonged harvest had to be
postponed as the first selective picking was due to start just before the rains
fell. However, the Sémillon grapes did have a good chance of developing
noble rot if the weather cleared (which it ultimately did), but not without the
risk of deteriorating in the meantime. The properties that harvested well into
October (as late as October 17) obtained the best results. Selection was crucial
for the finer wines though the general quality of the musts was high – grapey
and aromatic. As in the rest of the region the yields were severely reduced.

*Dry white: with the exception of top wines – drink soon. Sauternes: largely
disappointing. Drink soon.*

1993

Dry white★★★ Sauternes~ In spite of the heavy rains that affected the
region so dramatically, the production of dry white wines was comparatively
successful. The harvest for these wines officially began on September 10 and
the arrival of the rains resulted in the grapes being brought in very swiftly.
The harvest was twenty per cent smaller than 1992 and the resultant wines
were generally well-made, fresh, nicely balanced, and developed quickly.

However, mid-autumn wet weather was disastrous for grapes in the
Sauternes and Barsac districts, one of the worst ever vintages for these
great sweet wines. Beneficial botrytis scarcely appeared, black rot dominated.

Passable wines were made by growers who delayed picking until the weather finally picked up. Some de-classified.

Dry whites: drink up. Sauternes: sadly, a disaster. Some of the worst I have ever encountered, entirely due to the adverse weather conditions. Tread carefully!

1992

Dry white★★★ Sauternes★ Despite the enormous amount of rainfall and lack of sunshine, the few successes of this disastrous year were white wines. For dry white wines Sauvignon Blanc and Sémillon were harvested in the first two weeks of September, before the deluge that hit the red wine harvest later in the month. The plentiful results were light, fresh, and fruity, with elegant, balanced acidity, and an important commercial success after 1991's reduced harvest.

Almost disastrous in Sauternes. Very few sweet wines of any real quality due to lack of sunshine, and the cold, damp conditions which hampered development of botrytis. The wine of Château d'Yquem was declassified.

Dry white: drink up. Sauternes: give them a miss.

1991

Dry white★★ Sauternes★ Graves and Sauternes regions were even worse affected by the severe April frosts than the red wine districts to the north and east. It was a wet summer – August was particularly afflicted by heavy rain: 304 mm (12 in) in one and a half hours. Well-drained vineyards were least affected.

September was better, with exceptional heat on September 21, yet within a week the temperature had dropped to 10°C (50°F). The dry white harvest began on September 15 and those who picked early did best, though the crop was a fraction of normal. It then rained for eight days prior to the vintage in Sauternes. Due to the onset of rot, both noble and ignoble, picking in Sauternes was the earliest in recent years, ending by October 17. The problem was sorting grey from noble rot. Yields were severely reduced.

Avoid.

1990

Dry white★★★★★ Sauternes★★★★★ An excellent year, possibly the best sweet whites of the 1988, 1989, 1990 trio. The dry whites were soft and agreeable. The winter was very mild and vines flowered early, encouraging hopes for an early harvest. Uneven temperatures prolonged flowering, however, but after May the summer was long and hot until the end of August. Overall the dry whites had a better balance of acidity and alcohol than the 1989 vintage and are more exciting than those of the two preceding years.

A remarkable year for Sauternes and Barsac. At first the dry summer encouraged fears that there would be no botrytis, but the rainfall in August and September produced perfect conditions for the noble rot and botrytis appeared surprisingly early, developing exceptionally fast. Sugar levels were the highest since 1929 making vinification particularly difficult, the danger of volatile acidity being ever-present. The resulting wines, however, are superb.

The top dry whites still superb. Great Sauternes with an indefinite future.

1989

Dry white★★★★★ Sauternes★★★★★ The extreme heat this year resulted in very advanced growth. The vines flowered in May and picking in Graves began as early as the end of August. An abundant crop was harvested.

For dry wines, those winemakers who picked early, having anticipated low acidity and high sugar levels as a result of the heat, made impressive dry wines with a crisp finish. One of the most superlative-ever years for the two first growths, Château Haut-Brion *blanc* and Laville-Haut-Brion. By September the heat had given way to mild, misty weather, ideal for the development of botrytis. These are amongst the best Sauternes of the decade, and possibly of many previous decades.

Minor dry whites drink up, great Graves to 2010. Lesser sweet whites drink now, classed-growth Sauternes from now to 2025.

1988

Dry white★★★ Sauternes★★★★ A hot, dry summer was followed by a wet, humid, and ultimately stormy September, then an Indian summer. The hot summer benefited the dry whites and those who picked before the storms produced some good wines. The early autumn climate encouraged the spread of noble rot and provided ideal harvesting conditions for the sweet wines. Clearly an outstanding vintage for Barsac and Sauternes.

Dry white: don't wait. Sauternes now to 2015.

1987

Dry white★★ Sauternes★ A year of uneven quality. A cool spring resulted in an uneven flowering. The summer, though, was generally warm and dry, providing good conditions for the production of light, fresh, fruity dry white wines suitable for early drinking.

Much Sauternes production was marred by heavy storms in early October. Those estates where harvesting took place before the storms, with grapes affected by botrytis, produced some passable wines. But overall, not a good sweet wine vintage.

Drink up.

1986

Dry white★★★ Sauternes★★▷★★★★ An attractive and abundant year for dry white Bordeaux and another classic year for Sauternes. A good spring and a very successful flowering were followed by a perfect summer.

Heavy rains from mid-September, then humid, misty weather, unsuitable for high quality dry whites, better for the development of botrytis. The grapes were too diluted to make quality dry white wine at Château Haut-Brion. The Sauternes harvest took place in drier weather and a substantial quantity of grapes was brought in before the rains returned on October 19.

Dry white: drink up. Sauternes variable. Drink soon.

1985

Dry white★★★▷★★★★ Sauternes★★★ After a very harsh winter the weather improved and was fine and dry throughout the spring, summer, and autumn; September was one of the driest on record. The climate, providing such excellent conditions for the red wines, was not so kind to the whites. Many of the lesser dry whites lacked acidity and were rather clumsy, but the wines of the top châteaux benefited from bottle-age.

In Sauternes the drought resulted in highly concentrated sugar levels but insufficient moisture to encourage the development of noble rot. However, the

harvest took place in ideal conditions from October 1 and those who prolonged picking managed to make some very good wines.
Dry whites drink up. Sauternes at peak.

1984

Dry white~ Sauternes★★ Erratic weather patterns early in the year resulted in uneven flowering. Summer was fine, but heavy rainfall interrupted the harvest. Some light dry whites for early drinking, though most were unripe and acidic, lacking grace. The effects of hurricane Hortense in early October were, to some extent, dissipated by two weeks of windy weather which dried out the vines. Sauternes started their harvest on October 15 and managed to produce some passable botrytis-affected wines.
Dry white: avoid. Sauternes: drink up.

1983

Dry white★★★★ Sauternes★★★★★ The dry whites were lovely, stylish wines with good levels of acidity. Excellent and abundant Sauternes: beautifully balanced wines with great concentration of fruit. Certainly the best between 1975 and 1989. After a wet spring, conditions were hot and dry in June and July. Rain in August and early September caused anxiety for some, but misty mornings and fine, warm days were perfect for the development of good levels of botrytis in Sauternes which began there on September 29.
The top dry whites fully developed and still drinking well. Sauternes: perfection now and will continue to please well into the present century.

1982

Dry white★★★ Sauternes★★ A year which produced white wines of good quality, but not of the stature of the outstanding red Bordeaux. The vines flowered and grapes ripened fully under perfect conditions, perhaps too perfect for the dry whites which, though pleasant, lacked acidity. Moreover, botrytis forming in Sauternes was completely washed away by three weeks of torrential rain towards the end of September. The wines were sweet but, like the 1970 Sauternes, lack "golden" botrytis.
Dry white: drink up; Sauternes variable: drink soon.

1981

Dry white★★▷★★★ Sauternes★★★ Ideal weather conditions for dry whites and Sauternes. A hot, dry summer produced healthy, ripe grapes; autumn rainfall then encouraged botrytis development and harvesting took place between October 5 and November 13 during an Indian summer. Many attractive, elegant Sauternes: better than the 1982s but by no means great.
Dry white: should have been drunk. Sauternes: mostly at peak.

1980

Dry white★ Sauternes★ An average vintage. Cold, dismal weather early in the year resulted in a poor flowering. Conditions improved with a hot, dry August, but the weather broke, September being cold and wet. The dry whites were insubstantial but the Sauternes were saved by sunny weather at the end of October/early November; some quite pleasant wines.
Drink up.

1979

> **Dry white★★★ Sauternes★★★** A wet winter led to a cold spring and
> summer, a fine June provided good flowering conditions. A slightly larger
> than average crop was harvested, showers prevailing throughout. For
> Sauternes a late harvest with botrytis. Not an exciting year.
> *Drink up*

1978

> **Dry White★★★★ Sauternes★★** The long, sunny autumn which
> followed the cold spring and wet summer ripened the grapes and resulted
> in good quality wine full of alcohol and extract. Firm, long-lasting dry
> whites. However, due to the absence of botrytis, the sweet wines lack
> real character.
> *Top dry whites still at peak; Sauternes: drink up .*

1977

> **Dry white~ Sauternes~** The result of a cold summer and the driest September
> on record. A small crop of poor wines.
> *Avoid.*

1976

> **Dry white★★★ Sauternes★★★★** The year of excessive heat and drought;
> ripe grapes were harvested in late September. The dry wines, with the exception
> of those from Graves, were low in acidity, needing to be drunk quickly; the
> sweet wines show great style and opulence but will probably be overtaken by
> the 1975s.
> *Dry white: over-mature. Sauternes: very attractive but passing peak.*

1975

> **Dry white★★★★ Sauternes★★★★★** Spring frosts, then a hot, dry summer
> with some welcome rain in September and good harvest conditions overall.
> The top Graves châteaux made excellent wines. Perfect wines from Sauternes,
> well-constituted and firm.
> *Some of the top dry whites still drinking surprisingly well. The best Sauternes should
> keep indefinitely, all are lovely now.*

1974

> **Dry white~ Sauternes★** Miserable harvest weather resulted in mediocre
> Graves and poor sweet wines, Barsacs best.
> *Drink up, if at all.*

1973

> **Dry white★★ Sauternes★★** In common with reds: inoffensive, unimpressive,
> light wines. The better Sauternes quite good.
> *Drink up.*

1972

> **Dry white~ Sauternes★** A dreary vintage: many Sauternes were declassified,
> though some not bad.
> *Avoid.*

1971

Dry white★★★★★ Sauternes★★★★★ The best vintage of the decade. After a late spring and slow flowering, hopes were lifted by a pleasant, sunny summer and well-nigh ideal ripening conditions. There was botrytis on the grapes in Sauternes for the harvest which commenced early October.
Dry white: top châteaux still at peak. Sauternes: perfection now but with an almost indefinite life.

1970

Dry white★★ Sauternes★★★ These wines enjoy a good but, in my opinion, not entirely deserved reputation. Ripe grapes producing wines more generous in alcohol than acidity. In Sauternes an Indian summer further ripened the grapes but inhibited the development of botrytis. A bit four-square, lacking colour and zest.
Dry white: drink up. Sauternes: drink soon.

1969

Dry white★★ Sauternes★▷★★ A poor year; the damage was done during the wet spring, with poor flowering conditions. The white grapes in Graves were unripe and acidic but in Sauternes growers were just saved by an Indian summer. On the whole, rather skinny, short-lived dry wines with high fixed acidity, and variable quality Sauternes.
Drink up.

1968

Dry white~ Sauternes~ A miserable spring and summer: cold, wet, and sunless. Sauternes wholly declassified.
Avoid.

1967

Dry white★▷★★★ Sauternes★★★★★ After a late flowering, a hot dry summer and wet September, the grapes for the dry whites were somewhat unripe and acidic. However, in Sauternes the harvest began on September 27 in sunny conditions, resulting in well-structured wines of breeding, good proportion, and quality of flesh that gives richness and shape. A classic Sauternes vintage.
Dry white: with one or two exceptions (Château La Louvière still excellent) drink up. Sauternes: perfection now but all will keep. The top two of the vintage, Châteaux d'Yquem and Suduiraut, will keep indefinitely.

1966

Dry white★★★ Sauternes★★★ A cool, dry summer with no real heat until September. Both dry and sweet wines had a lean, firm, sinewy character and fairly high acidity.
The best Graves passing peak. Sauternes, though fragrant, lack flesh. Drink up.

1965

Dry white~ Sauternes~ Appalling weather conditions; a tiny crop of rotten grapes. Thin, over-acidic wines.
Avoid.

1964

Dry white~ **Sauternes~** A promising year, hot summer, ripe grapes. Early picking saved the dry whites but many lacked acidity and balance. Torrential rain ruined the Sauternes harvest.
Drink up.

1963

Dry white~ **Sauternes~** An abysmal vintage. The first of three disastrous years in Sauternes: little wine made.
Avoid.

1962

Dry white★★★★ **Sauternes★★★★** A fine summer with some rain. Good and firm dry whites. A classic vintage for Sauternes. The harvest began on October 1. An abundant crop. Well-balanced, long-lasting, elegant wines.
Dry white: the best still very good if you like Graves with bottle-age. Sauternes now beautifully mature, better than 1961s.

1961

Dry white★★★★ **Sauternes★★★** A small crop of stylish wines, but not of a comparable quality to the majestic reds. After poor flowering conditions reduced the potential size of the crop, an August drought and sunny September further pruned the yield. The Graves, picked early, had good acidity. In Sauternes the wines did not have the lusciousness of a great vintage, but nevertheless retain good shape and flavour.
Top Graves: interesting. Sauternes: drink soon.

1960

Dry white★ **Sauternes★** A good spring, but cold, wet summer. Graves better than Sauternes.
Avoid.

1959

Dry white★★★★ **Sauternes★★★★★** Good but somewhat solid Graves, lacking a little acidity. However, in Sauternes a monumental, heavyweight classic vintage. A long, hot summer with some rain just before the harvest, which started in good conditions on September 21. The grapes had a high sugar content, producing rich, powerful, massively constituted wines.
Sauternes: perfection now but will continue for many years.

1958

Dry white★ **Sauternes★★** Good summer, late harvest.
Of little interest now. Drink up.

1957

Dry white★★ **Sauternes★★★** A good spring, followed by perverse weather patterns – the coldest summer and hottest October on record – with variable results. The Graves very dry and acidic. Sauternes somewhat better: clean-cut wines with refreshing acidity, but lacking flesh.
Dry white: avoid. Sauternes: drink up.

1956

Dry white~ Sauternes~ Bad weather conditions at critical times, except for a brief improvement in time for picking; a poor, ill-balanced year.
Avoid.

1955

Dry white★★★★ Sauternes★★★★★ A classic combination of influences produced a great and abundant vintage for white Bordeaux. A fine July, hot and dry August made well-balanced dry whites, the best of the decade. Some beneficial September rain led to an early harvest in Sauternes on September 21, and to a dry October. Well-nigh perfect for Sauternes.
Dry whites: well past their best. Sauternes: at their peak of perfection.

1954

Dry white★ Sauternes~ A dismal, damp, and cold summer. Watery, ill-knit wines. Graves passable, Sauternes a wash-out.
Avoid.

1953

Dry white★★★ Sauternes★★★★ An outstanding August and wet September. Picking in Sauternes from September 28 in perfect weather. The dry wines pleasant, ripe, perhaps lacking acidity. Sauternes almost perfect, making up in finesse what they lack in weight.
Sauternes: drinking beautifully; most at peak, best will keep.

1952

Dry white★★★ Sauternes★★★ Well-balanced dry whites. Classic Graves. Barsac more successful than Sauternes: particularly attractive, rich, crisp wines. Hail completely destroyed the crop at Château d'Yquem.
Drink up.

1951

Dry white~ Sauternes~ An atrocious vintage. Yquem not made.
Happily few, if any, to be found.

1950

Dry white★★ Sauternes★★★ A better year for whites than reds. In Sauternes the harvest started in damp weather but developed into an Indian summer which ripened the grapes. Some very good sweet wines were made.
Sauternes: some extremely good wines showing few signs of fatigue; nevertheless, drink soon.

1949

Dry white★★★★ Sauternes★★★★★ A classic vintage with breeding and style. The crop was less abundant than in 1947 and less concentrated than the 1945s. In Sauternes harvest began on September 27 and continued into the driest October on record. Good botrytis.
Dry white: the top Graves still exciting to drink though deepening in colour, with ripe, honeyed bouquet. Sauternes: if well kept, superb.

1948

Dry white★★ Sauternes★★ A good though never popular year, rarely seen now. Sauternes not bad but on the lean side.
Drink up.

1947

Dry white★★★ Sauternes★★★★★ Despite the hot summer a good Graves vintage. A great year too for Sauternes, the harvest beginning early, on September 15, in intense heat.
Dry white: a few top wines, notably Château Laville-Haut-Brion, drinking well though untypically rich and honeyed. Sauternes: superb; rich wines still at peak.

1946

Dry white★ Sauternes★ A poor summer with wines to match. Sauternes saved by an extremely hot October. Rarely seen.
Hardly an option: neither dry nor sweet exist now.

1945

Dry white★★★★★ Sauternes★★★★★ The potential crop severely reduced by spring frosts. Hail, then a drought summer. An early harvest, beginning on September 10, produced small, ripe, concentrated grapes. A first-class classic vintage.
Dry white: firm, dry, well-constituted; very scarce, can still be excellent. Sauternes: rare, firm, and refined; drying out a little but perfect still.

1944

Dry white★★ Sauternes★★★★ Despite high hopes, a light and uneven vintage. Some very good Sauternes.
Sauternes: surprisingly good though rarely seen; drink up.

1943

Dry white★★★★★ Sauternes★★★★ A rich, vigorous, well-bred year. Sauternes now drying out a little.
Sauternes: the best still drinking well.

1942

Dry white★★★ Sauternes★★★★ Very rich, long-lasting wines with finesse and bouquet. Château d'Yquem was a great surprise.
Many dry whites still drinkable. Sauternes delightful.

1941

Dry white★★ Sauternes~ Poor vintage: lean acidic wines.
Drink up.

1940

Dry white★★★ Sauternes★ Rarely seen, indifferent vintage.

1939

Dry white★★ Sauternes★★★ Quite a good year generally.
Drink up.

1938

Dry white★★ Sauternes★★ A mediocre year, suffered wartime neglect.
Rarely seen.

1937

Dry white★★★★ Sauternes★★★★★ The high acidity, which sadly
spoiled the reds, produced long-lasting, crisp, dry whites. Classic Sauternes.
Dry whites now over the top. Best Sauternes are still superb.

1936

Dry white★ Sauternes★★ A mediocre, uneven year.
Rarely seen. Drink up.

1935

Dry white★★★ Sauternes★★★ A reasonably good vintage. Wines were
bottled just before the war and have rarely been seen since.
Château-Laville-Haut Brion and some Sauternes still good.

1934

Dry white★★★★ Sauternes★★★★ The second-best vintage of the decade.
The dry wines past best though interesting. The sweet wines delicious.

1933

Dry white★★★ Sauternes★ Not a great year for Sauternes.
Good Graves can surprise.

1932

Dry white~ Sauternes~ A disastrous year.

1931

Dry white~ Sauternes~ A poor year and worse market. Château d'Yquem
just drinkable.

1930

Dry white~ Sauternes~ A disastrous year.

1920s

1929 Dry white★★★★ Sauternes★★★★★ A consistently good, luscious
vintage; the best Sauternes since 1921. A particularly great vintage for Château
Climens. Superb wines.
Some dry whites good if well kept; Sauternes drinking beautifully.
1928 Dry white★★★★★ Sauternes★★★★ Firm, distinguished wines which
held well. Arguably, the best vintage of the century for the dry whites. Sauternes
totally different in style to the 1929: crisper, paler, and less luscious but with
better acidity.
Some top Graves good despite bottle-age; Sauternes superb.
1927 Dry white~ Sauternes★★★ The terrible reds and dry whites of this year
tarnished the Sauternes' reputation, which had benefited from late autumn sun.
Rarely seen. Sauternes can still be quite good.
1926 Dry white★★★★ Sauternes★★★★ A very good vintage.
Now drying out.

1920 to 1925 Sauternes only

1925~ poor year. **1924★★★** ripe attractive wines, which can still be very good. **1923★★★** a moderate, pleasant year, now drying out; and **1922★** a fairly early harvest of abundant grapes and wines which were light, but lacking quality. **1921★★★★★** an exceptionally hot summer which produced outstanding whites in all the European wine districts; arguably the greatest ever vintage of Château d'Yquem: deep-coloured, massively constituted wine, and, if well kept, still superb. **1920★★★** also a good vintage, though overshadowed by the 1921s: variable, some still drinking well.

1910s Sauternes

1919★★ variable; drink up. **1918★★** a fairly good year, the wines were firmer than those of the previous vintage. **1917★★** softer and riper than 1916, but not for long-keeping. **1916★** a difficult vintage, now rarely seen. **1915~** disastrous. **1914★★★** surprisingly good still, some drying out. **1913★★** drying out. **1912★** not bad. **1911★** at best fading but sound. **1910~** never seen.

1900s Sauternes

1909★★★★ a wonderful vintage; still drinking well if in top condition. **1908~. 1907★. 1906★★★★★** a classic Sauternes vintage; can still be superb. **1905★★.1904★★★★** a great vintage; powerful wines which can still be delicious. **1901 to 03~** not very good and rarely seen. **1900★★★★** a classic vintage; still rich, powerful wines.

Pre-1900 Sauternes

1899★★★★ not quite as sturdy as the 1900, now variable. **1896★★★★** an excellent vintage; **1895 to 94~. 1893★★★★★** an extremely hot summer; heavyweight wines, can still be very good. **1875★★★★★. 1871 to 72★★★★. 1869, 1865 to 64** all **★★★★★** and can still be fabulous.

Burgundy

Burgundy's heart, the Côte d'Or, occupies the lower slopes of an escarpment facing southeast across the broad valley of the Saône. A relatively small strip of vineyards, its soil, vinestocks, and climate differ completely from those of its major "competitor" Bordeaux. Of the quality factors and influences here, what the Burgundians call *climat* is crucial, embracing soil, subsoil, aspect, drainage, and microclimate. Because of multi-ownerships of vineyards the individual winemaker's approach and ability is also of fundamental importance. But above all, as elsewhere, the weather is the great dictator.

The Burgundy region is particularly susceptible to spring frosts and severe summer hailstorms which, though localized, can cause considerable damage to the grapes and taint the wine – at worst, stripping the vines of their leaves, grapes, and branches. Otherwise the usual weather variations occur throughout the growing season, producing distinctive patterns of character and quality in the wines.

RED BURGUNDY

The Côte de Nuits, at the top end of the Côte d'Or, is the most northerly of the great French classic red wine districts, producing at its best, well-coloured, well-structured wines capable of long life. Those of the Côte de Beaune are perhaps looser knit, broader – some, like the Volnays, with a certain delicacy. Continuing further to the south, the red wines of Mâconnais are modest and for quick drinking, whilst those of Beaujolais have a character and life all of their own, mainly due to the Gamay grape, partly to the different soils of this hillier area, the most southerly part being not far distant from Lyon and the upper Rhône Valley vineyards. Although most Beaujolais is produced to be quaffed young, within a year, even within months of the vintage, those made in the old-fashioned way have remarkable depth and staying power.

Classic red burgundy, however, is made only from the Pinot Noir grape and achieves its apotheosis in the famous village districts of the Côte d'Or.

WHITE BURGUNDY

Arguably the most successful, the most admired dry whites of the world. Demand exceeding supply, prices tend to be high. Nevertheless, made from the Chardonnay, the best white burgundies provide the yardstick against which the wines made from this now ubiquitous grape are matched.

Again, the heart of white burgundy is the Côte d'Or, this time the Côte de Beaune, where Meursault, the Pulignys, and the great Montrachet vineyard produce archetypal wines. Then there is Chablis, well to the north, halfway to Paris, with its classic, steely, bone dry whites – though in recent years more fruity and more oaky wines are emerging. To the south, the white Mâconnais and Chalonnaise wines are light, dry, and usually good value: Montagny, Rully, and Pouilly, of which Fuissé is the best known. All but the top Côte de Beaune whites should be consumed within one to four years after the vintage, good Meursault and Puligny-Montrachet from, say, three to six years, the bigger whites like Corton-Charlemagne and Bâtard-Montrachet from five to twelve years, and the scarce and concentrated Le Montrachet, of a good vintage, up to twenty years.

2002

Generally speaking, a relatively untroubled vintage. Most of Burgundy escaped the worst of the year's capricious weather with hardly any rain, making the vines easy to work and allowing the grapes to ripen. Fine weather in May and early June prompted early and successful flowering. Some areas experienced changeable weather conditions with too much heat at one time and too much rain at another, which stressed the grapes. July was cool and damp, and August saw dramatic swings in temperature, from lower to higher than normal. Dry conditions until early September, when some rain gave rise to early signs of rot, causing some anxiety and necessitating rigorous selection. The skies soon cleared and dry, mild, and sunny days and cool nights prevailed for the rest of the month, giving well-balanced, healthy fruit. Harvest dates spread throughout September, with the Côte Chalonnaise beginning as early as September 12. Most winemakers waited to pick until later in the month, making the most of the good weather.

Red★★★★ The lower than normal rainfall and deliberately restricted yields resulted in a smaller than usual vintage. Overall, however, the grapes were in excellent condition, despite the threat of rot in early September. Sugar levels were high and tannins ripe and well-structured. The maturity of the Pinot Noir in some regions, particularly Pommard and Volnay, was exceptional.

White★★★★ Chardonnay had low yields and rich sugar levels, with good acidity. The white wines are heady and intense, richly fragrant in their blend of fruit and mineral components, and express competently their respective terroirs. This vintage is comparable to 1990 or 1992.

Though not in the same class as 1999, an attractive vintage. The best reds have good keeping potential. The lesser whites are delicious, the leading Côte de Beaune whites, though drinkable now, will benefit from another two or three years bottle-ageing.

2001

Overall a disappointing vintage of small and inconsistent quality. Top vineyards produced clean, ripe fruit, but others were adversely affected by the changeable September weather. The key to success was hard work in the vineyard and at the *triage* stage. In Beaune ideal conditions prevailed until late May with early bud-break. Frost in early June lasted a week causing uneven flowering and fruit set, and much of the early growth had to be pruned. April frosts further hampered development, resulting in irregular ripeness. July warmed up towards the end and August was hot with violent hailstorms that caused considerable localized damage south of Beaune. Grapes were, however, picked in good condition in fine September weather. In the Côte de Nuits a cold and unsettled early September prevented the ravages of rot, but necessitated chaptalization and a severe *triage*. In the Côte d'Or and Côte Chalonnaise flowering started early, proceeding slowly but evenly; however humidity and the rain promoted mildew and *millerandage*, reducing the size of the final crop. In the Mâconnais and Beaujolais, a mild winter was followed by the wettest March on record (128.6 mm/5.1 in). July was challenging with outbreaks of mildew. Exceedingly cold and wet weather prevailed in September, and the *ban des vendanges*, which was set for September 6, took place in poor weather.

Chablis had a mild and wet winter and more rain in March, breaking the region's rainfall records. Some frost caused minor losses throughout the region on April 12 and 13 . A late flowering, which started on June 12 under fine conditions, lasting four weeks, and a bountiful quantity of fruit on the vines put back further the already late harvest. July was cool and storms and high humidity in early August caused sporadic outbreaks of mildew.

Red★★ Where yields were kept in check and healthy grapes maintained, the wines were well structured with good acidity, without being overripe. The reds are brightly coloured with firm acidity and tannins and well-defined fruit.

White★★ The crucial first weeks of September were cool and wet, diluting the sugars and acidity. Despite fine weather during the harvest, the damage had been done and late attacks of grey rot made things worse.

For me, the stars of the vintage are the village Beaujolais, drinking perfectly at the time of writing (Spring 2003) but doubtless remaining fresh and flavoury for a couple more years. Also the best whites of the Maconnais and Chalonnaise offer exceptional value for early drinking. The Côte de Beaune whites are soft and easy, not for keeping; the reds from the Côte d'Or make pleasant mid-term drinking.

2000

Growing conditions and weather patterns differed dramatically from one commune to the other, and sometimes even within a commune, but overall, an early spring led to a quick, uniform flowering, in turn heralding an early and substantial harvest. July was miserable with more than twenty days of rain; it was also one of the coolest ever recorded. Early September was sunnier, warmer, and drier than usual, until the storm on the 12th, which struck south of Beaune. Fortunately damage was localized and the Côte de Nuits was spared. A few more showers followed but after them the weather improved. However, 2000 was a disaster for growers who had not controlled their crop size and who suffered the full effects of the September rains, which severely hampered ripening and exacerbated rot, affecting the fragile Pinot Noirs especially. Colours were sometimes difficult to extract and flavours lacking, necessitating *triage* and *saignée* (or "bleeding") for a more satisfactory solid-to-liquid ratio.

Red★★★ In the Côte d'Or the vintage was progressively better from south to north. Volnays and Pommards better than Santenays, Savignys better still. The Côte de Nuits was more successful, with Gevrey-Chambertin the best of all.

White★★★★ The finest vintage for white Burgundy since 1996 despite a strenuous growing season and harvest. Chardonnay suffered some rot attack but the grape's thicker skin and other advantages (fine wines can be made from large quantities by top estates) helped to produce wines of finesse, elegance, and mineral purity. 2000 is a fine vintage for Chablis.

Lesser whites for early drinking though the best will benefit from bottle-ageing. Reds distinctly variable and should be drunk whilst the excellent 1999s are maturing.

1999

Dame Fortune has smiled on Burgundy; scarcely a poor vintage since 1984. In 1999, a generous harvest of high quality, probably the biggest ever. Weather conditions were generally favourable, with an early start; higher temperatures from mid-March encouraged swelling of buds, and it was warmer still in early April leading to good fruit set. There was some hail but it was with rain, so the vines escaped damage. Mid-May was cool and rainy. Despite later warmth, humidity persisted with early mildew to be combated. Chardonnay flowering began at the end of May, then Pinot Noir. Between June 2 and 14 flowering was regular despite some rain, occurring earlier and more evenly in the Côte de Beaune. It was a busy in the vineyards: trimming, disbudding, and spraying.

Mid-June was cooler, the rest of the summer alternating heat and mainly beneficial rain. *Véraison* took place end July to early August. The end of August and first two weeks of September were hot, with some timely rain on September 4–6. Thanks to sunny conditions there were record levels of maturity, high sugar levels for Chardonnay, averaging 180g/l and tartaric acid at 7.5g/l, both levels the highest at the start of harvest for ten years. In the Côte de Beaune, Pinot Noir in one vineyard achieved a sugar level of 230g/l. However, rain returned around September 18/19 and cooler weather persisted. Nevertheless, grapes were exceptionally ripe and healthy, and scrupulous growers who engaged in *vendanges en vert* (crop thinning), prior to *véraison*, vinified excellent grapes. Overall a huge crop.

Red★★★★★ at best. The red wines have good colour and luscious fruit, full-bodied with fine tannins. The vintage favoured early pickers and those who did not overcrop have made some fabulous wines. Others are attractive, with pleasant fruit but perhaps lack concentration.

White★★★★ The best have balance, freshness, and good acidity, all good keeping qualities.

Top quality whites for drinking now to 2008, the grands crus even longer; the finest reds from 2006 to 2020.

1998

Who would be a *vigneron*? 1998 had, unquestionably, a difficult growing season with severe frosts, hail damage, *oidium*, sunburnt grapes, and rot. Yet, some extremely good wines were made, both red and white, though volume was down. The winter of 1997/8 was wet but relatively mild with brief cold spells in January and February. Buds sprouted towards the end of March but there were widespread frosts over the Easter weekend. Chardonnay was, in the south Mâconnais, severely affected with temperatures dropping to -2°C (28°F) on April 14. Most unusually the frosts hit the lower slopes of the Côte d'Or, particularly affected being the *premier cru* whites, Meursault, Puligny, and Chassagne, and, even rarer, some of the *grand cru* sites of the Côte de Nuits, particularly of Gevrey. Little damage was done in Chablis as the vines were less advanced.

The rest of April was unhelpful but from early May the change to steady sun and higher temperatures resulted in an explosion of growth. Yet there were some storms, and Chablis' old enemy, hail, on May 14. Although flowering started early, as in 1996 and 1997, it was less even and spread over three weeks. By June 5 it was well underway in the Côte d'Or but the second week was cool, *oidium* appearing. Clusters and berries were small. Mid-June was warm and favourable. July started with a severe hailstorm in the Mâconnais on the 2nd, and the following day in the south Côte de Beaune, spells of cool and very hot weather followed, with temperatures reaching 38°C (100°F) on the 14th. A second heat-wave followed in August: the first week was over 30°C (86°F). Although there were no drought problems, the dryness and heat stressed the vines and singed the grapes. The first two weeks of September produced welcome rain, the sun returning on the 16th for a week – then rain again. Thanks to the summer heat, the grapes were ripe and, despite the rain, in surprisingly good health without mildew at harvest time which in the south started September 10 (Mâconnais) and in Chablis to the north on the 25th, early for that district.

Red★★★★ Ranging from good to great, the best have a good deep colour, supple tannins, good balance of alcohol, and acidity.

White★★★★ The phrase which seems to fit is pure and classic. The wines have good balance of varietal character, elegance, and good acidity, Chablis being particularly aromatic. Some producers in the Côte de Beaune think their whites superior to 1997. Some are concentrated but yields greatly reduced.

White Maconnais, Chalonnaise, and lesser Chablis drink now. Classic white burgundies for mid-term drinking, the grand cru *whites long living. All the top reds tend to have a tannic masculinity which demands bottle-ageing; even the respectable shippers' wines have a good future.*

1997

The third success in a row for this region, even in the face of a particularly variable year. The most important factor was lots of sunshine at the important times. Warm and dry conditions just before bud-break brought early development. Fears of a late frost were forgotten as the weather stayed fine for flowering also. Unfortunately, late June and July became unusually cold and wet which caused some flowering irregularities though *véraison* was ten days earlier than in 1996. By August it was hot, with some humidity and virtually no rainfall. This continued into September when a little rain occurred but obligingly stopped before the majority started to harvest.

Beaujolais commenced picking on August 31 – the earliest start many could remember. By September 13 the entire Côte d'Or had started to pick and Chablis followed on September 25. Unusually, the Pinot Noir had ripened before Chardonnay, but suffered a drop in yields due to poor fruit set. Total yields were down by thirteen per cent against 1996.

Red★★★★ Grapes reached exceedingly high maturity levels – so much so that chaptalization was redundant and some producers had to ask permission to exceed the usual alcohol levels. Results were variable and quality focused on tannic structure, as natural acidity was below average. Perhaps not as consistent as in 1996, but in general very satisfactory wines, some glorious.

White★★★★★ Stunning results here. The white wines also showed incredible degrees of ripeness, balanced, but with lower than average (but acceptable) acidity levels. The wines of this vintage will be the ideal complement to the 1996s – perfect to drink while waiting for the latter to mature.

After justified criticism of overall quality in the 1970s, growers in Burgundy swallowed hard and took note. It has paid off, for connoisseurs are homing in on the superb wines made, albeit at a high price, by the top growers. Both fleshy whites and fruity reds will make good mid-term drinking, the latter probably at best between 2005 and 2010.

1996

A vintage of good quantity – yields were between five and ten per cent above that of 1995, and of even better quality. Very dry, rot-free conditions and a long, cool ripening season produced both Chardonnay and Pinot Noir with maturity levels which were higher than that of 1990. This meant that chaptalization was not required in most areas.

Winter was cool until early April and a wet May prevented frost problems. June arrived with a burst of warm weather, which brought a quick and even flowering one week earlier than usual. This continued with a long, cool summer. Sunny days ripened the grapes and a cooling north wind helped maintain acidity levels. Some experienced a little rain in August, but elsewhere drought conditions loomed. Uniform health reigned in the vineyards, while quantities looked large. Harvesting began in the latter part of September in bright and cool conditions, continuing smoothly into October.

Red★★★▷★★★★ For those who pruned prior to flowering or in late summer, generous, charming, and seductive wines were made, the best with great balance of ripe fruit, good acidity, and silky tannins. In some areas, the wines suffered from dilution due to the summer rain; others had high acidity and low tannins.

White★★★★★ These wines definitely made a mark in 1996. Concentrated fruit needs time. The grapes were picked while astoundingly ripe, with balanced acidity levels. In Chablis the results were phenomenal – the vintage of the century? Perfumed, racy, and less fat than the 1995s but holding immaculate constitution and great ageing capability. Overall the best are unusually concentrated and are benefiting from bottle-age.

Wonderful white burgundies best between now and 2010. Reds variable, somewhat hard, and needing more bottle-age, the best drinking beautifully between, say, 2006 and 2012.

1995

A temperamental growing season resulted in another smaller vintage, but one of high quality. A very mild winter preceded a cool March and a subsequent late bud-break around the middle of April. Then, unusually low temperatures brought frost and as producers took measures against this the result was a slow and irregular flowering. Some damage occurred and *millerandage* caused a drop in yields, but then a consequent increase in concentration and overall quality. A hot summer followed, resulting in a fast maturation and the first grapes being harvested for *crémant* on September 9. Rain in the first half of September brought fear of botrytis. However, a fresh and early close to the vintage, around September 28 in Chablis, proved satisfactory.

Red★★★★ The Côte de Nuits wines benefited from their later picking, avoiding the rain. Small, thick-skinned berries from low yields; long malolactic fermentation and firm tannins gave supple, round wines with good ageing possibilities.

White★★★★ Yields were down nearly thirty per cent, but a touch of botrytis gave further concentration and some super examples. Increased sugar levels and good acidity created rich yet fresh wines with well-balanced fruit – very similar traits to the wines of 1985.

The top whites can still be hard though most are delicious now. Firm reds, some with considerable power and depth, probably best between 2005 and 2015.

1994

A relatively small vintage, the result of fifteen days of frost following a mild winter. Growers to the north, in Chablis, had to contend with snow in addition to severe frost. This retarded what had been rapid development of the vines. Considerably more damage was done in the Yonne than in the Côte d'Or.

Once into May the temperatures rose to more healthy levels. Flowering took place in early June in favourable climatic conditions and the beginning of the harvest was planned provisionally for September 20. The hot weather continued through the summer and by the end of August the potential quality of the crop was considered very high. Because of this the harvest began earlier than expected in mid-September but was almost immediately halted by the rains. Rot became a threat to both Pinot Noir and Chardonnay at this stage though it could be isolated. By September 20 sunny weather returned and picking resumed. The harvest was completed in favourable conditions – considerable sunshine with gentle winds.

Red★▷★★★ Rigorous sorting and low yields resulted in wines with generous fresh fruit aromas, some relatively lean but fragrant.

White★★★ Complex, heady, fragrant wines with personality for keeping. Chablis had more reduced quantities than elsewhere.

Unlike Bordeaux, since 1990 Burgundy's reds have ranged from passably good to excellent. The 1994 reds are drinking quite well now. The whites are more variable but the best are glorious now, yet will keep well.

1993

The year began well after a mainly dry winter. The final fortnight of March was hot and prompted early budding. Flowering was successful and even, taking place a few days earlier than usual at the beginning of June. Spring and summer were warm and wet until August – perfect conditions for the formation of mildew and, consequently, the vines needed twice as much attention as necessary. On June 19/20 a violent storm struck the central part of the Côte de Beaune and hail fell over St Aubin, Blagny, Meursault, and the most eastern part of Puligny. This had a drastic effect on yields – more than halving them within some of the better *premier cru* sites in Meursault (most notably Perrières, Genevrières, and Charmes).

The weather in August cleared and warm, dry conditions assisted the ripening, but as the heat increased towards the end of the month, its effects on both red and white grapes were quite different. The reds benefited greatly from accelerated ripening and by the time the rain fell in mid-September they had developed healthy thick skins. Chardonnay in the *grands* and *premiers crus* ripened well and was in good health for picking before the rain. At other sites the vines became over-stressed due to lack of moisture, which blocked the sap and halted the ripening process. Rain at the beginning of September brought about recovery of these vines, enabling them to ripen further.

When the major rains started falling on September 22, the grapes were generally in good health. Pinot Noir was cleared first along with the *grands* and *premiers crus* whites (due to their better exposure). The rest of the Côte de Beaune was then harvested in wet conditions – cool and showery rather than heavy, continuous rain; fortunately rot posed few problems.

Red★★★★ Quality is good to high – well ripened, intense, and complex. Tannins are strong and well structured giving considerable ageing potential.

White★★▷★★★ Quality is better than expected. The very best come from the hail-damaged vines in the Côte de Beaune where yields were so dramatically reduced. Unfortunately, many of the more generic whites suffered from over-production and higher than average acidity. In contrast, the results in Chablis are distinctly more uniform and favourable.

Red burgundy far superior to Bordeaux. Most are drinking well now, rich, fragrant. Lesser whites from the Côte de Beaune and the south – drink up; better Chablis drinking quite well now, storm-surviving grands crus superb but will get even better.

1992

This vintage was a remarkable success given the almost disastrous results in other parts of France. The only significant rainfall during the harvest was a downpour on September 22 which had little effect on the overall results.

The winter and spring were exceptionally mild. Budding took place as normal, but the vines advanced swiftly towards an early flowering at the end of May and the beginning of June. In some areas, *coulure* and *millerandage* posed a threat because of the limited rainfall. The up side was that it provided a natural check on what was clearly going to be an enormous harvest.

By early summer, growth was advancing at a precocious rate – around fifteen to twenty days ahead of usual – and necessary rain was provided by mid-June. At the end of July, some of the better growers green-pruned to keep a further check on the size of the crop. Ripening took place under perfect conditions as the temperatures were high throughout August. By September, the vines were at the pinnacle of health.

Sunny conditions persisted over the Burgundy region virtually throughout the harvest. The Côtes de Beaune and Nuits started their harvests on September 12 and 18 respectively. The rain in the third week of the month only affected the lesser sites of the Côte de Nuits and parts of the Côte Chalonnaise, as by that late stage, the rest of the Côte d'Or had finished harvesting.

Red★★★▷★★★★ Full and supple with good berry aromas, but many are lacking the necessary concentration for ageing. Generally, the better wines come from the Côte de Beaune.

White★★★ Fat, well-rounded with complex ripe fruit. Acidity is a little low.

The "middle-class" Côte de Beaune reds are delicious now, the top Côte de Nuits need time. Whites drink soon.

1991

Just about anything deleterious that can occur during the growing season did occur: April in the Côte d'Or was warm, with early bud-burst. May was colder with frost hindering development. In Chablis, the owners of the top vineyards managed to take effective action but the lesser vineyards were quite badly frost-bitten, the yield being reduced to roughly a third of normal.

Cold weather continued in June, retarding flowering, and both *coulure* and *millerandage* further reduced the crop, as did localized hailstorms. Thereafter the summer was hot and dry though severe hail on August 22 cut a swathe through vineyards at the northern end of the Côte de Nuits. Then in late September, 51 mm (2 in) of rain fell on the nicely matured grapes, just before picking was due to commence. After this delay the harvest got underway, but a week later there was more heavy rain causing some dilution and rot problems. Those who managed to time their picking right harvested healthy, ripe grapes which had the added advantage of concentration due to the reduced crop size.

Red★★ Overshadowed by the 1990s and very variable in quality.

White★★ Also variable.

Drink up.

1990

Yet another successful year for Burgundy. Climatically similar to the previous year, yet many feel that this will rank alongside the very best vintages of the 1980s; others, including me, think it is streets ahead. The winter was unusually warm in all regions of Burgundy; February and March saw temperatures as high as 24°C (75.2°F) in the Mâconnais, encouraging very early bud-break. However, April and June cooled down with wet, cold nights everywhere and frost in the Chablis area. Flowering was therefore later than usual, finished by late June in Chablis, the potentially huge crop being reduced by *coulure* and *millerandage*. The summer was hot and near-drought conditions led to an irregular *véraison*. Picking was early, beginning on September 17 in the Côte d'Or. Yields were up on 1989 and the grapes were generally small and healthy with thick skins. September was cooler than normal, making fermentation easier and allowing winemakers to extract excess tannins.

Red★★★★★ Côte d'Or reds are deep-coloured and concentrated with fine tannins. The Pinot Noirs have many of the ripe, raspberry fruit characteristics of the 1989s, but also have superior extract and tannin.

White★★★★ Growers throughout Burgundy were optimistic that this was a promising year. A surprisingly large crop of rich, elegant, well-balanced wines for relatively early drinking.

All but the finest whites, drink up. The reds are magnificent now, and the best Côte de Nuits will continue well into the present decade.

1989

The fifth consecutive successful year for growers in Burgundy. A mild winter was followed by an early spring in which growth was a fortnight ahead of normal. A long, hot summer resulted in an early harvest; exceptionally healthy, ripe grapes were picked from September 13 in ideal conditions.

Red★★★★ The harvest brought in a larger crop of red than white grapes. The Pinot Noir ripened well and produced high natural levels of alcohol.

White up to★★★★★ The Chardonnay, like the Pinot Noir, ripened well, producing high natural levels of alcohol. This is undoubtedly a good year, although there were some contrasting views among growers about the real status of the vintage.

All but the best whites should have been drunk. The top reds richly developed, many at peak.

1988

A very good year throughout Burgundy. For red wines this was the best vintage of the decade. The year had a poor start with a mild winter and long, wet spring. Despite this, however, bud-break was early and flowering and fruit set were problem free. Almost three months of dry and sunny weather followed, producing an excellent, slightly larger than average harvest which started on September 26 for the red grapes and on October 4 for the whites of the Côte de Beaune.

Red★★★★★ These are deeply coloured, rich wines combining a good balance of fruit, acidity, and tannin. Though attractive when young, they also had the capacity to age well.

White★★★ Ripe, fresh, well-balanced wines. However, yields were high and some wines lacked concentration as a result.

Minor reds from the Côte d'Or: drink up. Retain the top reds, particularly the leading estates, for drinking, say, now to 2020; the very best even beyond then. Minor whites drink up, higher quality white burgundies soon.

1987

Quite a small vintage; its reputation improved as it matured, particularly the reds. A cool and unsettled summer resulted in a poor flowering and fruit set, prompting caution among wine-growers. A particularly beneficial period of unusually hot September weather followed, and picking began on October 5 in good conditions.

Red★★★ The small yield of grapes had a high ratio of skin to juice, resulting in fairly concentrated, quite well-structured red wines for early to mid-term drinking.

White★★ This was a slightly less satisfactory year for the white wines. Firm and clean-cut, but perhaps a little on the mean side.

Lesser reds and whites: drink up. Best of both: drink soon.

1986

A very large crop of good wines. A cold winter was followed by a mild spring; flowering took place successfully during a hot, sunny June. Excellent conditions continued through the summer with the exception of some late August and September storms, encouraging rot. The harvest began on September 29 in good weather; those who picked late made the best wines.

Red★★★★ The size of the crop prompted concern as to its quality. Fortunately, this was largely unfounded, and where the grapes were not too swollen by the storms, quality was good. But, resulting wines lacked the charm of the 1985s, being rather tough and tannic. The best appear to have come from the Côte de Nuits.

White★★★★★ The whites were superb: dense and concentrated with excellent structure. Extremely good Pulignys; with increasing use of oak barriques becoming noticeable in Chablis.

Most reds fully evolved and are drinking quite well now. The firm, fragrant grands crus should develop further. Top quality whites now at peak.

1985

A phenomenally cold winter, during which the temperature fell as low as -25°C (-13°F) around the lower-lying vineyards of the Côte de Nuits in January, causing much damage. Nevertheless this was a consistently good year, partly because only the healthiest vines had survived the winter. Spring was cool, resulting in a late and often difficult flowering. However, between then and the harvest the weather was fine and warm, becoming glorious in September and October. Picking began on September 26 and a larger than average crop of healthy grapes was brought in.

Red★★★★★ Rich, ripe, clean, and fruity wines. Probably the best-balanced vintage since 1978.

White★★★★ Delightful wines. A late harvest of healthy grapes in the Côte de Beaune.

Whites drink up. The best reds are sheer perfection though some good 1985s are beginning to show their age.

1984

A dismal year, largely due to the difficult weather conditions that prevailed throughout the growing season. Spring arrived late, delaying flowering until early July. A two-month drought thereafter was followed by one of the worst Septembers on record, with ceaseless rain continuing into early October. Unripe grapes were harvested, the only consolation being that the cool weather prevented the spread of rot.

Red Low in natural alcohol and acidity, prompting widespread chaptalization. Unbalanced wines.

White★ Slightly better than reds.

Avoid.

1983

An extremely uneven year, even by Burgundian standards. A successful flowering followed a poor, wet spring. The summer was generally hot with the occasional period of rain and even hail in some areas. The grapes ripened well but frequently suffered from rot. A fairly small crop, with severe hailstorm damage around the Côte de Nuits.

Red★★▷★★★ May hailstorms in and around Chambolle-Musigny and Vosne-Romanée destroyed nearly one-third of the crop, though generally flowering was successful. An interesting and challenging year; rot and hard tannins were the only problems and the wines that outlive the latter will be drinking well into the present century.

White★★★★ Variable but often exciting wines with character and quality.

A controversial vintage, particularly the reds. Those from the Côte de Beaune are drinking well whereas some of the top Nuits are either tainted or so laden with tannin that it is hard to see them coming round. Drink up the whites.

1982

A mild winter was followed by a warm, early spring and correspondingly early flowering. The summer was generally fine; September and October were both hot and sunny and the harvest started on September 20. Many growers found that their cellars were too small to house their bumper Pinot Noir crop and also encountered the inevitable problems of quality versus quantity.

Red★★▷★★★ The excessive production of the red wines resulted in a lack of concentration. They were, however, healthy wines with ripe fruit, suitable for early drinking.

White★★★▷★★★★ Both very good and very poor wines, most at their peak during the mid- to late 1980s. Top *crus* worth keeping.

Most reds should have been consumed. Some of the leading whites can still be enjoyable. Best to drink up.

1981

Dismal weather almost throughout the year produced a very small crop of mostly poor wines. A cold winter ran into a warm spring, but frost attacked the vines once budding was underway and in Chablis this resulted in the loss of one-third of the crop. Miserable conditions did not relent until August during which there was some sunshine, but the harvest, which ran from September 24 until October 5, was continually interrupted by rain. Those who picked late, however, benefited from an improvement in the weather.

Red★★ With the odd surprise, this was a very poor year. The best were made from reduced crops of highly concentrated grapes.

White★ Mediocre. Some pleasing exceptions.

Drink up.

1980

A year of mixed results, but on the whole this was a good vintage. Bud-break was delayed by a cold winter and cool spring. A cold June led to extended and uneven flowering, though August and September temperatures were above average. Some rain fell before the harvest which ran from October 10. Those growers who picked late produced the best wines.

Red★★▷★★★ As a result of the small crop some deep, fairly concentrated wines, especially in the Côte de Nuits.

White★★ A disappointing and uneven crop resulting in acidic, austere, unbalanced wines, though some exceptions.

Most reds and all the whites should have been consumed. However, some of the best reds are still drinking quite well.

1979

An abundant vintage of mainly good-quality wines. Vegetation was delayed by a cold winter and spring, then frosts during early May coincided with budding. The summer was fair with the exception of several hailstorms, one of which caused particular damage between Nuits-St-Georges and Chambolle-Musigny.

However, the surviving grapes were healthy and a satisfactory harvest was brought in at the end of September.

Red★★★ Overall, quite good.

White★★★★ Attractive wines with a more obvious, easy charm than the harder, firmer 1978s. Very good in the Côte de Beaune.

Even the best reds should be drunk soon. The top whites can still be very good.

1978

An excellent year. The small crop of good quality wines came onto the market at a time of high demand, encouraging growers to open prices one hundred per cent above those of the atrocious 1977s.

Vegetation and flowering were delayed by an unusually cold spring and early summer; the weather turned on August 20 when the grapes were setting and an excellent autumn saved the vintage.

Red★★★★★ Well-structured wines; their strength is from ripe grapes with a good balance of fruit, tannin, alcohol, and acidity.

White★★★★★ The best year since 1971. All areas, even the minor districts, produced wines of high quality. Very firm, well-built, alcoholic wines, with fruit, extract, and acidity.

A highly satisfactory vintage for reds, most of which are drinking well now, but the best will open up further and probably last until around 2010. Top quality whites can still be superb, with a maturity span well into the present decade.

1977

Despite an ideal spring and perfect flowering, torrential rain throughout the summer, with a two-week break in August, and then further severe storms later in the month, brought this vintage near to disaster. However, by September the weather turned fine and the harvest started on October 4.

Red~ An abundant crop. Sandwiched between two far superior years the 1977s attracted little attention, though considering the conditions some drinkable wines were made.

White★ These were generally much better than the reds. Stocks were low, the crop small, and consequently prices were higher than they really deserved.

Red: avoid. White: drink up.

1976

This year had everything going for it: a mild, frostless winter followed by a summer of intense heat and drought. This relented slightly in time for an early September harvest.

Red★★★ A very welcome vintage, coming at the end of the recession and following three poor quality years. Wines of colour, fruit, extract, and alcohol, but with an excess of tannin which might never ameliorate.

White★★★★ The excessive heat ripened the grapes very early and, in order to avoid loss of acidity and an excess of sugar, the harvest was brought forward (to September 15 in Chablis). Some grapes were gathered slightly underripe. The result was variable, some wines lacking life, others too hard.

Most reds should be drunk soon. However, some are still very noticeably tannic, so, despite the risk of drying out, the best might be worth keeping. The whites are mainly consumed by now though the firmest can still be good.

1975

A disastrous vintage, the worst since 1968, though marginally better for the whites. After a fine late spring and early summer the weather was generally unpleasant and grapes suffered widespread rot. A small quantity of thin, mouldy wines coincided with worldwide recession. A year Burgundians prefer to forget.

Avoid.

1974

A mild but occasionally frosty spring, difficult flowering, and sunny summer were followed by the coldest September in years. Picking started September 21 in cold, wet, and windy weather.

Red~ Mainly dismal.

Whites★ Some passable wines made, though of no interest now.

Drink up.

1973

A successful flowering and dry start to the summer – the driest since 1945 – which broke mid-July, with heavy rain, particularly on the Côtes.

Red~ Light, watery, and unimportant wines. A late, wet, and extended harvest ran from September 22 until October 18. This was a miserable year – the size of the crop exceeded the permitted yield coinciding with a drop in demand.

White★★▷★★★★ Overall a good vintage for whites; comparable with, possibly better than, 1970, but the wines, though acidic, not as firm as the 1969s or 1971s. Wines of charm and fragrance, at their best when young.

Reds: drink up. Whites: one or two interesting survivors, thanks to high acidity.

1972

A severe winter was followed by warm weather at the end of March and the vines budded in April; summer was oddly cold but dry, and September mercifully sunny. A huge crop picked late under good, if cold, conditions.

Red★★★ Despite being unpopular with the English (due partly to being overshadowed by the three previous vintages, and partly to the association with the poor 1972 red Bordeaux) these were reasonably well-structured, pleasant, and interesting wines, though with a touch of bitterness. They have little appeal now.

White★★ Mediocre. Some of the grapes harvested too early resulting in over-acid wines. Others were light, lacking finesse. But, there were many pleasant results, though of no interest now.

Only the very best reds have survived. Drink up the rest.

1971

An outstanding vintage throughout Burgundy: vigorous, well-constituted wines. Apart from a slightly problematic flowering, the summer was settled. Some hail in August, and a poor final week, but conditions picked up with a beautiful first half of September. A small but well-nourished crop of grapes was picked from September 16 onwards. In the Côte de Beaune, the area worst affected by the hail, the quantities amounted to a mere fraction of the 1970 harvest.

Red★★★★ An impressive vintage, regarded as untypical by Burgundians. The severe pruning caused by the harsh weather resulted in unusually substantial wines. Overall, big, rich, and well-structured.

White★★★★★ One of the loveliest white burgundy vintages of the period. Dry, firm, well-balanced, and subtle; the Chablis, Meursaults, and Montrachets were particularly successful.

Reds still drinking well, best will keep comfortably into the present decade. Whites now mainly consumed though finest and firmest can still be good.

1970

Bad weather in April and May but thereafter conditions were generally fine through to October. A large, ripe crop was picked at the end of September.

Red★★ Sadly disappointing. Pale wines, probably due to over-production, many reaching full maturity within five years.

White★▷★★★ An uneven vintage which ranged from bad, somewhat dull, to good. The wines were often too soft, overripe, and lacking in acidity. Most, rightly, were speedily consumed.

Reds: fully mature, drink up. Whites: drink up.

1969

After a mild winter and cold, wet spring, the grapes budded late, but were then ripened by a fine, sunny summer. September was also wet, but fortunately sound, and ripe grapes were gathered from October 5 in fine conditions.

Red★★★★★ A superb vintage, not unlike 1949 in its style. The wines fell into two categories: light wines for quick drinking, and a higher class which had the body, tannin, and acidity for long keeping – being the first year of such quality since 1966. A vintage that constantly surprises and delights.

White★★★★★ A distinctly agreeable vintage. Firm, dry, and well-balanced classic wines, the best of which took a full ten years to develop.

The best reds excellent now and will keep, some well into the present century. Whites: drink up all but the very best.

1968

A very poor year. Such a catastrophic vintage that the Hospices de Beaune auction was cancelled. Some skilful winemakers who chaptalized their white wines did, however, manage to produce a few surprises.

Avoid.

1967

Favourable weather conditions, including a particularly sunny July and August, persuaded some vineyard owners to dispense with dusting the vines to protect them from disease.

Alas, ten days of rain in September produced some disastrous results. Many winemakers attempted to speed up fermentation; the wines produced were very uneven, some particularly high in alcohol.

Red★★ Variable, but the best, especially from the *grands crus climats* on the slopes, were delightful.

White★★★ A better year for the whites: highly attractive dry, refreshing wines with good flavour. Now well past their best.

Drink up.

1966

Crops were damaged by spring hail. The summer began poorly but conditions gradually improved. The harvest took place from September 28 in perfect conditions, the light September rain having gently swelled the grapes. At the outset growers were worried that the harvest would be small, but ultimately were pleasantly surprised by the good quantity and quality.

Red★★★★ Overall a firm, elegant vintage. The Côte de Nuits produced the best wines, and even the less good from elsewhere were attractive and lively.

White★★★★ Very high quality wines which combined austerity with fragrance, good firm flesh, plus sufficient fat and acidity to give them longevity. A very popular year which achieved consistently high prices.

Reds: the very best are perfect now, the greatest will continue to mature. Whites: most have been consumed though the very rare surviving grands crus *can still be superb, continuing to dazzle with style and richness.*

1965

A catastrophic year: rain waterlogged the soil and an appalling storm washed away some vineyards.

1964

A justifiably popular vintage with merchants. Record prices were achieved at the annual Hospices de Beaune auction.

After the hardest, snowiest winter in twenty years, conditions finally picked up, allowing a perfect June flowering. A hot, dry summer reduced the by then abundant crop. September alternated regularly between rain and sun, providing perfect pre-harvest conditions.

Red★★★★ Superb, meaty, open-knit wines.

White★★★ The grapes were high in sugar and low in acidity. A popular vintage but lacking finesse, and quick maturing.

Best reds can still be extremely agreeable though, of course, fully mature. Whites should have been drunk ages ago.

1963

A rather dreary summer but a sunny autumn produced a very large crop of mediocre wines.

Red★ Feeble and largely avoided.

White★★ Rather low in acidity; some good Montrachets.

Avoid.

1962

A very good year. A cold April preceded a summer which gradually improved and culminated in a sunny August and welcome rain in September, delaying the start of picking until October 8. Exceptional harvesting weather produced a smallish crop of ripe, healthy grapes.

Red★★★★ Fragrant, delicious, stylish wines. The best were slow starters but ultimately attractive, exciting, and well-balanced.

White★★★★★ Perfect balance of body, acidity, flesh, and crispness.

Reds are firmer than the 1964s, the best can still be superb and with years more life if well kept. Few whites remain but a grand cru, *if perfectly cellared, can still be delicious.*

1961

A mild winter and warm spring pushed the growth of the vines months ahead of normal. However, due to uneven weather patterns in June, the flowering took nearly three times longer than average and this, coupled with a bad summer, meant that the vintage reverted to its usual timing. Conditions for harvest were good and picking began on September 25.

Red★★★ A good, appealing, fragrant, and popular vintage.

White★★★★ A successful year, the wines were enormously popular.

Some of the reds still delicious but best drunk soon. The whites should have been consumed by now.

1960

Unripe grapes, poor wines.

Red~ Thin, almost all consumed early.

White~ Equally thin, very acidic wines, refreshing in early 1960s.

Avoid.

1959

Excellent for the reds but not the whites. Good growing conditions with a hot, dry summer and sufficient rain to swell the berries.

Red★★★★★ A magnificent vintage. From the first tastings these have always been highly flavoured, richly coloured wines with plenty of extract and tannin. The most dependable of the older vintages and the last of the great classic heavyweight reds.

White★★★ Growers experienced difficulties with vinification and the wine tended to lack acidity. The more substantial wines such as Le Montrachet and Corton-Charlemagne can still be very good. In the northerly areas the hot weather was most beneficial and produced some interesting Chablis.

The best reds are still superb. Few whites remain, drink up.

1958

The market was already inundated with high quality wines when this moderate vintage appeared.

Red★★ Rarely seen. Now fully mature; drink up.

White★ Not difficult to avoid: none to be had.

1957

Mild spring and early summer with extreme heat. Temperatures relented considerably with cool, grey July afternoons.

Red★★★ A good, flavoursome vintage, the acid levels adding zest to the wines.

White★★★ Disastrous May frost in Chablis destroyed almost all the vines, including those of the top growths. Elsewhere, wines were firm and fruity.

Some reds have survived, can be flavoury, but drink up.

1956

A disastrous year, menaced by disease and pests. Rarely seen.

Avoid.

1955

After a slow, cold start to the year, the weather picked up and harvesting took place under the best conditions in twenty years.

Red★★★ Sound and popular, though variable reds. The Côte de Nuits had depth and style but lacked length and finish; the Côte de Beaunes were light and at their best in the mid- to late 1960s.

White★★★★ A delightful vintage: elegant and beautifully balanced.
Reds fully mature, drink soon. Whites past best; drink up.

1954

Pleasant spring, successful flowering, but wet summer. A late, sunny autumn saved the harvest: abundant crop, uneven quality.
Red★★★ Overshadowed by the 1952s and 1953s, this vintage was undeservedly neglected.
White★ Unripe and a tendency to tartness. Few shipped.
The best surviving reds overmature but attractive. Drink up.

1953

Apart from a mild April, the weather was generally wet and cold until August/September when the warm sun ripened the grapes. The harvest started on September 29 under excellent conditions.
Red★★★★ Ripe, supple, attractive wines.
White★★★★ As with the reds, these were highly popular, and with good reason. Soft, pleasant, and very good value, though less firm than the 1952s.
Most if not all are fading. Drink up.

1952

A June drought, a hot July and August with some rain, then a cool September.
Red★★★★ Very reliable, tough, and concentrated as a result of the drought.
White★★★★ As is so often the case with burgundy, the whites were better than the reds. They all enjoyed great popularity, consequently few remain.
The best reds are still firm and excellent; whites are well past their best though can be interesting.

1951

With 1956, one of the two worst years of the decade. Rarely seen but some surprises, for example La Tâche.

1950

A vintage menaced by hail throughout the summer, the latter half was wet.
Red★ Feeble wines.
White★★★ A far better year for the whites. Good "useful" wines at the time.
Forget.

1949

A very wet start to the year, but worries were soon quelled by a dry summer with a little beneficial rain. Harvesting began September 27. This vintage was highly popular amongst the buyers and was bought at exceptionally reasonable prices.
Red★★★★★ First-class results. Compared to the 1947s, the 1949s were better balanced and closer knit, consequently they held for longer – burgundy at its elegant best.
White★★★★ Superb, supple, well-balanced wines which lasted well.
If well kept the top Côte de Nuits and Beaune reds still beautiful to drink; some great whites too though rarely seen and tiring.

1948

Cold, wet weather which gradually improved from mid-August.

Red★★ A variable vintage sandwiched between two superior years.

White★★ Virtually bypassed, despite being a moderately good year.

Some of the best reds have survived, tired but drinkable.

1947

Fantastic weather conditions throughout the year led to much well-founded optimism. The usual difficulties associated with winemaking in great heat affected some areas, but those who overcame them made outstanding wines.

Red★★★★ Immediately attractive, ripe wines. More stable than their counterparts in Bordeaux.

White★★★★ A ripe, delightful, early maturing vintage.

Some superb reds, "warm" and glowing; English-bottled wines are worth looking out for. Of the whites, the top Côte de Beaune wines can still be delicious if of impeccable provenance.

1946

Quite a good growing season. An abundant crop reduced by hail, followed by a cold rainy period and a warm decent harvest.

Red★★★

White★

Few ever seen. Drink up.

1945

An impressive year. Nature's severe pruning of the crop was undoubtedly the key contributing factor. Severe frosts in spring were followed by a cyclone on June 21 which devastated the ten principal villages of the Côte de Beaune, reducing their crop to one sixteenth of the estimated yield. Overall a small harvest of ripe, highly concentrated grapes.

Red★★★★★ Dry, firm, substantial, deep-coloured, well-constituted, concentrated wines of the highest quality.

White★★★★ A small crop of excellent wines with good finish. Few exported.

The greatest reds still magnificent, one of the most dependable of the older vintages; only a few whites have survived.

1944

This might well have been a good year, had it not been for the dismal rain which fell continuously throughout the harvest.

Red★ Light, washed-out wines.

White~ A poor vintage. None tasted.

1943

The best war-time vintage: well-nigh perfect spring, summer, and autumn. A shortage of labour, bottles, and corks.

Red★★★ Many of the wines had to be kept long in the cask, hastening decline and drying them out. Nevertheless, the wines had flavour, firmness, and ripeness.

White★★★ The best vintage between 1937 and 1945. Reds can still be delicious.

1942

After a good summer the vines around the Côte de Beaune were damaged by hail. The harvest began the following day on September 13 but was intermittent, taking four weeks to complete.

Red★★★ Good, stylish, little-known, and underrated wines.

White★★ Mediocre, light wines, quickly consumed.

Reds variable, from tired to still quite good.

1941

Healthy vines, but a cold autumn prevented full ripening.

Red★ A little-seen wartime vintage.

White★★ Better, crisper wines, some survived.

1940

Good growing season spoiled by mildew.

Red★★ Some good wines made but few remain.

White~ All consumed during the war.

1930s

Red Burgundy

1939★★ and **1938★★** were both mediocre years of little interest, few now remain. **1937★★★★★** was a rich, distinctive year, reported at the time to be the best since 1929 and far better than Bordeaux; the best still magnificent. **1936★** was a poor year of little interest.

1935★★★★ a very good, abundant year, though little was exported due to great interest in the fine, well-constituted **1934★★★★**, considered then to be the best of the decade. **1933★★★★** was another good year overshadowed by 1934. **1932~**, **1931~**, and **1930~** were uniformly disastrous.

White Burgundy

The 1930s, like the 1920s, produced some interesting whites. **1939★** and **1938★** were, however, not among them. But, undoubtedly the greatest vintage of the decade was the **1937★★★★** though only a very limited amount of it was shipped before the war. Once hostilities had ceased merchants were seeking younger wines. Passing over **1936★**, a minor and rarely seen vintage, the next-best years were **1935★★★** and **1934★★★★** both good to very good vintages, but now of course scarce. **1933★★★** another lovely vintage in Burgundy, was still showing well in the mid-1950s but has proved disappointing more recently. **1930~**, **1931~**, and **1930~** were all uninteresting.

1920s

Red Burgundy

A successful decade, including one of the best-ever Burgundy vintages, seven very good to excellent years, two mediocre and only one poor.

1929★★★★★ was a classic vintage of immediate appeal, combining quantity with quality which, if well-cellared, lasted remarkably well, though overtired now. **1928★★★★** survived the hazards of difficult weather to produce fine, firm wines; the best still lovely. Leaving aside the dismal **1927~** the other great year was **1926★★★★**, a small vintage, the best wines of which were fabulous, though few tasted recently.

1925★ a disappointing vintage; **1924★★★** very attractive despite the difficult weather conditions, although not as exciting as **1923★★★★** which produced a small quantity of very good wines. **1922★** was a moderate vintage following two more very good years: **1921★★★** and **1920★★★★** the latter despite having faced bad weather and disease.

White Burgundy

A decade that included some outstanding wines.

1929★★★★ was a magnificent soft, ripe vintage, but not as crisp as the excellent, firm, nutty **1928★★★★★** which was certainly the best vintage between 1921 and 1937. If well kept the 1928 whites can still be excellent.

The four mid-decade vintages, **1927★**, **1926★★**, **1925★**, and **1924★** were generally uninspiring, as was **1922★**; **1923★★★★** was very good for white burgundy, and even better was the remarkable **1921★★★★★** which was a magnificent vintage for white wines throughout France and Germany, though the few remaining white burgundies are now scarce and tiring.

1920★★★ was also a good vintage.

1910s

Red Burgundy

This was a decade which included three exceptional years of very high quality as well as its fair share of unexceptional years.

Favourable weather conditions leading up to an excessively hot August in **1919★★★★★** produced a fairly small vintage of outstandingly fruity, ripe wines, which can still be good. **1918★★**, **1917★**, and **1916★★★** were three moderate years, best of which was 1916. The second first-rate vintage of the decade was **1915★★★★★** which enjoyed an abundant quantity of superb quality grapes that made full, fruity wines.

Passing over the three years preceding 1915, the other great year was **1911★★★★★** a magnificent classic burgundy vintage, the perfect summer and early harvest yielding a small crop.

1900s

Red Burgundy

The first decade of the twentieth century included some remarkable vintages, although, inevitably, scarce now.

1909~ mediocre. **1908~** was generally a poor year due to unpredictable weather; **1907★★★** was a good year, producing light wines, few of which are now seen. The best vintage was **1906★★★★★** an ideal growing season and early harvest producing perfect wines; the best can still be lovely and even better than those of **1904★★★★** the other good vintage of the decade. **1905~**, **1903~**, **1902~**, and **1901~** of no interest. **1900★★** was not as good as its counterpart in Bordeaux, but did produce an abundant yield of moderately good wines.

1900 to 1919

White Burgundy

1919★★★★ was one of the three great vintages of the 1910s, the other two being 1911 and 1915. **1906★★★★** was the outstanding vintage of the preceding decade. Those well cellared remained more than just interesting for a long time.

Pre-1900s

Red Burgundy

The best vintages were **1898★★★**, **1894★★★**, and **1893★★★**, an interesting year which produced some extremely good wines in conditions of great heat, **1865★★★★★** and **1864★★★★** magnificent and can still be lovely to drink.

Rhône

Looking rather like an apple on a string, the narrow strip of vineyards along the banks of the Rhône eventually opens out across a broad plain. The division between the wine areas of the north and south is distinct: the microclimates differ, as do the vine varieties grown, and styles of wine produced.

RED WINE

The vineyards to the north are on steep slopes flanking the river, the two principal red wine districts being Côte-Rôtie, adjacent to Vienne not far south of Lyon, and Hermitage. Two lesser districts, St-Joseph and Cornas, are on the right bank of the Rhône, more or less opposite Hermitage; the vineyards of Crozes-Hermitage lie above and behind Tain L'Hermitage. In the key northern districts high quality, sturdy, long-lasting reds are predominantly made from one grape variety: Syrah. Vintages are important; the best repay keeping.

Châteauneuf-du-Pape is a small town just north of Avignon. Its vineyards, the most important of the southern Rhône, are on a wide plateau of stony soil upon which up to thirteen permitted vine varieties are grown. It is a hot district. The grapes can be literally sunburnt, the pigment extracted from their thick "tanned" skins resulting in deeply coloured wine. The hot sun, supplemented by heat-reflecting pebbles which act like night-storage heaters, produces a naturally high sugar content which converts into a proportionally high level of alcohol. Wines of power rather than finesse can result, with richness, softness, and depth of fruit. Wines designated Côtes du Rhône tend to be lighter in style, best drunk young. Even the best, like Gigondas, are best consumed within two to four years after the vintage. They are not individually commented on in the notes that follow: a good year in Châteauneuf will generally also be good in the Côtes du Rhône.

WHITE WINE

The three principal districts are Condrieu and Hermitage in the north, and Châteauneuf-du-Pape in the southern Rhône, all of these producing only relatively small quantities of dry white wine. A tiny amount is made in Condrieu from one grape variety, Viognier. Its most famous vineyard, with its own appellation, is Château Grillet. Most are best drunk young, within three years of the vintage. The white wines made in Hermitage, from Marsanne and Roussanne grapes, combine delicacy with sturdiness and the best keep well. White Châteauneuf-du-Pape often has a distinct touch of sweetness and, low in high natural acidity, should be drunk quite young. The weather conditions in the north and south of the Rhône can be taken as the same for white as for the preceding red. NB: 1989 and older whites: few to be seen. Drink up.

2002

Red★ White★★ A nightmare year for producers particularly in the south. Very heavy rains causing flooding which, in Châteauneuf-du-Pape, inundated vineyards. Though the picking officially started on September 11, because of the flooded soils, tractors were not able to reach the vineyards for two or three days, giving the rot a chance to spread.

White grapes picked early were of good quality, aromatic with good sugar levels. Red grapes fared worse, some vines uprooted and, again in the south, remaining under water for days. Cellars were also submerged. In the north, the situation, thanks to steep, well-drained slopes, was less traumatic, enabling producers in Côte-Rôtie to make passably good wines.

The wines of Côte-Rôtie are the most successful in this dire year. Hermitage, both red and white, should prove of useful "commercial" quality. The lesser Côtes du Rhône are light and fruity at best. Châteauneuf producers who salvaged their crops made light, undistinguished but pleasant enough wines. But it is not a long term vintage; wines for early quaffing, not for cellaring.

2001

Red★★★▷★★★★ White★★ In northern Rhône a mild winter was followed by a wet, warm spring without any frost, resulting in early budding. There was some irregularity in flowering, resulting in some *millerandage*, and *vendange verte* was practised regularly throughout the ripening season, to ensure even ripening and lessen the risk of rot. April was cold and dry, followed by a warm and damp May with flowering starting around May 21. While an early July brought warmer weather and ripening, a hot, dry August followed, and temperatures of 33°C (91°F) resulted in thick-pelliculed, small berries. There was, however, sufficient rainfall and the vines were not stressed. The white harvest began on September 17 and the red on the 18th, some pickers continuing up to October 6, the day before the rains set in.

2001 was more uneven in the southern Rhône. The region experienced a mild winter and a particularly warm yet wet spring. By the beginning of April the growth cycle of the vine was well under way, and continuous warm weather in May and June and heavy rainfall in July – with thunderstorms – accelerated growth. The grapes reached good maturity in a dry and hot August. In September the mistral arrived and continued over a period of eleven days at its strongest for thirty years, reaching speeds of over 50km/hr (31 m/hr). The wind's cooling effect and fresh nights and sunny days produced good concentration and maturity, even though juice yields were five to thirty per cent lower than in 2000 (depending on the grape variety). Châteauneuf-du-Pape starting picking on September 10. Syrah had good colour extraction and excellent fruitiness. Overall, 2001 was more favourable for the reds, but some very good whites were produced in the cooler regions like Côtes de Ventoux and Luberon.

The reds are variable, those from the northern Rhône being superior in concentration and extract, and with a good future. The best producers in Châteauneuf were as dependable as ever but their reds are mid-term wines. Rhône whites mainly for early drinking.

2000

Red★★★ White★★ variable Overall, a good vintage but not without its problems and determined by the growing north/south divide, hotter summers and lower rainfall in the south, and how growers handled yields.

In the northern Rhône, the climate played a greater role this year, perhaps suppressing some terroir and sense of place. Grey, dull weather, with a lack of sun in June and July, necessitated a late July/early August green harvesting to extract rotten bunches and cut excess crop. The weeks August 10–30 were too hot, and grapes with a south/southwesterly exposure toughened and their acidity levels dropped. Then rain in early and mid-September augmented alcoholic ripening but hindered tannic ripening and yields had to be restricted to avoid dilution. Some high quality growers bled their crop by the *saignée* method. Fine wines were produced but they were not of the same high standard as those of the south. In the long-term, the high crop effect is being aggravated by the use of over-productive clonal selection vines.

In the south, 2000 is compared to the classic 1998 vintage. Apart from a sudden spell of frost at the end of March, affecting parts of Châteauneuf-du-Pape, crops were generally rot-free, producing very healthy berries. There were some storms around September 20, but they were fortunately of little negative consequence thanks to a northerly wind that quickly dried the grapes, raising sugar levels, and leading to an early, large harvest. Even though large yields diluted some wines, many producers felt that this vintage produced wines of superb quality.

White wines for early drinking; reds variable but the best in the north need cellaring.

1999

Red★★★★★ White★★★★ As is frequently the case there are different situations in the north and the south of this major river valley. One has only to drive south from Lyon to Avignon to be visually aware of the tremendous difference, from the steep slopes and relatively narrow riverbanks of Côte-Rôtie and Hermitage to the broad expanse of vineyards on the stony plain of Châteauneuf-du-Pape. Microclimates and grape varieties, too, are different. It does not come as a surprise to read one brief report of the vintage "that ranges from the sublime to the mediocre", adding that Condrieu (whites) and Côte-Rôtie (reds) stand out as quality leaders. Despite some extreme conditions, including violent storms and large hail-stones, most were localized. The summer was generally dry but humid which resulted in a certain amount of botrytis and *oidium*. Nevertheless overall harvest conditions were excellent with major growers in the north and early pickers in the south ecstatic.

Summarizing the northern Côte du Rhône, the four best-known producers all agreed: "exceptional on two counts. Excellent in terms of quantity and quality", "at least as good as 1998", "comparable to 1995 and 1990", and one having no hesitation in comparing 1999 with the best vintages of the century. Reds with intense colours, ripe fruit aromas, good acidity, the whites well rounded and full flavoured. Very similar reports from the south despite heavy rains at the end of September.

Whites for early drinking; reds from the north for excellent mid- to long term drinking, from the south now to, say, 2010.

1998

Red★★★★★ White★★★ Unequivocally a great vintage and, with the exception of severe frosts in the north, a uniformly good growing season throughout this disparate and elongated region.

The winter of 1997/8 was wetter than usual, providing useful water reserves. Budding was relatively early but pleasant spring weather in the north of the Rhône Valley was, in parts disastrously, interrupted by severe frosts on April 13–14. As in Burgundy, instead of affecting mainly the lower vineyards and valley floor, the valuable hillside slopes were badly hit, especially Côte-Rôtie where the temperature fell to -5ºC (23ºF), a disaster not experienced for nearly half a century. As a result the crop was reduced immediately to thirty to fifty per cent of normal. Frost damage also occurred in Condrieu, St-Joseph, and Cornas, severely reducing yields. Happily the southern Côtes du Rhône and, mercifully, Châteauneuf-du-Pape were not affected.

Flowering throughout was early and regular. Thereafter the summer was hot and dry, with a smattering of rain at the beginning of August followed by intense heat and near drought, stressing the vines and reducing the potential crop. Well-timed rain during the first week of September was followed by mainly dry and sunny conditions for the harvest. Sun-thickened skins and ripe sugar levels resulted in deeply coloured reds with high alcohol content, sometimes in excess of a freakish fifteen per cent in the south, with rich, mature fruit yet fresh aromas. However, it is reported that some growers were tempted to pick too early, some too late, some wines left too long on the skins. The top estates made wines of superlative quality.

The reds vary from very good to excellent, the most impressive wines since 1990, particularly Châteauneuf-du-Pape. Condrieu and Hermitage *blanc* probably more satisfactory than Châteauneuf *blanc* which tends to be somewhat sweet and hefty in a hot vintage like this.

The reds, both north and south, will be long-lasting though the sheer richness of Châteauneufs will tempt the impatient. Whites: drink soon.

1997

Red★★★▷★★★★ White★★★ Uneven results in the Rhône Valley this vintage. The north enjoyed near perfect conditions and a straightforward, uniformly successful harvest. Conversely, further south unfavourable weather presented various problems and a far less consistent growing season.

In both areas the year started favourably with early budding. Flowering was also very prompt, when the south experienced some April frost and localized hail damage. This did not cause as many problems as feared but did reduce the yield slightly. Conditions were cooler during summer which slowed down the maturation process. A heat-wave then hit the region at the end of August, causing drought. There were a couple of sporadic thunderstorms before harvesting began and thereafter there were three perfect, sun-filled weeks.

The north started picking white grapes on September 15 and red on September 25. The grapes ripened slowly and evenly, but producers reported that the extreme heat had burnt some vines, causing some damage. But on the whole the red wines are very good and presage great longevity, some perhaps overripe. In the south picking started on September 8. A problem still remaining in this area is that many producers do not have temperature controlling equipment – vitally important when the grapes are harvested very hot. Both reds and whites have good colour and aroma, but slightly lack acidity as a result of the heat.

The best reds from the north, notably Côte-Rôtie, have ripe and supple tannins, drink say 2004 to 2010; those from the south are delicious now though some can disappoint, which applies also to the whites.

1996

Red★★▷★★★ White★★★ An inconsistent year and a difficult vintage, mainly due to rain during the summer and at harvest time. The start of the year saw a successful flowering, and producers who thinned out their crop in July greatly improved their chances of success. The beginning of August was cool and wet which hampered the natural sugar development. The weather then followed two different routes in the north and south.

In the north, late August became sunny and conditions were good until the end of the harvest. October 5 saw the start of the harvest, with the Mistral wind providing a cooling influence for the next three weeks. As a result the crop was healthy, rot-free, and abundant. Syrah found it harder to ripen so the reds are austere in style, yet good for slightly earlier drinking. Meanwhile, producers in Condrieu rejoiced after harvesting their Voignier grapes at fifteen per cent potential alcohol, with complementing acidity levels. Some even made Vendange Tardive wines, after harvesting as late as November 10.

The south suffered more as the rain continued into September, causing dilution in the reds. In mid-September the Mistral wind rescued the area from potential rot disaster, but a hard ripening had produced only a light and early drinking vintage. As in the north, whites fared better with excellent acidity.

Reds, notably from Côte-Rôtie and Hermitage now to 2009; Châteauneuf and the whites drink up.

1995

Red★★★★▷★★★★★ White★★★★ A good, clean, and fairly consistent vintage for the Rhône.

January was dry with average temperatures, caused by the effects of the longer than usual Mistral wind. February was dry and mild, then March turned fresh and windy. April was warm and rainy, notably during the final ten days. These conditions helped strengthen the vines. May was very warm, prompting rapid bud-burst, but then June brought cool nights and things slowed down again. Flowering began on June 7 without too many problems. July and August were hot and dry and the vintage started early on September 4. Ideal conditions prevailed and continued until the end of the harvest.

In the north yields were down by twenty per cent, due to *coulure* and *millerandage* during flowering. The reds are elegant and charming while the whites are more delicate than 1994s with good acidity. Some excellent Marsanne and Roussanne wines. The late September Mistral wind had a drying and concentrating effect in the south giving super-ripe reds with high sugar levels. Balanced with good acidity and tannin, these wines are delightful and comparable with those of the 1990 vintage.

Clearly a satisfactory year for red and white. Classic red Hermitage lovely now but will keep, Côte-Rôtie from say 2002, the blockbusters up to 2015; Châteauneuf-du-Pape until around 2010. Crisp whites pleasant now but don't keep long.

1994

Red★▷★★ White★★★ Not a great vintage but some quite attractive wines. Vegetation progressed quickly in the Rhône after a very mild winter and, unlike other French regions, the summer sun was so extreme that it scorched many of the grapes. Temperatures were as high as 42°C (107°F). The resultant wines are varied in quality and reflect the timing of their harvests in relation to the heavy mid-September rains.

In the north, budding took place early, around March 15. The temperature rapidly fell, retarding this growth. The end of May finally witnessed the flowering which was followed by some disease-related problems including a small amount of *coulure*. Grapes from steep slopes were not unduly affected by the rains that fell during the harvest, but those from the plateau lacked balance with too much acidity. The final grapes brought in were too waterlogged, and chaptalization was widespread throughout the region.

Further south similar problems at flowering occurred and *coulure* affected both Grenache and Syrah resulting in small bunches. Those who harvested most of their grapes before the rains were very happy with their results. Generally, the wines tend to have less colour but more tannin than 1993.

A "vintage of the century" dashed by heavy rain; yet the top producers, selecting only their best grapes, made good wines, particularly in the north. On the whole, not wines which will benefit a great deal with further bottle-age. Drink soon.

1993

Red★★▷★★★ White★★★ From north to south, conditions during spring and early summer were favourable, July and August reasonably hot and sunny However, mounting hopew of a great vintage were washed away by rains from mid-September. These resulted in very serious flooding, most notably in the south.

Reds from the north are light, early developing wines, with the best coming from old vines or from growers who cut their vines back significantly in August. Careful selection was necessary because of the prevalence of mildew and parasites. Chaptalization was required throughout. In the south, the red wines hold a little more promise as many grapes were harvested before the rains fell. Châteauneuf-du-Pape was the most fortunate in this respect, claiming better wines than in both the 1992 and 1991 vintages. Elsewhere in the south, many growers were able to get the crop in rapidly, managing to retain some fullness in the wines. The better wines have good levels of tannin and colour. White wines fared best, due to their earlier harvest. Hermitage, Crozes-Hermitage, and St-Joseph all produced agreeable wines.

Selected reds from top growers are drinking well now. Whites, drink up.

1992

Red★★▷★★★★ White★★★ Conditions were good during winter and spring, with normal temperatures and healthy levels of rain (after several unusually dry years). May was hot and a successful flowering took place. Unfortunately, this was followed by six weeks of wet weather which caused *coulure*, mildew, and eventually uneven ripening. The month of August was hot and consequently raised the hopes of the growers. Once into September dramatically wet and stormy conditions struck the region. Further rot had set in by the time of the harvest and in the north, the size of the crop was reduced by a quarter. Despite the extreme conditions, red wines from both north and south have fairly good colour and extract with soft tannins.

The white wines, although quite varied, were of satisfactory quality.

Reds: mainly for early consumption though some leading growers made exceptional wines. Whites: drink up.

1991

Red★★ White★★★ An uneven year, both climatically and for the resultant wines. Winter was unusually cold, March was mild and wet, April and May dry but cooler than usual – but, the region escaped the frost damage suffered elsewhere in France – and vegetation was delayed. Flowering was from May 25 to June 20, Grenache in the south being seriously hit by *coulure*. July and August were hot and dry, enabling the vines to catch up. However, mid-September rains in the north dashed hopes of a top-class harvest. Some rot in Côte-Rôtie but most grapes were fairly healthy.

In the south the surviving Grenache grapes had ripening problems. Late summer storms and humidity in September caused some rot. A small crop of mainly light red wines in Châteauneuf-du-Pape. In the north and south white wines were more successful, the grapes being picked before rain set in. *The reds from the south are lighter than usual, so drink up; Hermitage lack elegance, Côte-Rôtie fully developed. Whites, with good acidity, drink up.*

1990

Red★★★★★ White★★★★ Despite drought the wines were, like those of the previous year, powerful and promising, if a little less aromatic.

Throughout the north flowering was early and, where the weather turned cold, there was some *coulure*. Rain was localized, but the heat was less intense than in 1989 and July enjoyed some cool nights. Most growers started to pick in mid-September and the grapes were in ripe, healthy condition. Further south there was good rainfall during May and ripening was advanced. Harvesting of whites at Châteauneuf-du-Pape, where the rainfall had allowed the grapes to ripen fully, began September 5 and for reds September 10.

Overall, the wines were slightly lower in acidity than those of 1989, particularly in the south, but tannins were firm and alcohol levels high, indicative of wines slow to open up but full of promise and staying power. *Sturdy, long-lasting reds in north and south: Châteauneuf-du-Pape drinking well now. Hermitage also delicious now but will keep well, perhaps to 2020, Côte-Rôtie even longer. Whites: drink up.*

1989

Red★★★★▷★★★★★ White★★★★★ This was a very mixed year in the Rhône, ranging from very good to excellent. The long, hot summer which produced so many good wines throughout France caused serious drought in the Rhône region. Where rain did fall it was very localized. Some areas were, however, at a greater advantage than others: the older vines with longer roots were able to draw moisture from the subsoil, vines on clay-based soil benefited from clay's capacity to retain water.

The grapes harvested late produced better wines than where growers had panicked and picked early. Excellent wines were made in Côte-Rôtie – one of the few areas receiving some precious rain. Châteauneuf-du-Pape was also successful, producing rich, complete reds. Hermitage was less reliable, though the best reds are rich and complex and the whites are deep and full-flavoured. White wines from elsewhere were attractive but low in acidity. *Châteauneuf-du-Pape, some lovely Hermitage, even better Côte-Rôties, drink from now to around 2010.*

1988

Red★★★★ White★★★★ A very good year along the length of the Rhône, the wines from the north being excellent. Hail and rain around the Côte-Rôtie during flowering reduced yields and concentrated the crop. Excessive humidity during the spring and early summer caused problems in the south. Thereafter, the weather was hot and dry with sufficient rain in August to swell the grapes. Early picking avoided problems caused by later rains.

The crop was of average size and made rich wines with good levels of tannin and fruit. The white wines were generally of good quality. *Top reds drinking beautifully, whites past their best.*

1987

Red★▷★★★ White~ In the north of the region the weather was satisfactory and good wines were made at Côte-Rôtie. Hermitage was not so fortunate: rain fell during the spring and flowering, resulting in uneven fruit set. Stormy weather in August did not relent for the harvest (mid-October) and the vintage was less than perfect. Conditions in the south were worse – rain, storms, fog, even a mass invasion of caterpillars. Light, early drinking wines.
Drink up.

1986

Red★★▷★★★★ White★★★ An uneven and difficult year. Warm, dry weather during the summer. September dull, rain at the end of the month delaying the harvest which began on October 10. Those who selected carefully avoided pests and rot resulting from the wet weather. Further south the good weather held during a late and extended vintage.
Some good, long-lasting, tannic reds from Côte-Rôtie to Châteauneuf-du-Pape, drinking well now.

1985

Red★★★★★ White★★★★ After a severe winter and cool spring, the weather improved, with good flowering in early June. The summer was hot, dry, and sunny and harvest took place in good conditions from September 16 to October 11. Outstanding reds, rich, long-lasting.
Reds drinking beautifully now. The best Châteauneuf-du-Pape, in common with Hermitage and Côte-Rôtie, will continue unabated.

1984

Red★★ White★ A small crop of moderate quality wines. A late flowering took place in good weather, thereafter conditions were unsettled, becoming increasingly cool and wet. The harvest ran from September 19 to October 15.
Not wines for keeping. However, some, mainly from Syrah, are holding well.

1983

Red★★★★★ White★★★ The flowering took place during an unsettled June, and a magnificent hot, dry summer followed. The harvest was early and *coulure* reduced the Grenache yield to below average. The red wines from both the north and the south were excellent, rich, and concentrated with hard tannins which have softened with maturity.
Châteauneuf-du-Pape drinking well, Hermitage and Côte-Rôtie into this century.

1982

Red★★★★ White★★★★ A very large crop. As is often the case with such a big harvest quality varied considerably, but the best were excellent. Summer was long and very hot; heavy rains in August continued until harvest began on September 7. These conditions led to problems: the heat reduced acidity levels, fermentation was difficult and many wines seem "cooked" as a result. Pre-harvest rain also reduced grape concentration.

Growers who picked carefully and did not overcrop, and winemakers who controlled fermentation, produced the best wines. A vintage often paired with 1983: it is holding well but will not last as long.
Many reds are drinking well but "gamey"; fully mature.

1981

Red★★ White★★ Rain in the north during the flowering and the harvest seriously disrupted this vintage. Nevertheless some good wines were made, particularly those from the Côte-Rôtie. Further south, cold weather during the flowering resulted in an uneven fruit set and reduced quantities. After a summer drought the harvest began on September 14. This was a moderate vintage; rich, concentrated wines from Châteauneuf-du-Pape, which, like the better wines from the north, improved with time.

Though laden with bitter tannins the wines of Châteauneuf-du-Pape have survived but should be drunk soon. The wines of Hermitage are fully developed, the best Côte-Rôties are drinking well. Interesting but not great.

1980

Red★★▷★★★ White★★ In the north of the Rhône the year started badly with poor weather during the spring and flowering period. As a result not all the flowers set and the crop was small. The weather improved during the growing season and a late harvest began on October 8. In the south the weather was generally fine throughout the vintage. The largest crop ever recorded was harvested from September 25.

Fairly good, deep wines which, along with the 1979s, 1981s, and 1982s, were always overshadowed by the great 1978s.

Drink up.

1979

Red★★▷★★★★ White★★★ Favourable weather conditions produced wines of high quality. In the north temperatures were cool until late July; thereafter dry, sunny weather held for an abundant harvest beginning late September in Côte-Rôtie, while around Hermitage rains delayed the harvest until October 8. A good year for the south: after a late budding, flowering took place quickly in good conditions. Some variability in the wines can be found where the vines suffered from drought.

Overall, a moderately good vintage: wines from the north were concentrated with ideal levels of acidity and tannin, and ageing potential; those from the south were fragrant and soft.

Now fully mature. Drink up.

1978

Red★★★★★ White★★★★★ Terrible weather conditions made this a very difficult year, yet with excellent results, the best vintage since 1911. A cool, wet spring reduced yields; flowering was late and slow; the remaining summer hot and dry, too dry for some, through to the harvest. These were big, tannic, rich reds with acidity for long keeping.

Astonishing reds, packed with fruit, extract, and alcohol, the top wines from Hermitage and Côte-Rôtie absolute perfection and will continue for another twenty years.

1977

Red★▷★★ White★ A poor year in the north; bad weather produced thin, acidic, unripe wines. In the south, fine autumn weather allowed winemakers to produce light, attractive wines.

Drink up.

1976

Red★★▷★★★★ White★★★ A hot, dry summer produced ripe, concentrated wines in most of the north, at worst the whites lack acidity and are variable. The south enjoyed similar weather, but high hopes were dashed by rains during the harvest in late September. Good wines, but not for long keeping.
Best Côte-Rôtie and Hermitage fully mature.

1975

Red★▷★★ White~ A poor year in the north and south. In the south August rains had a disastrous effect on many of the grapes which had ripened too early, while benefiting those which ripened later. Problems were further exacerbated by a hot, dry Sirocco wind blowing in mid-September. Thin, astringent wines, lacking fruit and concentration: very short-lived.
Avoid.

1974

Red★▷★★ White~ The second of two large vintages in the Rhône. Early autumn rainfall diluted the grapes in the south. Overall, a mediocre year, the best wines coming from Hermitage and Châteauneuf-du-Pape where those made in the more traditional style were capable of ten years ageing.
Drink up.

1973

Red★▷★★ White★ Heavy rains in early September resulted in a huge crop throughout the region. The wines from the Côte-Rôtie had good colour but were a little light; best suited for early drinking. There was some hail damage in Hermitage, but the reds and whites from this district had good ageing potential. Further south the wines were light and low in acidity.
Drink up.

1972

Red★▷★★★ White★★★ A disappointing vintage in the Côte-Rôtie where wines were acidic and hard. A better year in Cornas and Hermitage where a small crop contributed both good colour and flavour. Some attractive wines in Châteauneuf-du-Pape.
Fully mature. Drink up.

1971

Red★★★★▷★★★★★ White★★★ An excellent vintage. The Côte-Rôtie produced big, full-bodied wines with real ageing potential. Harmonious, attractive, lighter wines from Hermitage. The south also had very good results, though with lower levels of acidity they have not aged quite as well or as long as those from the north.
Attractive reds, now fully mature.

1970

Red★★★▷★★★★★ White★★★ An excellent year in the south, and very good in the north: a vintage with real ageing potential. Hot, sunny weather during the growing season. Many rich and well-balanced wines were made throughout the Rhône.
Fully mature, the best still drinking well.

THE BEST OF EARLIER RHONE VINTAGES

Côte-Rôtie
1969★★★★ 1967★★★ 1966★★★★ 1964★★★★★ 1962★★★
1961★★★★★ 1959★★★★ 1957★★★★ 1955★★★★ 1953★★★★★
1952★★★★ 1949★★★★★ 1947★★★★ 1945★★★★★

Hermitage
1969★★★★ 1967★★★★ 1966★★★★ 1964★★★★★ and still amazingly good
1961★★★★★ perfection 1959★★★★ superb still 1957★★★★ 1955★★★★
1953★★★★ 1952★★★★★ 1949★★★★★ 1947★★★★ 1945★★★★★

Châteauneuf-du-Pape
1969★★★ 1967★★★★ 1966★★★ 1964★★★★★ 1962★★★★
1961★★★★★ 1959★★★ 1957★★★ 1955★★★★ 1953★★★ 1952★★★★★
1949★★★★★ 1947★★★★ 1945★★★★★

Loire

A relatively northern district of France, with a maritime climate at its western end, the well-spread vineyards along the meandering banks of the Loire and its tributaries mainly produce distinctly light, dry, and acidic wines, best drunk young. Most are white, some are rosé, just a few are red: Chinon, Bourgueil, and Sancerre Rouge. Vintages, of course, vary, some producing wine more acidic than others. Contrarily, the fairly rare very hot summer, such as 1989, does not produce the most typical Loire wines, though the reds and the sweet wines benefit from the extra ripeness.

The dry to bone-dry whites such as Muscadet, Sancerre, and Pouilly-Fumé should be consumed within one to three years after the vintage, as should Anjou Rosé whose main attraction is its pink colour and freshness. The dry whites and rosés do not feature in the notes on the older vintages. However, the semi-sweet (*demi-sec*) Vouvray and the glorious Vouvray *doux*, Coteaux du Layon, Bonnezeaux, and Quarts de Chaume which, in certain years, are beneficially affected by *botrytis*, the same "noble rot" responsible for Sauternes, all keep marvellously.

2002★★★★

Overall a very good vintage for reds, dry, and, in particular, sweet whites.

The start to the year was stormy but improved for an early bud-break at the beginning of April. The crucial flowering occurred quickly during a heat-wave in June though these higher than average temperatures made for a more difficult fruit set, reducing volume. Yields were further reduced by necessary crop-thinning and a drying east wind, so that the size of the harvest was twenty to thirty per cent lower than normal. Happily, the weather in September – the most important month for ripening – was excellent, particularly favouring those who had controlled yields through de-budding or thinning. Those that had not done so harvested a mixed bag of ripe, unripe, and even rotten grapes.

It was a fabulous year for Muscadet. Sugar levels were particularly high, excellent for the reds but perhaps a bit too high for the Sauvignon Blancs of Sancerre and Pouilly-Fumé.

The weather continued favourably into October, with dry, sunny days and cool nights, enabling growers to harvest healthy grapes not only at optimum ripeness but often with heavy, beneficial botrytis.

The dry whites for drinking soon, the reds will benefit from bottle-age but the real stars will be the sweet wines, notably of the Coteaux du Layon, which should have an excellent future.

2001 ★★▷★★★★

In the best of years quality can vary, which is hardly surprising considering the different, often quite contrasting, districts which are strung like washing on a line from the maritime climate of the Pays Nantais, best known for its Muscadet, to Anjou-Saumur and then Touraine, both of which districts produce red as well as dry and sweet whites, and to what are known as the "central vineyards", Sancerre and Pouilly-Fumé being the best known.

In all areas there was significant winter rain; the spring was generally mild though the Muscadet vineyards and part of Saumur's were, unusually, hit by severe April frosts. In Touraine the cumulative level of rainfall between the end of March and the last week of August was the fourth highest since 1959 though this was compensated for by periods of heat. Thereafter the weather improved and from mid- to end September it was dry with daytime temperatures around 20–25°C (68–77°F).

To sum up: a good year for Muscadet; the Cabernet Francs performed well for the reds of Chinon; Sancerre and Pouilly-Fumé wines were vivacious, and the later-harvested Chenin Blanc produced good *demi-sec* and *moëlleux* wines. *All the dry whites can and should be drunk whilst young and fresh but this seems to be a good year to cellar some of the reds, both Cabernet Franc, so often too acidic, and Pinot Noir. As always, the sweet Loire wines will provide much joy and should benefit from some bottle-ageing.*

2000 ★★★

Another French paradox: uncharacteristically uniform weather conditions did not fit the normal Loire season, yet overall the result was good quality grapes.

The spring was wet. July was atypical, cool with rain at the beginning and the end of the month with less sun than usual. Overall summer temperatures were below normal except in Sancerre and Pouilly. The rain then stopped and by late August the sun came out in force, ripening the grapes speedily. Sauvignon Blanc did well. Vineyard managers began picking in the last week of September, earlier than usual for these appellations. Only a little rain fell during the harvest and the grapes suffered little damage during picking.

2000 was perhaps the year of expressive wines, with Sancerre and Pouilly-Fumé both showing great terroir. In Chinon, despite a chaotic July, complete with mildew attacks, which were successfully treated, the results of the reds were quite surprising. The Cabernet Franc showed good acidity levels, which created supple yet lively wines with elegance and a lot of character.

Overall, yields were a little lower than in 1999, but they were still near average. The lower than usual summer temperatures meant that the sweet wines did not do as well this year though a few intrepid growers managed to make sweet wines from grapes picked in late November. *A good year for the dry whites and the refreshing reds of Chinon and Bourgueil. Few sweet whites.*

1999 ★★★

Following a mild winter the year started off well. From Muscadet to Sancerre – some 500 km (310.7 m) – an ideal spring, with no frosts, was followed by a successful early flowering and almost idyllically warm summer. By September there were hopes of another excellent vintage. Unhappily there was persistent rain from mid-September, though there were ten days of fine weather in early October. Some of the estates in Coteaux du Layon and Bonnezeaux, which need a combination of fully ripe grapes and noble rot, found it a difficult year necessitating up to seven *tries* to select the best botrytized grapes; some were still harvesting towards the end of November.

On the whole agreeable dry whites for early drinking, the classic reds of Chinon and Bourgueil varying from agreeable and easy, with low levels of tannin and acidity, to those with good colour, suitable for keeping. Good but not great sweet wines for early drinking.

1998★★▷★★★★

A fairly difficult year, particularly in the mid-Loire, with rain at some critical times. Distinctly variable. From winter to early spring the weather was relatively mild with temperatures above average, though some heavy rain in April retarded growth, and frost at the end of that month did considerable damage, hitting roughly fifteen per cent of the Muscadet vines. May was warm, speeding up development; June's warmth was a little below average, cool temperatures affecting flowering, with *coulure* and *millerandage* reducing the potential crop. Temperatures in early July remained on the low side. August, on the other hand, was very hot, *véraison* evolving rapidly. From the end of the month and into September the rains came, though relenting for the start of the Muscadet harvest on September 11.

The Sauvignon Blancs of Sancerre and Pouilly-Fumé were reasonably successful, as well as the Gamay, harvested between September 16 and 25. The later ripening Cabernet Franc (producing Chinon and Bourgueil) and much Chenin Blanc were picked in variable weather in October, but those who held out were rewarded by splendid conditions in early November, and harvested good, botrytis-affected wines.

Although not beyond its "sell-by date", Muscadets will and should have been drunk; the best Sancerres still drinking well. The reds for drinking from now until circa 2008, and the best sweet wines of Vouvray, Bonnezeaux, and Coteaux du Layon until 2010, perhaps longer.

1997★★★★★

Miraculously, a third very successful vintage. Bud-break ran smoothly in relatively good conditions, although there were some patches of local frost. Flowering was complete for most areas before hail fell in mid-June. The end of June did not improve and was the coldest and wettest in thirty years. The central vineyards did suffer from some uneven development. Fortunately a long and hot summer, punctuated by thirst-quenching storms in late August, ensured successful ripening and concentration in the grapes.

Picking started in Muscadet on August 29 and very high ripeness levels were recorded. This was also the case for the Chenin Blanc producers who achieved some record levels. The harvest for *moëlleux* wines lasted almost until the end of October.

Cabernet Franc triumphed again with a style very similar to 1996. Harvested at potential levels of thirteen degrees alcohol, the wines have dense colour and perfect balance of acid and tannins. Sancerre and Pouilly-Fumé experienced a small drop in yields and had to pick in stages after the uneven flowering.

However, they did achieve very good ripeness, with matching acidity levels and fine aromas.

Glorious wines, particularly the sweet wines which have that honeyed touch of botrytis and will have a long life. The dry wines such as Muscadet and Sancerre have passed their freshest acidic best but the latter can still be very attractive.

1996★★★

A very successful vintage the length of the Loire, the result of a dry and cool growing season and more sunshine hours than average.

Winter and spring were fairly cold, holding the vines back two weeks. The first half of June was warm, allowing the vines to catch up, but then cooled down towards the end, reversing the process. By late June a healthy and rapid flowering presaged a large harvest, though drought conditions during the summer decreased the crop potential. By September some welcome rain had swelled the small berries and the harvest started at the end of the month in dry conditions, with wind reducing the risk of rot.

Muscadet produced a large crop of lighter-style wines. Chenin Blanc did very well, with a high level of ripeness though botrytis found it difficult to break the thick skins. A cool, wet November did not help, though some very good sweet wines were produced by grapes left to dry on the vines. The red wines had an exceptional vintage: Cabernet Franc was harvested at 12.5 per cent potential alcohol and producers declared the wines similar to those of 1989 and 1990. Sauvignon Blanc yields were down by ten to twenty per cent, however very aromatic, vibrant, and concentrated wines with perfect acidity were produced as a result.

Dry whites: drink up. The sweet Chenin Blancs from Vouvray and Coteaux du Layon, though not benefiting from botrytis, both powerful and delicious now, and will keep.

1995★★★★

A most successful vintage. Most of the Loire valley enjoyed a long, hot, dry summer. These conditions continued through to the harvest followed by an Indian summer. The resulting wines were fine, rich, and of very high quality.

In Angers, a warm and humid autumn provided perfect conditions for noble rot and the production of stunningly deep and elegant sweet wines. Vouvray and Montlouis suffered slightly after some rain and many grapes required careful selection. The reds fared well, the top wines having both charm and firm structure, with good ageing capability. Central Loire vineyards experienced optimal conditions up to the harvest, and suspended picking for a few days to concentrate the grapes further. Generally, most wines are very good, especially the sweet whites.

A superb vintage. Sancerre and Pouilly-Fumé untypically rich – if any left drink up. Wonderfully ripe mid-term Chinon and Bourgueil, say now to 2010. Coteaux du Layon and Bonnezeaux superb, classic, will benefit from bottle-age, say 2005 to 2015.

1994★★

The conditions were favourable throughout the region during the winter months but the frosts of mid-April were more devastating than elsewhere in France. Touraine was the worst hit and in Chinon the red wine crop was half that of the previous year.

May ended on a cool note but the extreme heat from mid-June to mid-August consolidated the healthy, advanced state of the vines. Along with other parts of France, the Loire believed itself to be on course for a great vintage. The national pattern continued with the weather taking a downturn and Touraine in particular was unseasonably cold from mid-August until the heavy rains of mid-September.

Harvesting in the Loire took place very quickly due to the reduced size of the crop and was unprecedentedly completed in the main by the end of September. September 26 saw the return of fine weather offering ideal conditions for the development of botrytis. In general this vintage produced some reasonably good wines, but not the great wines many had hoped for. On the other hand, it was not the disastrous year some had feared.

Forget all but the sweet whites, but even these were upstaged by 1995 and 1996. Drink up.

1993★★★

The growing season began with early budding, but this was followed by a period of cold weather which delayed flowering until mid-June. Adequate conditions followed for healthy ripening, apart from hail which affected certain vineyards around Saumur-Champigny. Most of the central and western districts were able to complete most of the harvest before the rains fell in October. Sancerre and Pouilly-Fumé were the only areas affected as their harvests started on October 8.

In general, the growers were satisfied with their results – wines of modest to reasonable quality. The reds had good colour and structure but very few sweet wines were made.

Drink up.

1992★★

A productive vintage after the enforced rest imposed by the severe frosts of 1991; careful selection was, therefore, vital.

The growing season started well and vines advanced quickly. Prospects were good by the end of July. Unfortunately however, variable weather followed throughout the ripening season, and periods of rain and humidity were interspersed with warm, dry conditions. This resulted in the grapes swelling, inducing rot.

Dry whites from the length of the Loire were reasonably successful, and a few sweet wines were produced from grapes picked as late as early November. Chinon reds were also good, notably those resulting from careful vat selection which concentrated colour and structure. Bourgueil was less successful.

Drink up.

1991

A disastrous year climatically. Of all the French regions, this was the worst hit by April frosts which decimated the well-advanced shoots after an enticingly mild spring. Chinon and Bourgueil were virtually wiped out. Flowering in late June was also hampered by cold and, adding to frost losses, *coulure* and *millerandage* reduced the potential crop. A hot and dry summer raised hopes which were finally dashed by rain and rot-causing humidity at the end of September. By dint of careful selection, however, some passable wines were made, albeit in small quantities.

Avoid.

1990★★★★★

The drought of 1989 continued into 1990; results were good but acidity levels were a little too low.

Extremely mild weather during winter and spring, with the exception of a very hard frost in Muscadet at the beginning of April, encouraged an early flowering (mid-May), but cold weather in some areas, including Anjou, in early June meant uneven ripening. The desert-like heat scorched many of the grapes, especially in Vouvray, but the late summer rain then swelled them slightly. Picking began August 29 in Muscadet, September 24 in the central Loire and Sancerre, and October 8 in Vouvray.

In Anjou the crop was larger than the preceding year's, and this is destined to be an excellent year for the sweet whites of Coteaux du Layon, thanks to early morning October mists which encouraged botrytis. Also good for Vouvray.
Vouvray demi-sec, doux, and Coteaux du Layon fully developed but will keep.

1989★★★★★

An outstanding year for Loire wines; one which might well become the vintage of the twentieth century. A mild winter and exceptionally hot summer encouraged very early growth. Budding was in February and flowering three weeks ahead of normal in perfect conditions. Picking in Muscadet began in late August and Vouvray on September 20. The sun-ripened Cabernet Franc grapes in Chinon, Saumur, and Bourgueil produced beautifully rich, powerful red wines with high natural alcohol – perfect candidates for long keeping.

Growers from the Muscadet, Sancerre, and Pouilly vineyards produced plump, rich wines lower in acidity than normal, making this an untypical vintage, close to 1959 and 1964 in style. Chenin Blanc in Vouvray and Anjou came into its own this year, especially *demi-sec*. The sweet whites are classics.
The demi-secs drink up, the great sweet wines of Vouvray and Coteaux du Layon from now to 2020. The reds, usually dry and over-acidic, are well-constituted and still drinking well.

1988★★★★

An abundant vintage of very good quality wines throughout the Loire.

A mild, wet winter developed into a warm, sunny spring, pushing bud-break and flowering about ten days ahead of normal. Good weather continued throughout the summer and the harvest ran from mid-September into October for the Cabernet Franc grapes around Chinon and Bourgueil. These were rich, well-balanced wines with soft tannins.

Grapes for sweet whites thrived during the mild autumn and developed good levels of botrytis. Some growers harvested as late as November, producing wines of fourteen per cent alcohol. It is said that Coteaux du Layon, Quarts de Chaume, and Bonnezeaux stand comparison with the great 1959s. Though few are to be seen, *demi-sec* and *moëlleux* should keep.
Reds and sweet whites worth looking out for.

1987★

A very mixed vintage. A cool, damp spring led to late and protracted flowering and uneven fruit set. The weather improved, with plenty of sun between July and September, but broke during the harvest, necessitating careful selection of the grapes. Those who picked early and whose grapes had ripened fully produced good wines; elsewhere grapes were unripe and swollen by the September rains.

This was particularly the case for the red wines of Chinon, Bourgueil, and Saumur which produced quite attractive, but light, acid-deficient wines. *Drink up.*

1986★★★★

After a cool, wet start to the year, the weather improved and flowering took place only one week later than normal. Overall, this was a good year for the reds. Some good Cabernet Franc wines were produced in Chinon, Bourgueil, and Saumur where there was enough sun to fully ripen the grapes. The fine summer provided ideal growing conditions for the dry white wines. The Sauvignon grapes ripened fully, yet maintained a good level of acidity. A good year for Sancerre, and Pouilly-Fumé was reputed to be the best of the decade. A year of above average quality for the sweet whites from Vouvray: they were elegant wines with a flowery fragrance.

The top reds, though scarce, will have survived, but apart from some demi-secs, the whites will be "over the hill".

1985★★★★

A highly satisfactory year, particularly for the reds and the sweet whites. After a wet spring the weather picked up and remained hot and dry until the end of the vintage. The grapes were harvested in ideal conditions from September 30 until November 10. Pickers were able to go through the vineyards several times, allowing them to harvest the grapes at their optimum ripeness.

The reds were big, ripe, and attractive; well-suited for early drinking. In the districts where sweet wine is made, growers who waited were rewarded by the development of noble rot on the Chenin Blancs and produced some excellent wines. The Vouvrays were soft and dry with a perfect balance of sugar and acidity, with excellent ageing potential.

Reds deliciously mature, the botrytis-affected sweet wines still lovely.

1984★

A poor vintage throughout the Loire.

The wines on the whole were harsh, acidic, and out of balance. Not a vintage to remember.

Avoid.

1983★★

A large crop of passable wines. Spring and summer were wet and humid, but conditions improved mid-October in time for the harvest. The sweeter styles benefited from the good autumn weather; some were judged to be slightly too acidic but, for the Vouvray, this meant wines with good ageing potential.

Drink up, though some demi-secs can still be pleasing.

1982★★★

Good weather prevailed throughout the summer producing a large crop of commercially successful wines. But, on the whole, not a memorable year.

All well past best.

1981★★

A very small, modest vintage of little interest now.

Avoid.

1980★★

A good spring but protracted, very wet summer. The harvest in Anjou, Touraine and Vouvray took place under snow from October 11 to November 11. Despite all this, some pleasant *demi-secs* produced.
Drink up.

1979★★★

Dry, fairly well-balanced whites and light, agreeable reds; also some attractive sweet Coteaux du Layons.
Drink up.

1978★★★▷★★★★

A small crop, and a vintage which developed slowly, the sweet whites revealing themselves as remarkably well built.
The rare reds and best sweet whites fully mature.

1977

A poor year. Thin, dry whites and light reds.
Avoid.

1976★★★★

This was considered the best vintage of the decade. A cold, dry winter and early, warm spring. Flowering was advanced; summer was very hot and dry, but temperatures cooled in September. The harvest was, nevertheless, much ahead of normal, beginning early September. Unusually powerful wines: Pouilly-Fumé was more like a Burgundian Chardonnay; reds were well-built with long life.
Reds fully mature yet still tannic, and lovely Coteaux du Layons at peak.

1975★★★

Average sized crop of good wines. Fresh, supple whites slightly superior to reds.
Sweet wines still drinking well.

1974★

A large crop of mediocre wines.
Avoid.

1973★★

Some well-structured reds, and attractive Vouvrays and Layons.
Few remain. Drink up.

1972

A year to forget.

1971★★★★

A small crop of well balanced, elegant, and zestful wines.
Some good Vouvrays and Quarts de Chaume still lovely to drink.

1970★★

An abundant, pleasant crop of soft, though quite well-balanced wines. Not a year for the sweet wines.
Avoid.

OTHER GOOD/GREAT LOIRE VINTAGES

1964★★★★★ great sweet wines, still on top form; and **1959★★★★** fabulous Vouvray, Coteaux du Layon, and Quarts de Chaume. Excellent dessert wines were made in **1949★★★★** (at their peak now) and in **1947★★★★★** the greatest vintage for classic Coteaux du Layon, Quarts du Chaume, and Vouvray *doux* – still marvellously rich. **1945★★★★** also produced very good, firm, sweet wines. **1937★★★★★** was the best vintage of the 1930s: wines with excellent acidity. **1934★★★★** was very good too, though tiring now. And **1928★★★★** was another great vintage: the best sweet wines are still beautiful to drink.

Alsace

With the exception of small quantities of red wine and even rarer rosé, virtually all the wines of Alsace are white, the vast majority made to be consumed whilst they are young and fresh.

The dry whites made from Sylvaner and Pinot Blanc, and the now rarely imported Zwicker blend, should be drunk between one to three years after the vintage. However, when it comes to the major grape varieties, Riesling, Gewurztraminer, and the still too-little known Tokay-Pinot Gris, vintages are important, those of the highest quality achieving sublime heights and capable of remarkable longevity. Though close, geographically, to the Rhine wines of Germany and using German grape varieties, the wines of Alsace are totally different in style, fuller, less acidic, and with some remarkably high levels of alcohol, commonly 13.5 to fourteen per cent, even up to sixteen per cent though the latter is unusual.

2002★★★★★

In Alsace, the year began with an extremely cold January: the ground was frozen solid for a whole month. Spring was alternately sunny and rainy. Flowering and fruit wet in mid-June were even and successful, with neither *coulure* nor *millerandage*, and the forecast of a bumper crop prompted producers to embark on a severe green harvest programme in early July. Sunshine and showers alternated throughout July and August, and apart from five days late in the month, September had sunny, warm weather continuing into late October. Several days of strong, warm southerly winds at the end of October and the beginning of November allowed producers to harvest some of their best Gewurztraminer on record. Top vineyards in the *grand cru* Sporen reached Vendange Tardive levels, and there is even a fair quantity of Sélection de Grains Nobles (SGN) – something not seen since 1989. Weather conditions were excellent around September 30, the first day of the harvest, and there were only two days of rain during the following fortnight. Overall, ripeness levels were excellent, except for Muscat where the crop was too abundant. Pinot Noir and Gewurztraminer maturity levels were at around thirteen degrees potential due to rather high yields, while Pinot Gris was at above fourteen degrees potential. *"Everyday", inexpensive whites for early drinking. But this is a serious vintage and the high quality* grand cru *wines, particularly of Vendange Tardive and the rare SGN levels, well worth waiting for and keeping.*

2001 ★★★

Making great wine in 2001 was a difficult feat. Whimsical weather conditions meant that much depended on how vines were managed throughout the year.

The winter was mild, but changeable weather in May and June made flowering protracted. Although July and August were generally dry and sunny, average temperatures were slightly below normal. Rain in September dampened hopes of a great vintage and with an exceptionally hot, dry October, growers saw a rise in sugar levels with a corresponding fall in acidity. The harvest was about the same in quantity as the previous year and some producers were able to produce some Vendange Tardive wines.

Grand cru Rieslings are of anticipated high quality, ranging from soft and flowery to stern and austere, needing bottle ageing; Pinot Gris often surprisingly sweet, delicious, powerful; and the top Gewurztraminer perfectly scented, spicy but still austere. Wines to savour, buy, and keep.

2000★★★★

This year saw the introduction of new rules governing the production of Alsace *grand cru* wines. These regulations reduce yields and demand higher degrees of natural sugar, in an effort to curb high production and enhance quality. It was a relatively easy harvest for Alsace, less complicated than 1999 and 2001, offering good quality across the board, from the basic appellations to the *grands crus*.

Spring was sunny and warm, with early flowering. June was warm and dry, but July and August were cool and rainy. Warm, sunny days returned in September to provide ideal conditions for the harvest which began mid-September stretching into early October. The wines are precocious in nature, yet balanced and fresh, and ripe and dense, showing good levels of acidity. This is a good vintage for the Rieslings; they are mainly dry in style, supported by firm structures and mineral flavours.

The dry wines are fruity and fresh, and very typical of Alsace. Whereas the basic varietals can be enjoyed young for their juicy fruit, the lieux-dits, *or single-vineyard wines, and* grands crus *need more time to shed their youthful awkwardness. Some interesting late harvest and rare SGNs have been made for future drinking.*

1999★★▷★★★

Overall a good vintage despite some worrying weather conditions. As always, the most conscientious producers coped best. A pleasant spring with normal bud-break in mid-April was followed by a hot May and relatively early flowering, though extended, due to warm, humid, and wet conditions during the first two weeks of June.

Mildew had been a problem since mid-May, exacerbated by uncertain weather to the end of July. August was mixed but reasonably pleasant, and from the middle of that month to the third week of September the weather was hot and dry. At that stage, though, the average sugar levels and acidity were high, so was the size of the crop. Unhappily, from the end of September for some five weeks, encompassing the main harvest, the weather was capricious, humid, and rainy. Picking was stop and go, between heavy showers. Some growers reported the longest harvest of the century – from September 23 to November 30!

A potentially very good vintage was downgraded to good, quality depending entirely on the skill of the vine grower and his ability to cope with botrytis and wet conditions. The best producers reported an average-size crop of surprisingly good "elegant and racy" wines, with correct acidity and chaptalization not needed. Fewer top quality late-harvest wines.

Many decent wines for drinking now.

1998★★★★

The growers in Alsace consider themselves fortunate; they have had four really good and quite unprecedented vintages in a row, though whether 1998 quite matches the outstanding 1997 is debatable.

Weather throughout the year was uneven. Despite a cool April, the very hot and dry May encouraged development, and flowering was uneventful. July was damp but an extended heat-wave from early August to mid-September resulted in an earlier than usual harvest. There was rain at the start, but the main harvest began on September 24 in sunshine, quickly interrupted by a short rainy spell. Some of the major estates did not start picking until early October when the weather remained dry. The wines are generally considered excellent, with good levels of acidity in the Rieslings and Pinot Gris; some Gewurztraminer is merely good rather than great. A noticeable gap is widening between the run-of-the-mill producers and the half-dozen or so best, the latter marketing a surprisingly wide range of varietals and quality levels, and at corresponding prices.

At the lower, lighter quality end, Sylvaners and Pinot Blancs (do not confuse Pinot Blanc with Pinot Gris) should have been consumed. Muscats and Rieslings are excellent now but the individual vineyard and grand cru wines will benefit from more time. Pinot Gris, usually with alcoholic content in the 13.5 to fourteen per cent alcohol region, are archetypal food wines, the richer ones excellent with cheese. Gewurztraminer in 1998 can be extraordinarily powerful as well as intriguingly scented; one tasted recently had sixteen per cent of alcohol, higher than a fino sherry. SGNs will be for drinking from 2005 to 2013.

1997★★★★★

Record sunshine hours, double that of 1995, were soaked up by the vines this year. After some frost during a cold, dry winter, uneven bud-break, and *coulure* problems due to rain in June and July, producers were a little tentative. The weather then improved with a sunny August and September.

The harvest began on October 1, after the vines had taken full advantage of the exceptional conditions during September. This was another vintage for Riesling which achieved very high ripeness levels, though Gewurztraminer, again, had been affected the most by *coulure* and suffered crop losses. The harvest continued until November 4 and some early morning mists in October encouraged botrytis, but not enough. The grapes were harvested at levels equal to or higher than those required for the botrytized styles; however, without this the wines are never quite of the same quality. And so it was a year for the dry wines, with only a few top quality sweet styles produced. Some compared this vintage to 1949 and 1959: rather masculine wines with ideal sugar and acidity levels for ageing.

Some delicious racy Rieslings, pleasant, spicy Gewurztraminers and some surprisingly sweet, chunky Pinot Gris, all drinking beautifully now.

1996★★★★

A vivacious and healthy vintage, the third in a row. Yields were slightly higher than usual, except for Gewurztraminer which suffered some *coulure* during flowering. The best wines produced came from the Pinot family – Pinot Gris, Blanc, and Noir – all of which performed very well.

Winter was cold; spring arrived ten days late. Bud-burst started on April 19 but was uneven, leading to variations in maturity during the harvest. June was mainly warm and dry and flowering commenced on June 6, with similar conditions in July and August. Some producers felt drought was a threat; however a long, cool, and dry harvest began on October 7. Picking continued until November 11 for the late-harvest wines though due to the cold, dry weather botrytis was virtually non-existent.

Some producers used *passerillage* (drying the grapes on the vine, in the sun) to produce ripeness levels as high as those required for SGN wines. This is a year for the fine dry wines – aromatic, clean styles with high acidity and alcohol levels.

Attractive Rieslings, spicy Gewurztraminers, and impressive Pinot Gris, all drinking well now but the finest will develop well over the next five years.

1995★★★▷★★★★★

Declared a perfect Riesling vintage; Gewurztraminer did not fare quite as well.

Bud-break came late and a generally damp spring resulted in uneven flowering and problems with *coulure*. This was to limit the size of the vintage which was consequently down on average by twenty-five per cent. September rain and cool temperatures did not help matters, encouraging grey rot to spread widely, especially in vineyards where vines had not been thinned. Producers who had resisted picking early due to the rain were fortunate, as October witnessed a long Indian summer.

The official starting date for the vintage was October 5. Riesling and Pinot Gris had super-high sugar levels and above average acidity, with a ripeness comparable to that of 1983. Noble rot produced very good Vendange Tardive and a few SGN wines from these two varieties. Gewurztraminer did not achieve the same ripeness or level of quality. This vintage was very successful for those who had thinned and followed a strict regime. Their wines show superb glyceral texture as a result of noble rot. Depth, concentration, and a high residual sugar content were particularly evident in the late-harvest wines. These wines have substantial structure for ageing. Less fortunate producers' wines lack personality and grip.

Fragrant and characteristic Rieslings, substantial Pinot Gris drinking well now, though the top late-harvest and SGN qualities will not only keep but positively need bottle-age. Certainly up to fifteen years.

1994★★▷★★★

Vegetation progressed normally – budding took place in April, but was hindered by cold, rainy weather. The flowering took place soon after these wet conditions ended on June 8, and drier weather continued until early September. The rains came down in September and lasted thirty days – in that one month Turkheim experienced between 120 and 150 mm (4.7–5.9 in). Grey rot rapidly became a threat to the crop, particularly to Pinot, Auxerrois, and Riesling. The only crop remaining healthy throughout the deluge was Gewurztraminer.

The best wines are from growers whose patience held out until the beginning of October. Fine weather had returned and conditions were good both for harvesting and for noble rot. Some of the grapes picked at this late stage resulted in wines with a ripeness reminiscent of 1989 or 1990. The overall quality of these later-picked wines is significantly higher than 1993. The more basic wines should be carefully and thoughtfully selected but fine wines from later-picked low yields have excellent potential.

Lesser qualities should have been drunk by now but some superb Vendange Tardive Gewurztraminers perfect now and some hefty SGNs up to 2010.

1993★★★★

The heavy early autumn rain experienced by the rest of France had a less dramatic effect in Alsace thanks to the protection offered by the Vosges mountains. The volumes were lower but the quality higher than the 1992 vintage.

The growing season progressed healthily with an early budding. Flowering took place smoothly two weeks ahead of normal. As the harvest approached, hopes were extremely high for a great vintage. However, poor weather hit the region shortly before the harvest which started on September 23, the earliest date since 1976. Picking was carried out between showers.

Nevertheless, all varieties performed successfully with ripeness levels at times reaching those of 1988 and 1990. Dilution was not a threat due to healthy thick skins which also helped deter rot. The wines generally have good structure and ripe, round flavours though those from late-picked grapes were affected by the rain, few sweet wines being made.

Many satisfactory wines drinking well now.

1992★★★▷★★★★

Unlike the rest of France, the climatic conditions in Alsace were perfect for a really great vintage.

After a mild winter, budding was early and flowering was trouble-free. A warm, dry summer followed, with the hottest August since 1921, quite a contrast to more southern parts of Europe. The torrential rain that caused so much damage in the south completely bypassed the region and harvesting began on September 30.

Most growers reached the production limits imposed by the authorities, but better growers reduced their crops by as much as a quarter by green-pruning in July. If there is any criticism, it is that the acidity levels tend to be low, suggesting earlier rather than later drinking. Fine weather at the end of the harvest permitted the production of some glorious sweet wines, but overall, the wines have a full, round, opulent style.

An attractive vintage, most wines at or past their best now, though the great late-picked wines of the leading producers will continue to develop and delight well into the present century.

1991★▷★★★

After three years of drought the rains came, but not at the most propitious moment. Happily Alsace's vineyards did not suffer from the frosts that crippled other districts and the flowering took place in good weather conditions. However, due to lack of moisture in the soil, the grapes were small. Hail in August devastated some vineyards and heavy rain hindered development. More rain in September delayed the start of picking until early October and the protracted harvest ended a month later. A small crop of moderate and variable quality, though some pleasant surprises.

Some very good grand cru *Pinot Gris and Gewurztraminer. Otherwise avoid.*

1990★★★★★

The second of two excellent vintages. Very similar in style to 1989, but smaller in quantity. Particularly good for sweet dessert wines.

Alsace had no real winter, no frost or snow, and the vines began to grow in drought conditions three weeks ahead of normal. Budding began late May, but cold, wet weather followed, resulting in both *coulure* and *millerandage*, particularly affecting the more delicate Muscat, Gewurztraminer, and Tokay-Pinot Gris. September onwards experienced a mixture of rain, fog, and brilliantly sunny weather. The harvest began on October 4 and quantities were down by around twenty-five per cent from the previous year. The grapes were healthy, but the absence of botrytis meant no SGN wines were made. A very high sugar content and low acidity necessitated very careful winemaking. This was, however, the third successive year in which late-harvest wines were made.

Overall, the wines produced this year are characterized by their richness and roundness, due to a smaller crop than usual and particularly high levels of ripeness; especially for the Gewurztraminer and Muscat grapes. This vintage was considered by many to be comparable climatically, and possibly superior in quality, to the great 1961 Alsace vintage.

A good ripe year, most of the wines consumed with enjoyment whilst young and fruity. The top quality wines made from the "noble" grape varieties are now fully mature and still drinking well.

1989★★★★★

An admirable year, combining abundance and excellent quality. The vintage for late-harvest wines was the largest ever, producing extremely powerful wines, some reaching 214°Oechsle (thirty per cent potential alcohol).

A hot and dry summer provided ideal growing conditions, pushing the growth well ahead of normal. Some areas suffered from drought but early September provided adequate relief with a little rain. An unusually early harvest followed, beginning on September 27 in fine weather. The *grand cru* wines will keep well. The late-harvest and SGN wines will need considerable time to develop. Hailed as one of the greatest vintages ever.

The lesser wines drink up. The great late-harvest and SGN wines from now to 2010 and beyond.

1988★★★▷★★★★★

Excellent weather throughout the spring and summer raised hopes for a good vintage. However, heavy rains before the harvest disappointed many growers: as much as 50 mm (2 in) fell the weekend before picking commenced. For some growers, particularly those with well-drained sites, drier weather during the first week of the harvest saved the day. These areas produced some very good wines, including the top Rieslings and Tokay-Pinot Gris. Also some excellent late-harvest botrytis styles.

All but the top class late-harvest wines drink soon. Wines like Schlumberger's Cuvée Anne impressive but very powerful and demanding considerable bottle-age, well into the present century.

1987★▷★★★

Following a poor summer, the warm, sunny autumn saved this vintage from disaster. These were light wines, lacking the structure necessary for ageing.

Some of the late ripening Rieslings have developed complexity, but on the whole this vintage was for early drinking and all but the grand cru *and special* cuvée *wines should have been consumed by now.*

1986 at best★★★

A very good, if somewhat uneven vintage. An extremely cold, snowy winter was followed by a more temperate spring, providing ideal conditions for flowering.

There was hail in late July and the bad weather continued until September. Harvesting began late October/early November in misty, sunny, botrytis-inducing weather. Growers who selected grapes carefully during the harvest produced some excellent wines, particularly the Rieslings which have aged well. *The best at peak. Otherwise drink up.*

1985★★★★

A huge crop of good wines.

After a cold, wet winter and spring, with a particularly cool spell in April, conditions were fine and dry for the entire summer. Flowering was uniform and excellent, and picking began in early October and continued into December for the SGN wines. This vintage was an all-round success. Some really good wines were produced, including Gewurztraminers for early drinking. Those for laying down were also of fine quality, including some Rieslings and top-class late-harvest wines.

Excellent results at each end of the spectrum, but only the top SGN and Vendange Tardive wines, excellent now, warrant further bottle-age.

1984★

This was a dull year in Alsace. A mild spring was followed by a cool, wet summer and autumn. A dry October saved the day and the harvest yielded an average crop of wines, thin however, and lacking in fruit. The best were the light Rieslings and Pinot Blancs. Very few late-harvest wines made.

Drink up.

1983★★★★★

An abundant crop of excellent wines throughout Alsace. A very warm winter, wet spring, and dry summer which lasted into November, enabled growers to pick late into the month.

These were big, rounded, opulent, spicy wines, if occasionally a little overblown. The Gewurztraminer and Tokay-Pinot Gris are delightful and the top Rieslings are worth cellaring longer. 1983 was also an excellent year for the late-harvest wines and SGN.

Lesser wines should have been consumed a decade ago, but the best late-harvest wines are perfection now, yet firm enough for another decade.

1982★

Apart from a cold spell in January, the weather was fine throughout the year. Picking began on October 7 and yielded one of the largest crops ever – fifty per cent up from the previous year. Quality was low, with the exception of some of the better *cuvées*. Flat, dull wines tending to lack concentration.

Avoid.

1981★★★★

A good year throughout Alsace. The yields were high and this balanced out stocks after the small 1980 harvest. High humidity in the earlier part of the vintage gave way to dry, sunny weather during flowering. This lasted throughout summer until a hot, humid period in early September. The harvest took place in good conditions from late September. These were – with the exception of some light, inferior Sylvaners – well-balanced, attractive, fruity wines. An excellent late-harvest vintage.

One of the least-known of the really good vintages. Worth looking out for. Undervalued yet the finest at their peak now.

1980★

A small quantity of varied, but generally low quality wines.

1979★★

The wines were of good commercial quality but tended to lack acidity; suitable mainly for early drinking. Some remarkable exceptions.
Top Rieslings surprisingly good still. Otherwise avoid.

1978★★

A small crop of fairly good wines.
One or two of the late-harvest wines remain and can still be beautiful to drink. But don't wait.

1977★

A large vintage of mediocre quality.
Avoid.

1976★★★★★

After a cold, snowy winter, vines flowered during hot, dry weather in mid-June. The sunny, dry weather continued throughout the summer with the occasional rain shower in July and early October. Harvesting began early in October in good conditions and an average-size crop was picked.

The wines were excellent, with depth and concentration which, after a rather aggressive youth, have matured well. This year was also a successful vintage for the late-harvest wines and SGNs, which are still superb.
Most Vendanges Tardives now fully mature and perfection still; though the great SGNs will continue well into the present century.

1975★★★

An average-sized crop which produced some good wines.
One or two splendid Rieslings, otherwise of little interest now.

1974★

A disappointing year. After a mild, dry winter, bud-break took place in early April but further development was halted by freezing temperatures. The summer was mainly dry and growers forecast an excellent harvest. Hopes were dashed by non-stop drizzle for thirty days. This was the only year when October resulted in no increase in sugar levels. A small crop of poor wines.
Avoid.

1973★★★

After a mild winter, a cool, dry spring with bud-break in late April and a good flowering in mid-June. A splendid summer followed with very little rain from flowering through to the harvest, which began during the second week of October. Grapes for the late-harvest wines were picked by mid-November. The huge size of the crop would now be illegal, but did, nevertheless, manage to produce good Gewurztraminers, attractive Muscats, and dry but short Rieslings.
Even the best late-picked wines have passed their peak.

1972

A disappointing year. A large crop of thin, acidic wines.
Avoid.

1971★★★★★

The smallest vintage of the 1970s. Cool, misty weather in June caused *coulure* amongst some of the Muscats and even the Gewurztraminers. Overall the very dry weather, which extended through spring, summer, and autumn, produced some excellent late-harvest wines and SGN wines – especially Gewurztraminer. High temperatures during fermentation necessitated careful control. Careful winemakers were well rewarded.

Most now past their best, but fine, rich, late-harvest wines can still be delicious, though only the finest SGN wines warrant further bottle-ageing.

1970★★

A large crop of very ripe, commercial wines which tended to lack acidity.
Few remain. Drink up.

OTHER VERY GOOD ALSACE VINTAGES

1967★★★★ 1964★★★★ 1961★★★★★ 1959★★★★★ 1952★★★★
1949★★★★ 1947★★★★ 1945★★★★★ 1937★★★★★ 1921★★★★★

Only the rare dessert whites with a high Oechsle reading, and that have been well stored, will have survived.

Europe

Germany

The wines of Germany have many virtues: they are immediately enjoyable while young, fresh, and fruity; they are light and generally low in alcohol and even fine wines from the best estates need not be expensive – about the best value in terms of price and quality of any of the world's classic wines.

Yet, apart from cheap, fairly innocuous QbAs – wines of lesser quality to which sugar has been added before fermentation – the finer wines do not have the following they deserve. There are several reasons: first the labels and names appear, at first sight, to be dauntingly complicated, yet they are logical and more informative than most; second, they are not generally considered, apart from Trocken (dry) wines, food wines, for they are best drunk by themselves, not with meals; third, and most worrying, there is understandable confusion: a commercial Niersteiner Domthal sounding much like a Niersteiner Pettenthal of, say, Auslese quality from a great estate, inhibits the price that the latter can charge – a short-term advantage for the consumer but, long term, not the best inducement for quality wines to be made.

Vintages are important. Indeed, being a northerly European wine region, weather conditions are by no means as reliably satisfactory as more southerly wine growing areas. Yet experienced growers make wine of delicacy and charm, with perfect balance of fruit and acidity.

The harvest may take place in stages: early picked bunches suitable for chaptalization, riper bunches for Kabinett, Spätlese, and Auslese qualities; then, if the autumn sunshine persists, with beneficial morning mists, very ripe, sugar-laden grapes affected by *edelfäule* (*botrytis cinerea*, "noble rot") are individually picked to make sweet superlative Beerenauslesen and intensely concentrated Trockenbeerenauslesen (TBAs); and sweet Eiswein from frozen grapes.

Halbtrocken and Trocken, not to be confused with TBA, really do seem to take on flavour with food and need not necessarily be drunk when young, particularly those further qualified as Spätlese and Auslese. An Auslese Trocken, confusingly, is dry but rich, with length, whereas a straight Auslese will be semi-sweet and rich, best drunk alone. Auslese and higher qualities should be kept for eight to twelve years after the vintage, Spätlese from top estates best at five to eight years of age.

At long last, the Riesling, king of German grapes, is being acknowledged as not just one of the world's great white varieties but arguably the greatest. It reaches its zenith in the Rheingau and the Mosel: for sheer variety of style, of sweetness, unbeatable; for delight unmatched. The vintage notes that follow are concerned more with the higher grades of wine; the better the vintage, the finer the wines, and the longer they will keep. Not to be ignored is the excellent, firm, acidic Silvaner produced in Franconia and, increasingly impressive, some superb reds made from Spätburgunder (Pinot Noir) grape.

2002★★★★

Producers were on the brink of one of the greatest vintages since 1976, but the weather failed to play its part at the crucial stage; producers were particularly devastated because the microclimates in the main growing regions were in fact ideal. Nevertheless, there were some fantastic results, with good quantities of Kabinetts and rich Spätlesen, and smaller quantities of Auslesen.

May and June conditions were ideal, resulting in early, successful flowering mid-June. Heavy rainfall ensued in early July, but was followed by a warm summer with temperatures averaging 30°C (86°F). Storms with hail wreaked havoc on July 30, but no serious damage occurred and torrential rainfall swept across Germany until August 9.

Then, a warm and almost completely dry September followed with temperatures around 20°C (68°F) during the daytime. While the previous year's wines were influenced to a great extent by a "golden October," this year it was a sun-kissed September that was this vintage's saving grace. The warmer weather was interrupted by a severe hailstorm, which hit the middle Mosel on September 22, causing some damage, but afterwards, dry weather continued until October 12 .

In October total rainfall was fifty per cent above average. The berries, which were affected by noble rot, soaked up the moisture and could not dehydrate. There were many botrytis-infected grapes in top Riesling vineyards and in the Mosel as early as the first week in October, but producers held on to ensure higher must weights and for dry weather. Hopes were effectively dashed for Beerenauslese and Trockenbeerenauslese in many regions. The grapes remained surprisingly healthy, however, well into November, resulting in good quantities of excellent Kabinett and Spätlese musts. The average Oechsle levels were well above average, exceeding those in the 2001 vintage, the crop being twenty-seven per cent larger than the latter's small harvest.

With eight major regions, several grape varieties, thousands of producers, and styles and quantities from dry to sweet, ordinary to great, it is difficult to summarize the wines of any German vintage: the equivalent of encapsulating every district and producer in France!

2001 ★★★★★

An extraordinary roller coaster growing season, near to catastrophic with a rainy September but crops and quality were saved by a "golden October". Overall a highly successful vintage with firm, well-structured wines, those estates with well-drained prime vineyard sites faring best.

April frosts caused anxiety at bud-break, but damage was minimal. Flowering and fruit set in June were successful, and apart from a cool and wet few days in early August – and occasional hail and thunderstorms – the summer was dry and hot with temperatures hitting 35°C (95°F). Then, in September, temperatures dropped to 5°C (41°F) and the weather turned wet and damp, which resulted in the spread of rot, particularly in areas where the ripeness was most advanced. The rapid spread of rot through the vineyards in the Rhine valley mid-October made mechanical picking this year a poor option. Serious and unusual hail in early October caused damage in the Rheingau and hopes for a great vintage dwindled. Those that employed diligent spraying, careful working of the vineyards, and escaped the brunt of the hail, were rewarded with healthy, ripe grapes. The rest of October and well into November reverted back to warm and dry weather, helping the concentration of flavours in riper grapes. In the Mosel growers who delayed the harvest until October and November were rewarded with the best results since 1959. Had the rains of September continued for another week or so, then even in the Mosel, rot could have been destructive.

Acidity levels were higher this year, while physiological ripeness was as perfect as in 1997. In Rheingau some growers reported yields down by about fifty per cent on last year, due to hail, but most of the later-picked fruit was of Spätlese quality and above; one major estate, for thirteen years running, succeeding in producing high quality wines of every Prädikat level. Rheinhessen and the Pfalz produced well-balanced, healthy, ripe grapes, again of Spätlese quality and above, but yields were lower than in previous years.

As always, drink the minor wines whilst refreshingly fruity and acidic but, if humanly possible, give Rieslings of Spätlese and Auslese qualities significant bottle-age; the transformation will be well worth the wait. The few TBAs produced will be of supreme quality and high price. Finally, take note of the German red wines which have changed out of all recognition over the past few years, and in 2001 the Spätburgunder Spätlesen are excellent.

2000★★▷★★★

On the whole an "average" vintage, difficult for the producers owing to an extremely rainy summer. It was a year when strict pruning, green harvesting, and very selective picking produced the best results, the best being aromatic Rieslings grown on classic vineyard slopes.

An unusually early blossoming of the vine at the end of April and beginning of May was followed by a hot summer, which accelerated the growth of the vines in early June. Until the arrival of the rain, the harvest looked very promising, and there was a good chance for top quality sweet wines. Then continuous rain towards the end of the summer in July and August led to mildew in the Rheingau, though rigorous selection in the steep vineyards proved beneficial, resulting in wines with better acidity balance than in the previous two years. The Mosel vineyards escaped the full force of the September rain due to their steep slopes and good drainage, but ripening was severely hampered. There was a thirty to fifty per cent attack of botrytis, and through botrytis selection, Auslese level was reached, albeit in small quantities. The rest of the grapes were used to produce a Spätlese. The Pfalz was not too badly affected by the rain, with Pinot Gris and Pinot Noir attaining good acidity levels. Generally, growers who protected their berries suffered less.

A vintage for early drinking, with some useful Trocken and Spätlese/Trocken Rieslings – ideal restaurant wines in style and price. Though there are exceptions, the higher Prädikat wines lack the requisite firmness and elegance but will prove agreeable to drink within the next two or three years.

1999★★★★

No doubt about it: Germany has enjoyed the longest string of really good vintages in history. 1999 was splendidly successful despite rain throughout the harvest. A good summer, and skilful work in the vineyard, produced quite remarkable results.

Spring was normal, flowering average despite some colder spells in May and June, with adequate rainfall. Summer however was long, warm, and exceptionally sunny, advancing the ripening of the grapes. Well-drained vineyards avoided the danger of drought stress. September was miraculous, said to be the warmest of the century, but from September 20 the rains came and continued throughout the harvest resulting in a larger crop than anticipated. Late-harvest grapes benefited from a "golden October". Well-drained soils were least affected by the rains but flatter vineyards with insufficient drainage resulted in high yields and diluted fruit character. A particular success in the Saar and Ruwer. All regions in Germany reported very ripe fruit and unusually low acidity: distinctly unclassic, but pleasing and very drinkable.

Most attractive wines, many drinking well now though the top Auslesen will benefit from a further four to ten years bottle-ageing.

1998★★★★

"A great vintage despite the weather" to quote from a VDP newsletter of January 1999. It was certainly not an easy year. The paradox is explained away by the exceptionally long growing season between early flowering and a very late harvest, and the fortitude and survivability of that greatest of all white wine grapes, the Riesling.

An early bud-break, too much rain in April, but a hot and sunny May led to an early flowering, two weeks earlier than normal in the Mosel, excellent in the Rheingau and elsewhere around the first week of June despite low temperatures. This was followed by extensive rain and a cool early summer, July warm and dry though lacking sunshine. The rest of the summer was noticeably hot with record highs up to 40°C (104°F) in the Rheingau and Germany's all-time record at Brauneberg in the Middle Mosel: 41.2°C (106.2°F). Some growers were faced with sunburnt grapes, rare enough in Europe's most northerly classic wine area. Thanks to the sun and heat, most districts saw their grapes ripening healthily right into early September when weather set in for a long haul of rain. The Mosel enjoyed one sunny week in October and, shortly after, on October 24, suffered from storms and flooding. Happily, the rain slid off the steep slate slopes and thanks to that and the resilience of the Riesling, the crop remained amazingly ripe and healthy throughout the wet harvest.

Picking began in the Rheingau in the second week of October, vines there also benefiting from the drying northerly winds blowing over the Taunus hills; ninety-five per cent was of Prädikat quality. The redoubtable Robert Weil estate boldly reported that its harvest took place between the middle of October 1998 through to February 1999, a small amount of frozen grapes being picked on February 14 to make an Eiswein! In Rheinhessen careful selection was necessary because of rot. Baden to the south reported a good healthy crop; Franconia compared the 1998 to the excellent 1975, and the Pfalz was able to produce wines with good fruit and elegance, with particularly successful Rieslings up to Beerenauslese quality. The Nahe harvest was "sensational" despite 100 mm (3.9 in) of rain in October. Picking in the Mosel continued well into November and, though the wettest year since 1982, managed to make good wines. However, its tributaries, the Saar and Ruwer, not the easiest of districts, were less successful, though excellent Eisweins were made.

The year of the miracle? Almost. Apart from some excellent Prädikat wines (Kabinett wine and above) the volume produced was sufficient to replenish stocks after a series of small harvests.

1997★★★★

Good fortune held for these northern producers, with the tenth successive top-class vintage.

The season did not start smoothly as much of the winter was freezing and frost in April disrupted the bud-burst. Low-lying and flatter vineyards were affected the most and Riesling, as so often, proved to be the most resilient vine.

Flowering was hampered by cool conditions in June and local hailstorms. By August the whole country was treated to ten weeks of perfect ripening weather, with essential rain falling on September 12 and October 13 to 15. The Indian summer brought clear blue skies and lengthened the growing season. The harvest began around the beginning of October and was complete by the second week of November, producing the most healthy grapes growers could have imagined.

Ripeness levels were high and acidity was slightly lower than previous years. The result was that no adjustments were required to the final wines. Yields were down again this year due to the problems at the start of the season, some producers experiencing losses of up to fifty per cent. *Edelfaüle* was nearly non-existent so the sweet styles are very rare, though some producers did manage to produce Eiswein.

The quality is generally high, mostly at Kabinett and Spätlese levels. The wines have fine structure and will be slightly earlier maturing due to the lower acidity levels. This is the year of the Riesling. Drink now to 2010 depending on quality.

1996 ★★★★

Unusually, for German wine districts, the problem in 1996 was not too much rain but too little. Indeed, by September doom and gloom hung over Germany in the expectation of a failed vintage. Luckily fortunes changed and the results were actually quite remarkable. The one downside was a drop in yields of nineteen per cent compared to the ten-year average. The Mosel and Pfalz had the smallest yields, but of fine quality.

Snow in February during a long winter pre-empted a mild spring and early bud-break on April 18. May was unpleasant. June started well but the weather then broke, causing delay, uneven flowering, and *coulure*. July and August were warm, and a cool but sunny period from September running into October lengthened the harvest period and facilitated ripening. A little rain in September also boosted strained water supplies.

The harvest began on October 2, two weeks later than usual, and was finished by mid-November. The later-picked grapes were the best, having more ripeness to balance high acidity levels. Mosel and Pfalz producers did not pick until the end of October. This was another year of mostly QbA and Kabinett wines due to the late ripening, but they possess good concentration and depth. A Christmas vintage for the Eiswein wines, between December 24 and 26, triggered by Arctic "Tom" and freezing temperatures.

On the whole, well-structured, dry, and "fruity" wines, drinking well now. ("Fruchtig", fruity, in German wine lists indicates slightly sweet, as opposed to "trocken", dry). Also many Auslesen of high quality which will benefit from further bottle-ageing, and outstanding Eisweins.

1995 ★★▷★★★★

A labour-intensive and tricky vintage, but generally it was very successful and for some even exceptional. Many good QbA wines, mostly Kabinett QmP wines and a few Eiswein wines were produced. Production was below average, approximately ten per cent down, though some producers experienced up to fifty per cent loss as a result of poor vintage conditions, necessitating crop thinning, multiple *tries*, and strict selection.

Summer was very warm with some refreshing showers during August which helped to control ripening. Nackenheim in the Pfalz experienced some near-disastrous summer hail. September was wet and awkward with rot causing most of the problems. October warmed up and, encouraged by these weather fluctuations, *edelfäule* occurred resulting in grapes with extremely high levels of sugar and acidity. Producers who hung on until mid-October, especially in the Mosel and Mittelrhein, made stunning wines. Two cold days, November 5 and 6, produced some Eiswein.

Riesling performed exceedingly well, with thick skins offering protection from excessive *edelfaüle*. Despite a tricky vinification, with stuck fermentations, intriguing and beguiling wines with good, dry extract, very high acidity levels were made, many with potential for ageing well.

Some really lovely wines for drinking now. Rheingau and top Mosels of Auslese quality are delectable, yet with more to offer.

1994★★★▷★★★★

A good to very good vintage and in some regions, notably the Mosel-Saar-Ruwer, as remarkable as 1990. The percentage of Prädikat wines was surprisingly high, so much so that in some regions, such as the Mosel, better producers downgraded wines to QbA level for the sake of sales. The sugar and acidity levels of late-picked grapes were generally very high and have great potential for longevity.

Winter and spring were mild and fairly wet but offered favourable conditions for early budding and flowering. By June the onset of high summer temperatures confirmed the potential of a great vintage. Many of the leading properties chose to green-prune to avoid excessively high yields.

Heavy rains fell throughout Germany during September but failed in the main to affect the crop. Warm, misty autumnal weather in conjunction with damp conditions proved ideal for the development of *edelfaüle* and helps to explain why wines of Spätlese and Auslese quality were in profusion. Riesling in skilled hands performed splendidly throughout Germany at all Prädikat levels but none more so than those from the Pfalz and the Mosel.

Drink up the QbA wines but enjoy the ripe and ready Spätlesen and Auslesen now. The very best will keep.

1993★★★★▷★★★★★

This year came extremely close to being great, particularly in the Rheingau and Nahe but, as in the rest of western Europe, rains fell in September resulting in a distinctly varied vintage which made life difficult for the grower. Those prepared to take the gamble and harvest late (benefiting from a warm sunny autumn – most notably in the Mosel) and who selected carefully, produced some excellent wines, with a high proportion of Prädikats, most notably at Auslese level.

The winter was mild and an early, warm spring provided optimum conditions for early budding and flowering, which took place three weeks ahead of usual. Hopes for a very fine vintage rose quickly, but were dashed by regional drought conditions and a cold August. From mid-September until the first week of October the weather was poor and heavy rains fell – three times the monthly average. These proved to be beneficial in the better-drained sites (particularly the steep slate hillsides of the Mosel valley) but caused rot in parts of the Rhine. Many growers had started picking but decided to stop and wait for more clement weather. The better estates gambled and only started picking once the rains had passed. This paid off enormously as throughout Germany producers and their vines basked in late autumn sunshine. Grapes rapidly dried out and the warmth and early morning mists encouraged widespread *edelfaüle*.

Vigorous and time-consuming selection was required in order to retain only the most healthy grapes but where the yields were low, some very fine wines were made; generally, the harvest was about one third that of 1992. The best wines have intense fruit, healthy acidity, luscious sweetness, finesse, and great elegance, with the ability to age beautifully for many years.

Minor wines, QbAs, drink up – or ignore. Take advantage of the late-harvested Rieslings which are approaching their best and will continue well into the present century.

1992 ★★▷★★★★

This schizophrenic year neatly demonstrates the conflict in standards in German winemaking. On the one hand this vintage is comprised of sensationally good, long-living wines from super-ripe grapes, and on the other, weak and watery wines (even at QmP levels). Attitude, perhaps, is more the culprit than nature.

The conditions were good throughout the winter and spring; budding took place a little later than usual, but things caught up and flowering occurred two weeks ahead of the average. The summer consisted of very high temperatures, humidity, thunderstorms, even hail (in the Ruwer) resulting in over-stressed, unhealthy vines. Overcropping was a problem and many of the better growers chose to green-prune, though many did not.

From October 20 there was frequent interruption by rain. The beginning of November was dry, but rain resumed on November 9 which had a further diluting effect. In general, the best wines were those picked before the first wave of rainfall. *Edelfaüle* did affect a few sites and there was even some Eiswein made, but overall, the drier wines were more successful.

With such good vintages in the years up to 1990, and some attractive wines more recently, it would be tempting to give 1992 a miss, but don't; many estates in all districts managed to produce some excellent wines.

1991 ★★▷★★★

After the unprecedented successes of the previous three vintages it would be easy to dismiss 1991 as a failure. This is not so, though the results are highly variable, depending on the district and the times of picking. In any case, after so much quality wine, a large harvest of QbAs proved useful commercially.

In the Saar and Ruwer, the severe frost of April 20/21 halved the crop. Perversely, this increased the concentration of the remaining grapes and enabled them to survive the summer drought that affected most other regions, and which inhibited ripening. There was also frost as late as early June, but flowering, though delayed, was generally successful. The weather remained hot and dry until mid-September: those vineyards on water-retentive soils, such as the eastern parts of the Rheingau, survived better than those on light sandy soils, as in the Pfalz. Hail in August decimated some parts of the Rheinhessen.

Because of the weather conditions, picking time was critical. The rain was too late, and optimum harvesting conditions only lasted for one week. Those who picked before October 27 and after November 4 missed out. Nevertheless, in certain districts *edelfaüle* was taken advantage of, and some growers in the middle Mosel managed to make wine at every quality rung up to TBA. An Eiswein from the Rülander grape was made, for the first time, at Castell in Franconia on December 13.

The inexpensive QbA wines, drink up. Rarer and expensive, Auslesen and Eiswein drink soon.

1990★★★★★

An excellent vintage; never before has Germany had three consecutive years of outstandingly top quality wines, although everywhere quantities were down on 1989.

Leaf development was very early but stopped for two weeks during a cold April. May was mainly warm and dry, interrupted by occasional hailstorms and showers. Very cold, sometimes freezing nights extended blossoming over almost four weeks, particularly in the southern regions. The result was incomplete fertilization, or "blossom-drop", and an irregular development of the small berries. Berries remained small throughout the hot, dry summer. Heavy rain in late August, followed by storms in many areas, resulted in rot reducing the crop size. Picking was advanced for the early varieties, many of which made wines in the Prädikat range. Everywhere this was described as an "ideal" autumn. Contrary to expectation, acidity was higher than in the 1989s and many growers felt that this would be the firmer, better, more consistent vintage of the trio.

A classic Riesling vintage: some estates reported harvesting only Spätlese and Auslese-quality Rieslings with excellent acidity, and in the Rheingau the wines promised to keep well. Growers from Baden were optimistic for their excellent red wines. The only disappointments were in the Saar and Ruwer where the grapes were less ripe and *edelfaüle* did not develop well, consequently few late-harvest dessert wines were made there.

Minor wines drink up; those of Spätlese and Auslese quality from now until well into the present century.

1989★★★▷★★★★

A huge vintage of very good wines. An average of fifty per cent of the crop was declared as Prädikat wine, and this increased to as much as sixty-six per cent in the Rheingau.

Near perfect weather prevailed throughout the year. A mild winter and warm spring prompted an early bud-break, followed by flowering in ideal conditions. The summer was warm and dry, only interrupted by occasional thunder and hailstorms, the effects of which were severe but very localized. The grapes ripened well and picking began early at the beginning of September. Most growers selected carefully, and so avoided the usual disappointments associated with overproduction. Some Rheingau estates enjoyed their best vintage since 1971: the grapes had benefited from elevated *edelfaüle* levels and made highly concentrated wines.

Lesser wines at or even past their best but virtually all the higher quality Prädikat wines are lovely now and will continue to evolve in bottle; the TBAs, very sweet, mammoth, and glorious. A classic Riesling vintage.

1988★★★★

Excellent summer weather prompted hopes that this would be a classic year for German wines. However, unfortunate pre-harvest rain, fog, and, in the Saar and Ruwer, hail, dampened expectations. But this did not prevent it from being a good vintage. In the Middle Mosel the weather remained fine throughout the harvest and some classic Auslesen wines were made, especially in the region between Erden and Bernkastel. Many of these will last well. Frosts during the harvest in the Nahe on November 7 enabled growers to make superb Eiswein. Rheinhessen and Pfalz produced some good wines – top Prädikats being real classics. Perhaps the weakest wines came from the Rheingau, but even here many reached Kabinett level and above.

QbA and Kabinett wines drink up; Auslesen still drinking well.

1987

A severe winter, during which temperatures sank to -15°C (5°F) causing some damage to the vines. April was warm but temperatures fell again during May and June and heavy rain caused rot in some areas. Considerable pessimism resulted from this – one renowned Mosel grower declared that he would not be bottling his 1987s at all. Warm, dry weather from mid-September until the harvest alleviated much anxiety. The Rieslings were harvested from October 28, although many growers held off for as long as possible so that picking continued until the end of November. The crop was quite large, but of this only fifteen per cent was QmP (quality wine), the majority being only QbA.

Drink up.

1986★▷★★★

Problems caused by difficult harvest conditions made this a vintage of mixed quality. An exceptionally severe winter, during which temperatures fell as low as -20°C (-4°F) was followed by a mild spring, then warm weather during May and June. Flowering was early, starting mid-June.

The hot summer gave way to a poor September but this did not dispel optimism among growers. However, violent storms hit in late October, stripping many vines, and made harvesting particularly difficult.

Those sites which had escaped the storms produced some top quality wines, the best of which were the Auslesen, Beerenauslesen, and TBAs produced in the Pfalz region. Elsewhere the wines were of average quality.

Top quality sweet wines at their peak.

1985★★★

Severe frosts and hail during the winter considerably "pruned" the eventual size of the crop, but the quality was generally high.

In the Mosel flowering took place in late June and poor weather continued until September. An Indian summer saved the day, providing good conditions for late ripening, and the harvest began on November 17. The better sites here made some excellent, well-structured, acidic wines with good keeping qualities.

After a poor start to the year, the Rheingau enjoyed more equable weather conditions than the Mosel; the summer was hot and dry and picking began on November 4. The dry weather reduced the size of the crop and winemakers produced some excellent wines. At worst, sometimes dull, short, and lacking.

Most should have been consumed by now. The very best still delicious.

1984

A cool spring delayed flowering until mid-July. Vine growth was on average three weeks behind normal, and problems were exacerbated by poor weather throughout the summer. The harvest started in late October for the lesser grape varieties and mid-November for the Riesling. The grapes were unripe and the wines were excessively acidic.

Avoid.

1983★★★★

The year got off to a bad start with a cool, wet spring which caused flooding along the Rhine and Mosel. Fortunately, the vines were not damaged and fine, warm weather in June accelerated the growth. The flowering took place at the end of the month, and the excessively wet spring was counterbalanced by one of the hottest, driest summers on record. Early-harvest grapes were picked in September. A period of rain followed by sun then swelled and ripened the Rieslings and their picking began later in October. Virtually no *edelfäule*.

The wines of 1983 combined quality with quantity. Over forty per cent of the huge crop was of Prädikat standard, the best since 1976. Those from Saar and Ruwer and the Nahe fared best.

An all-round success and one of my favourite vintages. The top grades from leading estates are still drinking beautifully.

1982★

A huge vintage – the biggest ever recorded in Germany – producing 165 million cases. The quality, however, did not match the quantity. Fine, warm weather during spring encouraged an early flowering during the first week of June. The gloriously hot summer prompted much optimism among growers, but hopes were dispelled by wet weather in early October which diluted the grapes and caused rot.

About twenty-two per cent of the wines were of Prädikat quality, only the top sites producing modestly good results, the best coming from the steep, well-drained sites of the Mosel – JJ Prüm's Wehleners for example.

Drink up.

1981★★

A warm spring prompted early growth. Unfortunately, progress was checked by severe April frosts, damaging the newly grown shoots – most seriously in the Rheingau, Saar, and Ruwer.

May and June were warm and wet, and flowering began fairly early (June 8) but was interrupted by rain causing damage in all areas, particularly in Rheingau. The remaining crop ripened well in good weather during the last part of the summer, only to encounter the hazards of rains during late September/early October. Rieslings were picked from October 12 and growers who held out longer and harvested later were rewarded by drier weather towards the end of the month.

This was a small crop of mixed quality wines. The best were the fresh and racy Kabinett and Spätlesen from the Mosel.

In winemaking there is both life-supporting acidity and tart acidity. The 1981s have a lot of each. The best quality wines can still be attractive, otherwise avoid.

1980

A disastrous year for German wines. A cold wet winter, cool spring, then lovely warm weather through May to early June; wet weather and the latest flowering in memory then followed, finishing at the end of July. The vines also suffered severe *coulure*. Poor weather throughout the summer prevented the grapes from ripening and picking was delayed until early November. However, this enabled winemakers to produce a reasonable amount of Prädikat wine (thirty per cent of total output). But overall, this was a thin, hard vintage.

Avoid.

1979★★★

Severe January frosts, following a hard winter, caused widespread damage to the dormant vines. The full effects were seen only in May, especially in the Mosel-Saar-Ruwer and parts of the Rheinhessen. The Rieslings, however, did not suffer greatly and the Mosel in particular produced some light, easy, enjoyable wines.

A largely forgotten vintage though many very attractive wines were made. Some, thanks to good acidity levels, can still be delicious.

1978★★

Bad weather during the spring, a late flowering, and wet summer weather finally gave way to a fine, dry, sunny September which pruned the crop, especially in the Mosel. The harvest was late. Pleasant enough wines but lacking in length.

Drink up.

1977★

A mediocre, rather uninteresting year. The vines started well but flowering was hampered by a cold April and May. The summer was changeable but generally inclement until a delightful October. Conditions were ideal for the development of *edelfäule* in the Rieslings and a small quantity of Eiswein was made. Some passable wines from the southern Pfalz, but all past their best.

Drink up or avoid.

1976★★★★

A gloriously ripe vintage, thanks to an exceptionally warm summer. Blossoming and growth was extremely early – by as much as three weeks along the banks of the Rhine and Mosel. Late August rain swelled the grapes; September to mid-October was warm and then damper conditions encouraged the spread of *edelfäule* amongst the late ripening grapes. The best year since 1971 produced a fairly small crop of fruity, well-balanced wines; perhaps less ripe than the 1971s and less fat than the 1964s and the 1959s, but very appealing. Many Auslesen, Beerenauslesen, and TBAs, all lovely, the best developing well in bottle, some, though, lacking acidity.

All are fully mature; but surviving great bottles still glorious.

1975★★★★

Except for a cold April, the weather was warm, flowering speedy and successful, and summer was hot, culminating in a scorching August. Early September was wet but autumn sun ripened the grapes for the harvest beginning on October 17. An undervalued year, the buyers being more interested in the 1976s as soon as they came onto the market. The 1975s however were firmer and more acidic and they have, in many instances, overtaken the 1976s. A vintage also notable for increasingly widespread use of new grape varieties and unusual crossings. The Auslesen wines can still be lovely.

Upstaged at every turn by the 1976s, yet now more than holding their own. The very best are still delicious and, if you can find them, undervalued.

1974

A dreary, wet vintage. Heavy rains during harvest time washed out the crop.

Avoid.

1973★★▷★★★★★

The largest crop on record. A late spring was followed by an unusually hot summer, some September rain and then more sun until November. The wines were of variable quality, ranging from some very pleasant examples which, however, lacked acidity and extract (perhaps due to overproduction), to uninteresting. A vintage for quick drinking.

Mostly consumed in the mid- to late 1970s. Too late now except for a few excellent Eisweins.

1972★

An unexciting year that nevertheless produced useful commercial wine which restocked the trade cellars depleted after the sales of the outstanding 1971s.

Avoid.

1971★★★★★

A magnificent, classic year of great abundance. The overall quality was so great that producers and merchants moaned about the dearth of commercial wines available for everyday drinking.

The vines flowered early and well, then a wonderfully sunny summer lasted right through to the autumn. The resulting grapes were small, ripe, well-nourished, and immensely healthy. Best of all were the Rieslings from the Mosel which had absorbed the moisture from the early morning autumn mists and achieved a most wonderful balance. All in all, soft, delicious wines with perfectly balanced, ripe sweetness, and fruit acidity. They had none of the flaccid quality of the 1964s or the almost overwhelming richness of the 1959s, but were closer in weight and charm to the 1953s and 1949s.

Auslesen and the great dessert wines are not only delicious, some are still continuing to evolve.

1970★★

A moderate year. The vines blossomed late and a dry summer followed. Those who picked late were able to make high quality wines; some picking continued right through to December and even January, enabling Eisweins to be made. Some good wines but they were overshadowed by the 1971s.

Just a few quality wines holding on; but drink up.

1969 at best★★★

The best were good, firm wines, especially in the Mosel. Forgotten once the 1971s arrived.

Some excellent Auslesen from the Mosel and the odd Pfalz Beerenauslesen, otherwise drink up.

1968

An abundant quantity of poor-quality wines.

1967★▷★★★★★

After a mild winter the spring suffered a combination of sun, rain, terrible cold, wind, and thunderstorms. Summer was better but disastrous harvest rain washed out some districts. Those who delayed picking were able to enjoy some late autumn sun and made excellent TBA wines. The results ranged from a few poor, thin wines to some excellent dessert wines. The top estates were excellent yet the vintage underrated.

Some TBA magisterial, "Wagnerian" wines. Otherwise ignore.

1966★★★

Good, stylish wines. Cold, wet weather in early November delayed harvesting and limited further ripening. However, a few good Eisweins were made.

Over the top now. Drink up.

1965

A very poor year due to uneven weather conditions.

1964★★★★

The best vintage of the 1960s, much welcomed and very popular, coming after four rather uninteresting years. Fine, dry weather continued right through the spring and summer pushing the growth of the vines ahead of normal. The lack of rain, coupled with an increase in production in some areas, caused concern amongst growers. An enormous crop was harvested and picking continued through to the end of November. The finest and longest-lasting wines were those from the northerly, steep slate slopes of the Mosel-Saar-Ruwer where the acidity counterbalanced the unusually high sweetness of the grapes. Overall, these were soft, ripe wines. The best vintage between 1959 and 1971.

All but the very best wines from the Mosel-Saar-Ruwer well past their best.

1963★▷★★★

Cold, hot, wet – and an Indian summer. Overall, roughly equal quantities of below- and above-average wines.

Of little interest now.

1962★▷★★

A year which included a long cold spell and a long period of drought. Picking continued into December and much Eiswein was made – the best 1962s. The rest pleasant but very light.

All but the Eisweins long since faded.

1961★▷★★★

A small crop of very uneven quality which achieved, but perhaps did not merit, very high prices. No great sweet wines.

Drink up.

1960★

Large crop of raw, unripe, mediocre wines.

1959★★★★★

An outstanding vintage. Rarely has such a prolific crop produced such consistently high quality wines. An exceptionally fine summer: hot, dry weather right through to October. Anxiety was caused by almost unprecedented heat at vintage time, the unusually high sugar content, and low acidity of the grapes. The wines produced were excellent, full-bodied, naturally sweet and ripe, and developed slowly. There were a record number of Beerenauslesen and TBAs made in the Mosel-Saar-Ruwer.

As in Burgundy, I consider 1959 the last of the heavy-weight vintages. Many great wines from Auslese to TBA are still superb to drink. The latter will keep.

1958★★

A huge crop, the biggest for twenty years, but only of moderate quality wines.
Avoid.

1957★★

Mediocre wines mostly consumed by the early 1960s.
Avoid.

1956

A disastrous, cold, wet year. Small quantity, very low quality.
None tasted.

1955★★

With few exceptions, a small crop of uneven, commercial wines. Some good reds.
Pass.

1954

Very poor quality wines due to appalling weather conditions.

1953★★★★★

An outstanding vintage – the result of good weather throughout the year except for some severe frosts in May which damaged the vines in the lower-grade areas. Healthy grapes were harvested in excellent, sunny conditions. Wines from the Rheingau reached perfection – elegant, firm, and supple. Many soft and pleasant wines, not meant to last, were produced in the Mosel; the best from the Saar and Ruwer. Open-knit, easy wines were made in the Rheinhessen, the Silvaner grape producing the best. Overall, a ripe and fruity vintage which varied in character from district to district. Incidentally, the quality of corks used in the mid-1950s was poor, some failing to withstand the test of time.
Only the finest Auslese to TBA have survived. They can, however, be glorious.

1952★★★

This would have been a great vintage had it not been for rain in September and October. Some well-constituted wines were made in underrated vintages.
Firm wines with good acidity, a few of which still retain a vestige of freshness as well as honeyed bottle-age.

1951

Poor, thin wines.

1950★★

A pleasant year of commercial quality. Of little interest now.

1949★★★★★

A great classic year – and the best Mosels since 1921. Apart from early spring frosts, which pruned the crop size, conditions were excellent. These were firm, well-balanced, refined wines which lasted well.
The top quality wines can still be delicious.

1948★★

An average vintage of little interest.

1947★★★★

A warm but too dry summer produced an average-sized crop of grapes which lacked the moisture necessary for full ripening. The wines were low in acidity and many only short-lived. The finest were nevertheless soft, rich, and of high quality.

TBA wines from great Rheingau estates are still magnificent.

1946★★

Unfairly considered an "off" vintage. Upstaged and ignored.

1945★★★★★

Coming at the end of the war, the vines suffered from disease and a lack of labour to combat it. There was also much looting by released Polish and Russian prisoners. Consequently, despite the fine summer, a tiny crop was harvested. However, those that were made were excellent.

Even the finest now drying out. Some rare and still fabulous wines exist.

1943★★

Best of the war vintages. Beerenauslesen still remarkably good.

DECADE OF THE 1930S

The 1930s produced some interesting vintages, though after 1937 German wines were, understandably, rarely seen outside their own country.

1937★★★★★ was magnificent: an early flowering; hot, dry summer and September rain swelled the grapes and made this the best year since 1921. My favourite German old classic vintage. The best can still be fabulously good. The second-best year of the 1930s was **1934★★★★** some wines even merited five stars. Few to be found now and likely to be over the top. **1933★★★** produced an abundant crop of soft wines; some Rheingau wines were drinking well in the late 1970s, demonstrating how natural, unsugared, well-cellared wine can still be delightful at forty-five years of age. The first three years of the decade were, sadly, of poor quality.

1920s

1929★★★★ was the first really good vintage after 1921. Spring frosts were followed by a hot, dry summer which lasted well into September; a small crop of healthy, ripe grapes was harvested. If cellared carefully, these wines lasted well, but now are very rare. **1925★★★** was good, though rarely seen. The best vintage of the decade was undoubtedly that of **1921★★★★★** arguably the greatest of the twentieth century. Spring frosts and a summer drought reduced the size of the crop and disease-free grapes were picked in good conditions. Those from the Mosel, Rheinhessen, and Rheingau were the best. Some have survived. **1920★★★** produced variable but mainly good wines. Some late-harvest wines were outstanding.

1910s back to the nineteenth century

1915★★★ a good, abundant vintage. **1911★★★★★** excellent, particularly for the wines from the Rheingau: the end of an era. **1906★** modest vintage.

1900★★★★ considered by some to be an even better vintage than 1893.
1897★★★, **1895★★**, **1893★★★★** probably the best of the century, after 1865
and 1811. A small quantity of very rich wines after an exceptionally hot summer,
and, incredibly, some Rheingau TBA still superb.

Austria

Mozart, Strauss, Vienna, and the Danube; mountains for skiing and *The
Sound of Music*. All most evocative. And wines to match, with their easy-to-
drink charm and reasonable prices. Apart from the unfortunate so-called
"anti-freeze" scandal in the early 1980s, good wines have been made for
centuries in the Wachau, Styria, Burgenland on the Hungarian border, and
around Vienna, the only major European capital city to have such a wealth
of vines on its doorstep. Although some good red wines are now produced
it is the light, dry to medium-dry white wines of Germanic style that are the
best known: Riesling, Müller-Thurgau, the highly scented Muskat Ottonel,
Traminer, Ruländer, Weissburgunder (Pinot Blanc), and the ever popular
Grüner Veltliner, best drunk young. Excellent late-harvest wines are made,
rich Auslesen, outstanding "Ausbruch" and luscious TBAs.

After years of being taken for granted there is a new awareness of the –
frankly – brilliant quality of the top producers' white wines, particularly the
firm, steely Riesling; also, at another level, some quirky but equally brilliant
sweet whites. As with most other white wines, the lighter, drier styles should
be drunk within a year or so of the vintage (though the Viennese flock out to
the suburbs to drink the new wine shortly after it has finished fermenting),
only the finest Riesling and late-harvest wines having a good cellar life.

2002★★★★

A very good vintage in this increasingly popular and well-respected country.
Drought in Burgenland and extensive floods and hailstorms in lower Austria,
particularly in the top white wine-producing regions of Kamptal, Kremstal,
and Wachau, in early August were particularly severe. Fortunately, they had
little impact on overall production. Alternating heavy rain and warm sunshine
and breezes encouraged an early maturation and harvesting started during
the second week of September. Producers owe much of the vintage's success
to stricter than usual crop thinning to remove any grapes affected by rot, shoot
thinning to reduce yields, and improvements to the vine. In addition, wind
arrived immediately after the rains and quickly dried the grapes, helping to
prevent the spread of rot. The result was fruit-packed grapes, with spicy notes
for Grüner and a super clear fruit definition for Riesling.
*The white wines are aromatic, elegant, and show good extract. The reds also have
aromatic qualities, with a good balance between power and fruit, partly due to an
extensive green harvest during the summer. Lesser whites for early drinking, the finest
Rieslings say from 2004 to 2008.*

2001★★★▷★★★★

The winter was dry and mild, with minimal frost damage. Flowering and
fruit set were successful, though the unusually cool weather in June delayed
ripening until a hotter July and August fuelled the growing process. September
was wet, and although the cooler temperatures and wind restricted rot, the
heavy rains hindered ripening and significantly diluted the grapes. The Indian

summer of October and early November reversed this process, concentrating the grapes rapidly as they finished ripening. The weather, as if to oblige, remained fine for the last days of picking, helping those who picked late and selectively to yield top quality grapes. Most of the Grüner Veltliner was picked during October, but the Riesling harvest only got underway in early November. In contrast, the red wine harvest was rushed in during early October to minimize rot resulting from the September rains. The acidity of the later-picked Riesling and Grüner Veltliner grapes was good, the waiting definitely paid off. Some good botrytis affected wines from Burgenland and a few Eisweins produced in December.

The lesser whites ready now; the reds variable, probably best 2004 to 2007. The best dry whites have good fruit and varietal definition, the top Rieslings 2006 to 2010.

2000★★★

An exceptionally dry spring and summer resulted in smaller grapes and a yield that was around ten to fifteen per cent lower than in 1999. Some producers had to drip-irrigate their vineyards to ensure stability in the ripening process. Fortunately there were no significant losses from hail or frost. The grapes were extremely healthy and ripe, and early maturity meant that the harvest started two to three weeks earlier than usual in all Austria's wine regions. Picking in the Burgenland was finished by September 20 except for the sweet botrytized wines and the harvest for dry whites and reds was completed by mid-October. The warm weather created high levels of concentration and gentle acidity, while the cool October nights gave excellent aromatic definition to white grapes. The reds were also of surprisingly high quality. The dry weather and lack of essential autumn fogs led to fewer sweet wines being produced this year.

A useful, very agreeable vintage for the dry whites and reds, the latter warranting some bottle-age.

1999★★★★★

Of all European wine-producing countries, Austria claims – with some justification – the most uniformly successful results in 1999, each district reporting a great vintage, with quantity above average. A frost-free spring, successful flowering from the middle to end June, and a warm, rainy summer encouraging good growth though some severe localized hailstorms affected Styria and Lower Austria. August was variable but an unusually mild and sunny September advanced maturing, the early ripening varieties being harvested in excellent health by the end of the month. Fine weather continued into October enabling all the grape varieties to develop fully. In parts of Austria, such as the Wachau, wine growers traditionally wait until the beginning of November before picking the Grüner Veltliner and Riesling grapes on their top sites. Those fortunate growers anticipate some outstanding wines. Happily, botrytis appeared at the right time enabling the superb sweet white wines to be made in traditional regions in Rust and Neusiedlersee.

Clearly a highly attractive and eminently drinkable vintage with some superb Grüner Veltliners and racy, acidic Rieslings. Austrian reds, which have improved out of all recognition over the past ten years, should be good as they will ever be, richly flavoured and well structured, probably drinking best between now and 2008. The glorious TBAs, often such good value, are lovely to drink now but will keep and develop well over a decade.

1998 ★▷★★★★

After three short vintages, production in 1998 was back to normal. However, the harvest itself was considered difficult though most producers were reasonably pleased with the outcome. Growing conditions started off well. Unlike 1997 there was little frost damage. Flowering occurred from early to mid-June and was completed two weeks earlier than the previous year, with very little *coulure*. July was warm, but wet, encouraging good foliage growth, followed by a hot, sunny August, greatly advancing the fruit's ripeness. September started off with a period of rain followed by a week of warm weather, helping the early ripening varieties. Thereafter, changeable weather during the harvest, bouts of rain interspersed with lengthy periods of sunshine which, happily, dried the grapes for the patiently waiting pickers. The quality of the whites is very good, the reds ripe with potential.

Austrian whites are extremely attractive to drink when young, particularly Grüner Veltliners. But some noble Rieslings, firm, with bottle-ageing capacity, are worth looking out for, some, notably from Styria, being racily acidic. The reds of 1998 will be for mid-term drinking. The sweet whites, often of exceptional value, can be enjoyed at virtually any age.

1997 ★★★★★

An exceedingly cold winter and late frost, especially around the Niederösterreich area, was followed by a relatively late budding. Subsequently, flowering was problem-free and ran smoothly. July was very wet until August when the weather improved and growing conditions were ideal right through to the end of the harvest.

A very high proportion of sunshine hours and exceptional weather in September produced healthy and balanced grapes. These were harvested between the end of September and the end of November, starting in Burgenland. Yields were down compared to 1996 and sweet styles were very rare after minimal botrytis, although some Spatlëse and a few Eisweins were produced. The wines, both red and dry white, were of very high quality with excellent extract and balance.

One report claimed this to be "one of the finest vintages this century in Austria", so take note! Unless you have inside information, stick with charming dry whites and the surprisingly enticing sweet whites and drink them whilst young and fresh.

1996 ★★▷★★★

A very complicated vintage, requiring great patience and strong nerves. The producers saw a twenty per cent drop in yields compared to 1995. Winter dragged on causing the growing season to start late. Most were spared frost, except near Lake Neusiedlersee. May and June were fair and flowering was over quickly. By mid-August the rain had arrived and did not relent for the harvest.

A warming *Föhn* autumnal wind raised temperatures, but yields had been reduced and quality was in doubt. This was compounded by a high incidence of botrytis. For those who held back from picking, fourteen sunny days blessed November and late-picked wines were rich, with pronounced acidity. In a year more suited to dry wine production, many wines affected by botrytis, but acidity is high and the best will benefit from some bottle-age.

Drink the dry whites now; botrytised sweet wines now to 2006. The better than ever new-style reds still do not have a track record and might as well be drunk fairly soon.

1995 ★★▷★★★

The summer was inconsistent, but on the whole it was warm and sufficiently sunny to allow good development. Unfortunately, rain fell quite heavily at the beginning of the harvest which took its toll on the early ripening varieties. By October an Indian summer had settled in and created perfect conditions for the rest of the harvest. The weather had reduced yields by one third compared to those of 1994, but quality was good, with a significant production of TBA wines. The cool summer had a positive effect on the acidity and concentration of fruit in the grapes.

Regional differences did occur: the region around Vienna produced finely balanced wines; Burgenland experienced the favourable botrytis and made elegant Prädikatswein, while Styria's wines were highly fragrant and fresh.
All but the late-harvest wines drink now.

1994 ★★★★

A successful vintage for both dry and sweet wines, which benefited from the intense summer heat. Although some areas experienced drought during the summer, harvesting began early in mid-September. The fruit had excellent ripeness levels, resulting in good concentration and finely balanced acidity. Some of the best examples come from Burgenland – excellent reds and dry whites, the latter having very good acidity. Styria had more balanced climatic conditions than elsewhere with frequent light showers. Many wines are of Spätlese level with a few TBAs.

In 1994, Austrian reds were still scarcely known outside their country of origin but have continually and greatly improved in quality. Their whites on the other hand are a sheer delight, almost all, except the remarkable and good value TBAs, best drunk young. The Styrian whites often have a penetratingly high acidity, a style of its own.
All more than ready for drinking.

1993 ★★▷★★★

An unbalanced vintage of variable quality and quantity. The best wines were from Burgenland due to severe frosts at the beginning of the year which heavily reduced the crop. The worst damage occurred east of Neusiedlersee, which in parts lost as much as ninety per cent of its normal yield. Spring began early and was remarkably hot until the end of May when cooler weather followed. Ripening progressed well throughout Austria. Reds and dry whites from Burgenland are near excellent. Grüner Veltliner was more successful this vintage with the re-emergence of its enjoyable vivacious character.
Charming, easy wines, mainly consumed by now.

1992 ★★▷★★★

Following a cool, dry start, favourable conditions encouraged growth, resulting in a large proportion of healthy bunches. So perfect was their condition that when torrential rains fell in June, no detrimental effect was experienced. By the end of the month drought conditions had set in and remained until the harvest, the summer being one of Austria's hottest ever. By the time of the harvest at the end of September, temperatures were generally still over 25°C (77°F). The vintage is considered perfect for red wines. Few botrytis wines were made due to the summer's aridity, but Spätlesen are common, particularly from Wachau. Here, growers picked early to retain freshness and made some successful wines.

Lack of acidity is apparent in many wines, notably from Burgenland. A little rain fell at the end of October but rot was minimal.

The sort of vintage to tempt one to try Austria's lesser known reds in their present state of maturity. The whites were easy and agreeable but should have been drunk by now.

1991 ★

A bitterly cold winter and late spring. The flowering was also delayed by cool weather and a poor June. July was warm and sunny but August was heralded by torrential rain causing flooding of cellars and low lying vineyards. The latter half of August was fine but the vines were too far retarded, and the harvest was delayed and hampered by wet weather and rot. Nevertheless, in Burgenland, growers who waited took advantage of a late Indian summer and, around Rust, made some exceptional botrytis-affected sweet wines.

Best to avoid, except for the richer dessert wines which are still drinking pleasantly.

1990 ★★★★

After a normal spring, summer brought the same drought which affected large tracts of Europe. Areas of light and sandy soil suffered the most, especially the younger vines where the rootstock was unable to find sufficient water, but irrigated estates (in the Wachau for example) fared well. In general, good winemakers made superlative wines but overall quality can be patchy. Quantities were good. There were some excellent wines in Wachau and Kamptal-Donauland, with some good dry Spätlesen from most properties. A long autumn promoted quality including many high Prädikat wines. The long growing season also came as a god-send to the Styrian growers, for whom cool conditions sometimes prevent the grapes from ripening fully; Sauvignon Blancs and Morillons (Chardonnays) were particularly fine. In Burgenland there were many top Prädikat wines made, including some Ausbruch. In the Weinviertel one grower even picked an Eiswein on the first day of the Gulf War.

Minor whites drink up. Late-picked quality dry whites which often benefit from a little bottle-age can still excite; the dessert wines now at peak.

1989 ★★

A mild winter was succeeded by a cold, damp spring. The summer was variable with frequent rain. Finally, in mid-October, some good sunny weather set in and lasted until the first days of November. The variable quality of the vintage put paid to hopes of another superlative "niner" (an old peasant tradition in Austria holds that the best years for wine are those ending in nine), but patient growers who picked late made very good wines, particularly in Burgenland and Styria.

Drink up all but the best late-picked wines.

1988 ★★

This was the first year in five not to be affected by severe frosts. The result was a potentially bumper crop. A good spring was followed by a hot summer, but rain came in September. Those who picked early made wines on the dilute side, others were rewarded by an Indian summer. Quality is variable. The vintage seems to have been best in Lower Austria. One grower in the Langenlois region harvested an Eiswein as early as November 5. Many Styrian wines betray a taste of rot.

Drink up.

1987★

After a generally abominable year in the vineyards a good autumn came to the rescue and in general the 1987s are good if occasionally on the sharp side. One or two excellent red wines were made in Burgenland.
Drink up.

1986★★★★★

Prior to 1990, 1986 was considered the best vintage in Austria since 1979. One or two Austrian wine-writers even came out with that dangerous phrase "the vintage of the century".

Frost damage reduced the size of the crop to below average, but otherwise growing conditions were near perfect. Wines to look out for are the reds from Burgenland; Styrian wines; Wachau Rhine Rieslings. High Spätlesen were harvested in the Weinviertel and one or two Auslesen in Vienna. One grower in Langenlois even picked his Grüner Veltliner on October 5 and fermented it in new oak! The wines were high in extract and had good acidity.
The best dry whites, from low-yielding vineyards, were firm and acidic but past their peak now.

1985★★★★

Spring frosts killed up to ninety-five per cent of vines in parts of Weinviertel, and elsewhere the damage ensured that the harvest was not even half the average. Flowering took place under exceedingly difficult conditions. The rest of the year was good, if not excellent: "a great year" as one Langenlois uttered perversely.

There were some very good reds from the Burgenland region, impressive, long-living Sauvignon Blancs from Styria, and a small amount of botrytized wine was produced in the Thermen region.
An attractive vintage, but well past their prime. Rare reds are still worth seeking.

1984★★★

Originally thought of as the post-war *annus mirabilis*, but later denigrated for a lack of acidity in the wines. Near perfect weather in summer and autumn led to a large crop. Growers who ensured that their wines had sufficient acidic backbone produced wines with the best potential. In Burgenland, 1983 produced the best quality reds to emerge prior to the 1990 vintage. Elsewhere areas not normally noted for Prädikat wines yielded musts high in residual sugar. Auslesen produced in Styria and the Weinviertel, and high Spätlesen in the Wachau. Most were vinified dry.
Drink up.

1983★★★★★

A great vintage. Outstandingly ripe wines, notably excellent TBAs.
All the soft, dry whites will have been drunk by now but the exceedingly sweet and concentrated TBA wines are still superb.

1982★▷★★★

The biggest crop on record. An excellent summer and early autumn was rounded off with a miserable, wet October. Those producers who picked before (or after) the rain, produced wines of quality. Good levels of botrytis in the Thermen region and there were some luscious Prädikat wines from Rust.
Even the top-class sweet whites well past best.

1981★★★

Notable only for late-picked sweet wines. These were quite widespread, with wines of TBA levels in Rust and Seewinkel; good, high Prädikat levels in the Thermen region; one or two rare Ausbruch wines from Vienna; and, one of the rarest of all, a Beerenauslese from Styria.

Ausbruch and TBA wines still drinking well.

1980

A bad vintage pretty well everywhere.

1979★★★★★

An excellent year which began with a perfect flowering and continued through a hot summer and a sunny autumn. This was the last of the great "niners". The long autumn produced Auslesen in Wachau and Krems, Beerenauslesen in Styria, Ausbruch in Vienna and Klosterneuberg, and TBAs in Rust and Seewinkel.

Drink up all but the top dessert wines, which have excellent, life-preserving acidity.

1978★

Cold, dry year; generally mediocre.

1977★★★★

Excellent year.

Few, if any, remain.

1976★▷★★★

Some good TBA and Ausbruch wines from the Burgenland.

The Ausbruch and TBA wines can still be superb.

1975★★

Average quality only.

Drink up.

1974

Very poor.

1973★★★★

Very good year.

TBA and Ausbruch wines can still occasionally be encountered from the Burgenland region.

1972

A very poor year.

1971★★★★★

An excellent year. Long-lasting wines.

Some top Rieslings from Vienna and even one or two Grüner Veltliners from the Wachau still on top form; also scented, honeyed Beerenauslesen from Rust.

1970★★

Mediocre.

MORE REMOTE AUSTRIAN VINTAGES

1969★★★★★ was one of the great "niners"; some top TBA wines from Rust can still be found and are superb. **1967★★★** produced good Prädikats from the Burgenland: look out for Ausbruch and TBAs. **1966★★★** fine Rieslings from lower Austria, some surprisingly good wines from Styria, and rich, fat, powerful TBA wines from Langenlois. **1963★★★★** some very attractive Prädikat wine from the Burgenland. Look out for the **1961★★★★★** *raresimme* TBAs or Auslesen from the Burgenland; excellent wines were also produced in **1959★★★★★** though all but the richest and best are drying out. **1955** was chiefly memorable for the departure of the Allied armies, notably the Russians. **1949★★★★★** a great year. And **1945★★★★** the year when all the old stocks of Austrian wine disappeared down the throats of the invading Soviet troops. Older vintages are so rare, one might as well say that they do not exist.

Hungary (Tokaji)

Hungary is a surprisingly big and successful wine-producing country. Its best known regions, growing red and white table wines, are around Eger and on the gentle slopes bounding Lake Balaton. Until the final disintegration of the Iron Curtain, basically only two qualities were produced: everyday inexpensive quick-consumption wines, and wines of slightly superior quality for the many excellent local restaurants.

The better known wines such as Badacsony Riesling and Egri Bikaver (Bull's Blood) in good years are sound, but essentially for early consumption. Vintages do vary but do not feature commercially. Several other local grape varieties are used, making passably appealing wines for a mainly local market.

Tokaji, or Tokay, is the odd man out amongst the great classic wines of Europe. Happily, there has recently been a renaissance with an influx of outside investment and influential winemakers. Tokaji makes not only an unusual style of wine, it has quite remarkable ageing potential. Indeed, in common with madeira, the finest and the richest Tokajis have an almost limitless cellar life. For this reason this section of the pocketbook is devoted solely to Tokaji vintages.

However, Tokaji appears in various guises. Szamorodni or natural table wines can be dry or sweet in style; both, in good vintages, will keep though the dry is something of an acquired taste. The Aszú wines, to which measures of a concentrate made from overripe grapes are added, range from medium-sweet three-*puttonyo*s to a very sweet, Sauternes-like, five-*puttonyo*s. Following exceptional years intensely sweet and long-lasting Aszú-Eszencia will be produced (the pure Eszencia or Essence – it has various spellings – is rare and very expensive, but it has an almost limitless life span).

2002★★★ variable

A warm spring was followed by an early flowering (a week earlier than usual) and then a long, hot, and dry summer with temperatures hitting the mid-30°C (95°F) mark. The Zéta and Muscat grapes – both early ripening varieties – were picked after the onset of the morning mists in early September; they were ripe with good sugar content. Furmint and Hárslevelü, late season varieties, were put under severe stress by rainy and damp weather throughout the second half of September and most of October. Winemakers in Hungary's Tokáji region were ecstatic on November 3, when bright sun, clear skies, light breezes, and fairly mild temperatures broke through. Expectations of high quality botrytized grapes for Aszú were, however, horribly dashed when freezing temperatures set in that evening and by the next morning, snow had covered the ground. Aszú yields were much lower this year, due partly to the hot, dry summer that resulted in small berries and partly to the autumn rains and cold spell in November. The Aszú grapes picked in October and early November had fine botrytis and better flavours than those gathered in September as they had more time to ripen, although they did not have a lot of acidity. Intensive grape selection was crucial this year. The vast amounts of rain diluted the flavours of the botrytized grapes and caused incidences of *penicillium* and grey rot. Renowned winemaker István Szepsy, whose own winery produces mainly the extremely sweet six-*puttonyos* Aszú, believes that the 2002 vintage overall is "not excellent, but looks good."

Early days but clearly not a great Tokaji vinyage. Wait and see.

2001 ★★

A difficult vintage for Hungary. Although flowering and budding of the vines occurred at the usual period, the summer was rainy and cooler than average, resulting in a slower maturation. Rain in September caused abundant grey as well as noble rot and part of the harvest was lost. The weather in October, however, improved substantially, allowing the grapes to mature well and preparing them for a second onset of botrytis. Good weather continued throughout the harvest, with the best grapes still on the vine, and picking was underway at most estates by mid-November. The extended autumn saw a prolonged maturation and botrytization, meaning that the grapes were still less shrivelled and concentrated than at the same time last year. Although sugar and acid contents were high and in good balance, there was less concentration of sugars than last year. The Muscat musts had lovely flavour and balance.

The new investors in this remarkable region must have started to worry as theirs is an all or nothing situation; they are in the business to make and market only Aszú quality wines which arise as a result of singularly appropriate weather conditions, hot sunny autumns with ripe grapes affected by botrytis. 2002 proved disappointing though some attractive wines were made – but not of the classic five- or six-puttonyos quality.

2000 ★★★★★

A great vintage combining abundance and high quality Aszús. The vines flowered and ripened early due to some of the hottest and driest weather the region had ever experienced. The temperatures in July and August were high, and the rains followed on at just the right time. By the time the essential botrytis arrived the grapes were totally ripe – in some cases overripe – and a concerted effort was made in the vineyards to pick at their peak. The unusually high sugar content prompted a slow and delicate development of the botrytis, and with a hot, sunny autumn as well, the berries shrivelled to a good concentration. However, due to a lack of rain, botrytis affected mainly the densely bunched Furmint, with just a few Hárslevelú grapes.

Watch out for these when they come on to the market. The five- and six-puttonyos Aszús and Aszú-Essencias will be superb and long lasting, very much in the style and quality of 1993, 1983, 1972, and 1947, and with a life span to match.

1999 ★★★★★

Hungary normally benefits from a benign continental climate, with long, hot summers and warm, dry autumns. 1999 was no exception. In the Tokaji region, despite hailstorms in August which reduced somewhat the size of the crop, it also had the effect of concentrating the flavours in the remaining grapes. Most of the botrytis-affected Aszú grapes were picked in perfect condition in late September and early October, some of recently recognized "first-growth" status even later. The 1999 vintage is considered the finest in the Tokaji region since the excellent 1993.

Tokaji Szamorodri dry for early drinking – something of an acquired taste; the various grades of Aszú can be drunk as soon as they appear on the market but the Aszú of five-puttonyos and higher in a great vintage like this are best with some bottle-age and will drink beautifully for well over twenty years.

1998★★

The much heralded renaissance of the wines of this venerable classic region suffered a setback in 1998. It was a disheartening year: small crop, quality lacking – sparked off by an unanticipated severe attack of downy mildew. Following a relatively normal spring, there was heavy rain in June and July which, combined with warm weather, provides conditions favourable to the development of fungal diseases. Unfortunately, few farmers failed to counter the spread of mildew, not recognizing the first appearance of *perenospera*, the most dangerous of all vine diseases. It spreads like wildfire, causing the leaves – the lungs of the vine – to fall off, stifling the production of sugar. The same conditions re-occurred in September, with warm rain on September 6–7, 19, and 20. Black rot and other problems set in, resulting in badly affected grapes and cluster-dropping. Those vineyard owners with capital and expertise did take remedial action. Overall, however, the dry wines are a disaster and only a small amount of Aszù berries were harvested, without the benefit of the benign botrytis, resulting in thin wines, low in alcohol, lacking in acidity.

Avoid the dry whites. A small quantity of Aszú three-puttonyos for early drinking.

THE REST OF THE 1990S

1997★★★ a small vintage. **1996★★★★** very good, ripe, round, and balanced wines. **1995★★★▷★★★★** good to very good, average yields. **1994★** poor. **1993★★★★★** excellent year for Aszú, drinking well now. **1992★★★★** small crop, very good Aszús. **1991★★★★** very good Aszús. **1990★★★★** a good all round vintage.

1980s

1989★. 1988★★★★ one of the two best vintages of the decade. **1987★★** moderate. **1986★★** average. **1985★★** average. **1984★★** average. **1983★★★★★** excellent, at peak. **1982★★. 1981★★★★** and **1980~** a wretched vintage.

1970s

1979★★★★ 1978★ disappointing. **1977~** poor. **1976★★★ 1975★★★★ 1974~** poor. **1973★★★** good Aszús. **1972★★★★★** wonderful Aszús: excellent, will keep. **1971★★ 1970~**

1960s (Aszus only)

1969★★★ 1968★★★★★ the Aszú-Eszencia is lovely, but will develop further. **1967★★ 1966★★★ 1965~ 1964★★★★** the first post-war vintage of Aszú-Eszencia to be imported and marketed in the UK. **1963★★★★★** drinking well. **1962★★★★ 1961★★★★ 1960~**

1950s (Aszus only)

1959★★★★★ perfect now. 1958★★★ 1957★★★★★ 1956★★★ 1955★★★
1954~ 1953★★★★ 1952★★★★★ l951~ l950★★★★

1940s

1949★★★★★ 1948★★★ 1947★★★★★ perfection; magnificent concentrated
Eszencia. 1946★★★ good. 1945★★▷★★★★★ 1944~ 1943★★★ l942★★
1941~ 1940~

THE BEST PRE-1940 TOKAJI VINTAGES

1937★★★★★ 1936★★★★★ 1935★★★ 1934★★★★★ 1932★★★★★
1931★★★★★ 1930★★★ 1927★★★ 1924★★★★★ 1923★★★★★ 1922★★★
1921★★★★ 1920★★★★ 1919★★★★★ 1917★★★ 1916★★★★★
1915★★★★★ 1914★★★ 1912★★★★★ 1910★★★ 1907★★★ 1906★★★★
the last great vintage of the Austro-Hungarian Empire, high Aszús and
Eszencias still superb. 1905★★★ 1904★★★★ 1901★★★★ 1900★★★★★
Great Tokay Vintages: 1889, 1865, 1834, 1811– the most renowned vintage
of all time. (All these old Eszencias will be more than drinkable:
concentrated, fabulous.)

Italy

For sheer volume of wine produced, and for variations of style and quality, Italy
is unmatched. It is also an impossible country to deal with in a general way as
climatic conditions vary widely: from Sicily, with its North African influence,
to the foothills of the Alps. Classic French grape varieties are starting to intrude,
changing the nature of some wines, though winemaking methods alternate
between primitive and highly sophisticated.

Once undependable, now far less so; unpredictable, perhaps. But enormous
strides were made in the 1980s and 1990s. A combination of new attitudes, much
improved winemaking, and amenable weather conditions have enhanced the
quality of much Italian wine out of all recognition. Undoubtedly, the development
of *vini da tavola (vdt)*, with strong Cabernet input, helped draw attention to these
new and highly successful *vdt* wines, which became known as "Super Tuscans".
Within the last few years the Chianti Classicos have risen to this challenge and
a new breed has emerged, reverting to more traditional grapes.

Two major districts have long been, and still are, regarded as the homes
of the great Italian classics: Tuscany, with its famous Chianti region, between
Florence and Siena, and to the north, Piedmont, producing sturdy long-living
Barolo and stylish Barbaresco in the hills around Alba and Asti. These two
districts not only set the standards but, amongst Italian wines exported, are
the best known in the quality field, which is why they are featured principally
in the vintage notes that follow.

But it is not merely a geographical convenience; few other regions make
wine which even Italian connoisseurs consider worth cellaring for any length
of time. For these lesser wines, vintages tend to be irrelevant as most are
speedily put on the market and as speedily consumed.

2002★★▷★★★

A problematic year. The volume of production was twenty per cent lower
than in the previous year, qualifying it as the most meagre crop in Italy for

half a century. As for quality, "heterogeneous" sums it up best, with instances of both mediocrity and excellence.

Piedmont Barolo, La Morra, and Castiglione Falletto were devastated by a hailstorm on September 3. What was not damaged by hail was attacked by rot, necessitating rigorous selection. Luckily, a final burst of twenty warm, sunny days saved a potentially disastrous harvest. Some producers battled with fragile grape skins, which risked splitting before reaching maturity. Piedmont's wide range of microclimates also contributed to varying degrees in quality.

Tuscany The alternating sunny and rainy days from July onward prevented water stress, but caused overripeness, very high sugar values, and excessive concentration in the grapes. In some instances the warm, humid conditions encouraged diseases, inducing many growers to harvest early, despite a certain lack of ripeness, creating wines with unusually green tannins and uppish malic acid. A few sunny days graced September. Those that risked harvesting later were more successful. Alcohol levels were lower than last year, but sugar and acidity levels good. The whites show interesting aromas and freshness, and are pleasant. Reds have good alcohol levels, fruity aromas, and elegance.

Early days, but the usual advice: drink the dry whites whilst young and fresh – this applies to all the Italian regions, from Friuli to Sicily. It is impossible to generalize about the reds. Tuscany appears to be the more favoured and the Chianti Classicos should prove to be good, early to mid-term wines, best perhaps between 2007 and 2010. Piedmont is more variable, the better Barolos and Barbarescos from 2008 to 2012.

2001 ★★★★

A mild winter and spring allowed even flowering and good fruit set. Summer was hot and dry, but without the intense heat which can stress the vines and scorch the grapes. Frost in April, followed by hail, cut yields. Many areas were also hit by drought over the summer. Rain and below average temperatures, interspersed with sunny days over the harvest caused diluted and uneven ripening for some. A good October in most regions gave greater ripeness resulting in high sugar levels and good natural acidity.

Piedmont The most successful northern region as most of September's rains fell further east. On the whole, the reds are very phenolic and ripe, with high colour and tannins. The Barbera was high in acidity with potential alcohol levels of 13.5 per cent, the Nebbiolo benefited from an Indian summer and achieved great ripeness.

Tuscany Most of the best hillside sites escaped the worst of the April frost, which served as a natural pruning device, lowering the yield but contributing to the grape quality. The Sangiovese had powerful, persistent tannins, while the Cabernets were very fruity with great character. Due to Tuscany's diverse terroir and microclimates picking started in August and finished around October 15. The grapes benefited from a slower maturation bringing out well-balanced tannins with alcohol levels between twelve and fourteen degrees.

I confess to being an admirer of the white wines of northern Italy and in 2001 Trentino, Alto Adige, and Friuli regions made attractive wines, delicious, as always, for early drinking – from now to, say, 2005. Red wines from most regions are successful, particularly Piedmont where the classic Barolos and Barbarescos, fairly massively proportioned, will benefit from bottle-ageing, reaching an extended plateau from 2010 to 2016. In Tuscany the later-picked classics, with considerably reduced yields because of weather conditions, should prove good to very good mid-term wines, the Chianti Classicos probably best between 2008 and 2012.

2000★★★▷★★★★

This year extreme conditions alternately advanced and hampered the ripening cycle, resulting in uneven quality and reduced quantity. Spring was very hot, summer early and very cold, mid-summer scorching and drought-like, and the autumn extremely stormy.

Piedmont There were strong expectations for Piedmont even after the late season rains and intense heat in August had concentrated the sugars and phenols of the slow ripening noble Nebbiolo grapes before they reached normal maturity. Torrential rains in mid-October and water stress caused problems, resulting in very low yields; and quality in Barolos and Barbarescos was severely diminished by the late season downpours. Producers still expected to make good wines, despite the extreme August heat that raised fears of overly high sugar and alcohol levels. Those who harvested early reaped small quantities of good quality grapes. They had a lot of fruit, concentration, and aroma and there are many *vins de garde*, with high tannins and good structure.

Tuscany A similarly variable but perhaps more difficult vintage in Tuscany. The intense heat-wave in mid-August combined with October rains to yield Sangiovese grapes which, in many cases, were either out of balance due to overripeness and raisining (particularly intense in Montalcino) or diluted in character. Top estates produced grapes with high potential alcohol levels, but lacking in even development and complexity of flavour.

Not an easy year to sum up; variable, to say the least. Described by some as "great", the best of Piedmont's classic reds do approach this, with tannic Barolos needing considerable bottle-age. Tuscany equally variable but on the whole, mouthfilling and agreeable for the mid-term, say 2006 to 2010.

1999★★★★

It is worth reminding ourselves yet again that it is impossible to generalize about vintage conditions in Italy, whose very many and diverse wine districts span latitudes that stretch from North Africa to southern Burgundy, from Sicily to the Alps, not to mention altitudes (I am reminded by Nick Belfrage MW) that rise from sea level to over 3,000 feet! (914 metres) For this reason I shall continue to concentrate on what I consider the two principal classic regions, Piedmont in the north and Tuscany in the heart of Italy.

Piedmont Despite variable weather conditions and heavy humidity in August, causing problems with rot, it was a successful vintage, the fifth in a row. Excellent early ripening Chardonnay and Dolcetto, and the late ripening Nebbiolo; Barolo and Barbaresco very good, on a par with 1995 though not quite up to 1996 and 1997.

Tuscany Also very varied weather conditions, including high temperatures. Yields are high and some producers consider that they have made the best wines of the decade. It was certainly a Sangiovese year, those wines made from grapes picked before the end of September rains having good, deep colour and high sugar levels.

The dry whites and lighter red wines are drinking well now; Chiantis from 2005 to 2010, Barolos from the top estates 2008 to 2012.

1998★★▷★★★

It is difficult for a vintage, however good, to follow so hard on the heels of one as superb as the 1997. Nevertheless, some good wines were made though overall quantities slightly down. The spring was cool and wet, delaying growth ten to fourteen days behind normal. Contrastingly, the summer was hot and dry, many areas suffering from drought. Rains in the last week of September and the first week of October brought the drought to an end but interrupted the harvest in some areas.

Piedmont May started with perfect conditions for flowering, though rain later hindered blossoming and resulted in some fruit drop. Some reported small but adequate light rains to temper the overall summer heat and dryness, also that sun happily interrupted the rain at harvest time. Reds are good enough, whites above average.

Tuscany Mixed results following mixed conditions: hot and dry summer, uneven ripening, and rain, though not continual or excessive, at harvest time. The Brunellos of Montalcino are good, with Chianti Classicos tending towards the tannic, resulting from the summer heat and lack of rain.

Drink the lighter, less important whites though the serious Chardonnays from Barbaresco need bottle-age, as do the reds. Both the latter and the classic Barolos will probably be at their best from around 2005 to 2012, perhaps longer. Chiantis will develop sooner, though the tannic Chianti Classico Riservas from, say, 2004 to 2010.

1997 ★★★★★

Shouts of jubilation from producers all over Italy after their most successful vintage in fifty years. Certainly the best since 1990. Growing conditions ran in near text-book fashion, with a mild winter and spring giving clear and temperate days. The only small upset resulted in slightly reduced yields after premature budding and flowering were affected by late frosts in April and May. Conditions then became warmer during August and continued until October, with cool nights and rain falling at the required times. By harvest time most vines were around one week ahead of their growing cycle and producers were ready to start picking up to two weeks earlier than scheduled.

Piedmont The only area to experience an increase in yield, mainly due to the Dolcetto which did not achieve such high quality. Harvesting did not start early but was rapid and nearly over by late September. Nebbiolo ripened before Barbera – almost unheard of. The grapes were small and of optimal weight and size, providing complete harmony and balance of every constituent. This has only occurred in four other vintages this century. The main difference was slightly lower acidity, which was beneficial as sometimes this can be too assertive.

Tuscany Quality was exceptional after grapes had developed almost identically to those in Piedmont, and comparisons were made to the 1947 vintage. However, more directly affected by irregular flowering, yields in Tuscany were significantly lower – twenty per cent compared to 1996. This did not help the continuing price rises for the top quality wines.

Drink delicious Barberas now; Barolos 2008 to 2025; Chianti and the fashionable vini da tavola now to 2015 – if you are fortunate enough to have bought them early. They are now hard to find, and expensive.

1996 ★★★★

Another seriously good vintage. Compared with 1995 yields were up by five per cent, though still ten per cent below that of 1994 – again a result of the grubbing-up programme which eliminated many vineyard sites.

The first two weeks of June witnessed extremely high temperatures of 30°C (86°F) and above, causing a quick and uniform flowering. The summer temperatures were slightly lower than the Mediterranean average, but conditions were constant and the ripening was slow and even. September and October were wetter but low temperatures protected vines from rot. The harvest started at the beginning of October and continued in favourable conditions.

Piedmont Good results in Barolo and Barbaresco. Thick skins and late-picked grapes produced lush, opulent wines with quality comparable to 1990. Quantity was down, due to the vines still recovering from hail damage in 1995. Asti: great results with good, early ripening Dolcetto. Barbera: not such high quality.

Tuscany High quality and fine aromas, Chianti and Montalcino producing wines of deep colour and great ripeness. Montepulciano experienced a few problems. Producers were undecided as to whether quality was better than in 1995.

Classic Barolos say 2004 to 2012. Chianti now to 2008.

1995★★★▷★★★★★

Another unpredictable year, becoming typical of the 1990s and possibly one of the most fickle of the last thirty years. A warm spring raised hopes only to be dashed by rain at bud set and during flowering, resulting again in decreased yields. A hot July followed by a cool August upset the vineyard cycle further, with rot causing problems. The bad weather continued into September, changing to Indian Summer conditions from mid-September through to mid-October. New EU grants available to producers for grubbing up vines in an attempt to reduce overstocks of wine did in fact result in an overall small vintage.

Piedmont After the rain at flowering, hail in August caused extensive damage. Some producers, especially in Barolo, lost between fifty and seventy per cent of their crop. For those that survived, a long growing season ended with one of the latest harvests in two decades, at the end of October. Barolo was particularly successful.

Tuscany Following similar tumultuous growing conditions, the skies cleared on September 15 heralding forty-five rain-free days with temperatures up to 27°C (80°F). This continued into October, and patient producers, especially in the Chianti Classico region, harvested slowly ripened grapes with deep colour and firm structure. This vintage can be compared with 1990.

Long-lived Barolos, well into the present century. Chiantis from now to 2010, vdt *perhaps even longer.*

1994★★▷★★★★

Piedmont Spring conditions were good with precisely the correct level of rainfall. Severe frosts struck fairly late into flowering, reducing the harvest by ten to thirty per cent. In July Barbaresco was badly hit by hail. Summer was dry and hot and the grapes ripened healthily two weeks ahead of usual. The ripening process slowed down in mid-September when heavy rains fell for 17 days. Harvesting went ahead in reasonable conditions with favourable results. Medium-bodied wines, but in reduced quantities.

Tuscany Climatic conditions were particularly good, almost certainly the best seen in Italy this vintage. The ripening season started early and temperatures were consistently high. Summer was long and hot with light rain during June and July. Chianti Classico produced the best results, with a high proportion of Riserva wines. Montepulciano and Montalcino produced concentrated and characterful wines. Conditions also proved ideal for Cabernet-based *vdt* wines and even more so for rarer Merlot-based wines.

Not a great vintage for Barolo or Barbaresco: drink soon. Some attractive Tuscan wines drinking well, but the best will develop further.

1993 ★▷★★★

Piedmont Considering the torrential rain that fell during the harvest, the condition of the fruit was good due to the heat and aridity of August. The quantities are small and the quality is reasonable. As a result of the rainfall sugar levels are unfortunately outweighed by acidity, producing early maturing wines. Barolo and Barbaresco have very pleasant fruit and aromas.

Tuscany The further south, the more satisfactory the results, seems to be the trend in this sodden vintage. Tuscany, therefore, fared much better than Piedmont though more rain fell in the two weeks before harvesting than during the previous eleven months. Fortunately the hot, dry summer resulted in very small grapes with thick skins that withstood the rain. Quality was good to very good.

The above summary tells all, or nearly all. From both north and south: wines for early consumption, not laying down, though top producers provided some pleasing surprises.

1992 ★★▷★★★

Throughout Italy the weather had been satisfactory during the growing season, despite a cool and wet early summer. What eventually dashed all hopes of a fine vintage were the storms and torrential rains of late September which lasted until mid-October.

Piedmont Ripeness was the main problem. The earlier ripening Dolcetto fared much better than Nebbiolo; only relatively light-weight and early drinking Barolo and Barbaresco were produced.

Tuscany Here growers were able to make more successful wines due mainly to the earlier harvest and selective picking. A tiny quantity of Riserva wines was made in Chianti after October 16, once the rains had finished. Further south in Montalcino and Montepulciano, where picking started even earlier, weightier wines were possible. Some interesting Brunello and Vino Nobile di Montepulciano were made.

Drink soon.

1991 ★▷★★

Piedmont A cold spring; late and irregular flowering; and a long, hot, and very dry summer followed by heavy rain at vintage time. An average crop, variable in quality, mainly light wines. Some good late-picked Barolos and Barbarescos.

Tuscany A poor spring: cold and wet with damaging frosts; then a dismal May to mid-June alternating with rain and too little sun. The summer was hearteningly hot and dry but the rains returned for the late harvest. Variable quality, lower than average production. Also some pleasant surprises.

In general: drink up.

1990 ★★★★★

The hot, dry summer produced grapes of exceptional quality. Yields were very low everywhere and the small bunches of concentrated fruit encouraged growers to predict a top-class vintage, ranking beside those of the best in the post-war era.

Piedmont The third year of almost perfect weather conditions in Barolo and Barbaresco. Rainfall was better distributed than in 1988 and beautifully healthy grapes were picked two weeks ahead of normal. The quantity, however, was around ten per cent down, producing well-balanced wines which are ageing well.

Tuscany The weather was perfect here too, providing intense heat, light rain to nourish and ripen the grapes, and cool evenings to conserve their acidity. Showers during early September helped to produce healthy fruit, and as in Piedmont the grapes were brought in early. Even the late ripening Sangiovese had been harvested by the end of September; the last of the reds were in by mid-October. Full, deeply coloured, flavoursome wines with round tannins and good acidity.

Chianti Classicos, which tend to be drunk too young, are delicious now. Barbarescos showing well but will continue to develop; the finest, classic Barolos between 2010 and 2020 or beyond.

1989 ★▷★★★★

The exceptionally good weather throughout much of Europe was unfortunately not experienced in Italy. Wet, often tempestuous conditions characterized the summer and disastrous rain fell intermittently during the harvest. This was the smallest vintage of the decade.

Piedmont Apart from a violent hailstorm in June which damaged vines around Barolo (some growers lost as much as sixty per cent of their crop), Piedmont largely escaped the bad weather. Conditions were satisfactory and sound red and white grapes were gathered. Overall, the yield was down by fifteen per cent. Perhaps the best reds of the decade.

Tuscany A very mixed year. Some areas had too much rain while others had too little and suffered drought. The Chianti was better than the Chianti Classico and few Riservas were made. Best wines came from Montalcino and Montepulciano. Overall, light wines and early developers.

Barolo and Barbaresco from now to well after 2010. Chianti drink soon.

1988 ★★★★▷★★★★★

Generally, an excellent vintage for Italian wines. The yield was very small – Tuscany brought in its smallest crop for twenty-five years.

Piedmont Cold and wet weather during flowering resulted in an incomplete flower set. Then warm, damp weather followed, encouraging the development of mildew in late June. Thereafter, the summer was hot and dry, aiding the development of ripe and healthy grapes. However, rain during the harvest caused problems, especially with the Nebbiolo and the later-picked grapes in Barolo and Barbaresco. The Barbera, however, was picked just before the rain and made wine of good quality.

Tuscany As in Piedmont, a cold start to the year impaired the flower set, and yields were further reduced by severe heat and drought. However, the harvest, which began on September 22 for the Cabernet grapes and October 1 for the Sangiovese, produced high quality wines. Riservas were fruity with firm tannins. The best wines came from Montalcino where weather conditions were less severe, with an early harvest and above average size crop.

Chiantis and the good vdt *drinking well now, Barbaresco, Barolo, and Brunello di Montalcino 2008 to 2020.*

1987 ★★▷★★★

Variable quality, overshadowed by the superior 1988 vintage.

Piedmont A cold winter was followed by a cool but dry spring. Conditions were generally fine throughout the summer, with the exception of a rather cool July. August and September saw some welcome light rain and the harvest began in early October. The crop was of average size and decent quality.

Tuscany The vines flowered under excellent conditions but their progress was then hampered by a long, dry spell which lasted from July until late September. The harvest, which began on September 23, took place in many areas during damp, rot-inducing weather. In Montalcino, however, the grapes were picked earlier and a large quantity of excellent quality wine was produced. Overall, these were light and enjoyable wines, but not candidates for Riserva status.

All but the very best reds, drink up.

1986 ★★★

A good year which provided better drinking than the 1987s but shadowed by the tiny but excellent crop produced in 1985.

Piedmont The winter was unusually cold and spring was wet. All of Italy sizzled under a heat-wave during May which broke at the end of the month with unsettled weather and sometimes violent localized hailstorms. Some growers lost their entire crop, while others miraculously escaped altogether. Unfortunately and sadly, affected areas included the top sites, including Barolo where growers lost up to forty per cent of their crop. The rest of the summer was hot, dry, and humid. Rain during the first ten days of September fleshed out the grapes which were then fully ripened by two weeks of hot weather. The harvest began during the last week of September and a small quantity of good quality grapes was picked, mainly producing wines for mid-term drinking, though some outstanding Barberas.

Tuscany A large crop harvested after a hot summer which, with the exception of the odd burst of rain in July, was mainly dry. Some good, fruity Chiantis were produced, but few Riservas. The Brunello and Vino Nobile di Montepulciano were of average quality but the top *vdt* were notably elegant.

All fully mature. Drink soon.

1985 ★★★★★

An extremely good vintage throughout Italy but, perhaps even more importantly, the year in which a shift of attitudes was perceived and a new era of more serious winemaking began, particularly in Tuscany.

Piedmont An exceptionally cold winter gave way to a warm, dry spring. A rather uneven summer followed, yet superb wines were made, particularly by the best individual producers in the best districts. Those from Barolo were very successful, making deep-coloured, richly tannic, long-lasting wines.

Tuscany Even better than Piedmont. Similar weather conditions.

One of my favourite vintages. Wonderful wines: great depth of fruit; mouthfilling without being coarse. The big Barbarescos, Barolos, and Brunellos, though delicious now, are still developing. Chiantis are still drinking well.

1984 ★

A poor year throughout Italy, with the possible exceptions of Sicily and Sardinia and northern Piedmont.

Piedmont Cold, wet weather in May and June led to a late and incomplete flowering. The weather was cool and unsettled throughout the summer and the grapes were not fully ripened in time for the harvest. The wines were thin and unripe.

Tuscany A similar story to Piedmont, with almost continuous September rain. Ironically, this was the year in which Chianti was promoted to DOCG status. *Avoid.*

1983 ★★▷★★★★

An uneven year: disappointing for some, excellent for others. It was the vintage which awakened my interest in Italian wines.

Piedmont The vines flowered during rain, July was hot and humid and some growers experienced problems with rot. Uneven weather in late summer improved in time for the harvest in October. The crop was of average size and the best growers, who selected their grapes rigorously, made very good wines. Elsewhere the quality was often poor.

Tuscany A good year. Spring was mild and the vines flowered in early June. Summer was fine with just the required amount of rain. In Chianti the weather continued unbroken until the harvest which began on September 22. Riserva Chiantis made delightful drinking. In Montalcino the weather deteriorated during harvest, and careful selection was needed.

Drink up, though the "new wave" of Chiantis can still be delightful and the classic Barolos, as always needing time, now pretty well mature.

1982 ★★★★★

An excellent vintage throughout Tuscany and Piedmont.

Piedmont Mild, dry weather during the spring pushed growth ahead of normal. Some vineyards were damaged by hail in late April but overall there were few problems. Summer was hot and dry with some rain in late September through early October prior to the harvest. An average crop of rich, ripe, flavoury wines.

Tuscany A long, cold winter relented with a sudden change in the temperature in May. Apart from the odd wet period and hail in early September, the weather was hot and sunny, approaching drought conditions. Picking began on September 20 and the quality of the wine was consistently good for all of Tuscany. The top Riservas were outstanding.

A most attractive year. Drink up the Chiantis but the classic Barolos and Barbarescos are still laden with tannin.

1981 ★★★

An uneven and generally disappointing year.

Piedmont Winter was long and cold. Vines then suffered rot during a hot, humid June and July. Apart from a wet patch in late August/early September the weather was cloudy but dry until the harvest, beginning in late September. Careful selection of grapes was essential. The best wines were the Barbarescos.

Tuscany Overall, a much better year for this part of Italy. Spring was late but hot and the good weather continued almost without interruption through the summer. The harvest, beginning on September 20, was staggered due to rain midway. As a result, the wines made from grapes picked before the rain are of superior quality to those made later, elegant with good ageing potential.

Some very rich wines but overall variable. Drink soon.

1980★

A moderate year, though inevitably with good, if not outstanding, exceptions.

Piedmont A mild winter ran into a cool spring which lasted until June. Growth was retarded until July when the weather suddenly became hot and dry. These conditions lasted until late September when rain fell until early October. The harvest started extremely late and was interrupted by snow on November 4. An average sized crop was picked.

Tuscany Similar weather conditions. Picking started in early October but was delayed by rain and many growers found that they did not finish until November. On the whole the grapes were ripe and healthy and some very good wines were made.

Drink up.

1979★★★★

Piedmont Very good early maturing wines from Barolo and Barbaresco.

Tuscany A huge harvest of good to very good quality, generally not, however, for long keeping.

Chiantis can still be superb. The great producers' Barolos are very good now though will age further. Sassicaia is perfection.

1978★★★★★

The best all-round vintage of the 1970s.

Piedmont Damp, cold weather in spring and early summer brought the vintage near to disaster. A warm, dry autumn saved the day: small crops of fine Barolo and Barbaresco, for ageing.

Tuscany Similar conditions to those in Piedmont produced a small vintage with some outstanding, long-lived wines, especially in Brunello di Montalcino, Carmignano, and Chianti Classico.

Superb reds, the best perfect now.

1977★▷★★★

Piedmont Not a good year: small crop, generally poor wine.

Tuscany Some very good Brunello di Montalcino, Vino Nobile di Montepulciano; and some good Chiantis.

Drink up.

1976★

Piedmont A vintage of uneven quality.

Tuscany Disastrous year.

1975★▷★★★

Piedmont A mediocre year, yet some delightful wines.

Tuscany A fair year. Particularly good for Brunello, Vino Nobile di Montepulciano, and Chianti from the Siena area.

Even the best reds fully mature. Drink up.

1974★★▷★★★★

Piedmont An excellent, abundant vintage for long keeping.

Tuscany Except for some very good Chianti Rufina, this was generally a poor, unreliable year.

Only the substantial reds, Barbaresco, and Barolo worth looking out for. Drink up.

1973★★▷★★★

Piedmont An uneven year, mostly only fair.
Tuscany Also uneven; some excellent wines from Carmignano.
Drink up.

1972

A disastrous year.
Avoid.

1971★★★★★

Piedmont For Barolo and Barbaresco this was possibly the best year since the war.
Tuscany Overall, a very good though uneven vintage. The best wines were from Chianti, some disappointments in Montalcino and Montepulciano.
The top Barolos, Barbarescos, and Brunello still at peak. Top Chianti Classicos need drinking. The "new reds", Sassicaia, Tignanello, Rubesco Torgiano, all superb, fully mature.

1970★★★▷★★★★

Piedmont A large-sized crop of excellent wines.
Tuscany A good year: excellent Brunello and Vino Nobile.
Fully mature. Only the top Barolos have time in hand. The rest, drink up.

OTHER OUTSTANDING ITALIAN VINTAGES

Piedmont Barolo: **1964**, **1961**, **1958**, **1952**. **Tuscany** Brunello: **1967**, **1964**, **1961**, **1955**, **1945**. Chianti: **1968**, **1967**, **1964**, **1962**, **1957**, **1947**. Vino Nobile di Montepulciano: **1967**, **1958**.

Spain

For over a century and a half sherry was the only quality wine of Spain, table wines being indifferent to execrable, or if good, relatively unknown. The dramatic upturn began in Rioja in the 1960s, and a decade later one family in Penedès, Torres, experimenting – as they still are – with different grape varieties grown at different altitudes, and superb winemaking and marketing, carved a niche which raised the whole conception of what Spain can produce commercially. Rioja has become fairly complicated with a wide range of styles and qualities. Coming more recently to the fore is Navarra, a district on the northern border of Rioja producing some excellent reds.

The Ribero del Duero, once noted only for Vega Sicilia, (the "Lafite" of Spain, renowned in fame and price) more recently became better known with the more amenable Pesquera which has spawned Duero lookalikes of varying quality. It needs to be stated that Vega Sicilia spends up to ten years in wood, so, for drinking dates, one must add at least twelve years to the vintage. La Mancha, to the south of Madrid, still produces fifty per cent of Spain's total production of table wines. But wines from this area, and nearby Valdepeñas, are not in the same league as the districts mentioned above.

The white wines of Spain, sherry excepted, were once uniformly atrocious, but tend now to range from passable to good though few are exceptional and hardly any, in my opinion, warrant cellaring for more than a year or two. The following vintage notes refer only to the red wines from three major districts.

These have the added advantage of still being very reasonably priced for their quality. Really old vintages, particularly of Rioja, can occasionally be found. They seem either cheap for their age or wildly overpriced, but can be very good in a somewhat idiosyncratic way. Interestingly, but not to my taste, there are now a number of impressive, small production, and expensive "cult" wines of which Pingus is an example.

Please note that as weather conditions in Navarra are frequently similar to neighbouring Rioja, vintage notes apply generally to both of these northerly districts.

2002★★★▷★★★★

A difficult year resulting in irregular quality. Producers were faced with sudden frost in April, a short, cool summer, sporadic rainstorms during the harvest, and the lowest annual average temperatures in the last thirty years. The low temperatures slowed growth, leading to lower yields, although the grapes did have concentrated acidity and sugar.

Rioja Drought conditions in March and two bouts of April frost at bud-break caused low cluster counts and small cluster size. Higher than normal summer rainfall led to the swelling and splitting of grapes resulting in rot in some regions. Warm, sunny weather from the weekend of September 14–15 cleared most of the rot and allowed healthy fruit to ripen well. Rains returned during the third week of September, producing a twenty-five per cent lower crop. There are some excellent wines with good alcohol levels and colour.

Penedès Early maturing varieties Macabeo, Chardonnay, and Tempranillo were affected by botrytis after a rainy August and early September. Selection was rigorous with losses of twenty-five to thirty per cent, and maturity did not reach the usual limits. From September 7, for two weeks, the weather changed and maturing of the grapes took place in splendid conditions. The early harvest in the second week of August was mainly due to rot infestations in lower-altitude vineyards.

Ribera del Duero A rainless winter, frost in early May, and a cold and overcast summer caused growers to despair. Sorting tables were an absolute necessity to obtain quality wines, leading to a small harvest. There was, however, a broad range in quality, differing from producer to producer. Overall, quality is good, but not great.

Whites drink soon. The reds very variable. Most will be drinking well from 2005 to 2008.

2001★★★★★

The vintage can be summed up as high quality, low yields. At their best the concentration of the reds was "spectacular", depth of colour superb, and tannins smooth. In short, the wines were extraordinary.

Rioja Earlier than usual budding, flowering, and setting, due to an exceptionally warm spring and early summer. A hot, dry summer was punctuated by timely but limited rainstorms in August and September and provided ideal weather for the harvest which, in some cases, was up to fifteen days earlier than the usual date. *Coulure* in Garnacha and *millerandage* in Tempranillo was prevalent in higher, older vineyards on arid soils, but overall, small berry size, good skin-to-pulp ratios, and high alcohol levels were indicative of high quality. The second biggest harvest in Rioja's history. Great wines were made.

Penedès An early and small harvest due to a combination of hard-hitting spring frosts (a severe case occurred on April 21, affecting Chardonnay and Pinot Noir in the mountain vineyards), which hindered flowering, and drought. Thankfully, the summer was hot and dry, with providential rain at the end of July, just before *véraison*, resulting in extremely high quality. Intense rain in October enabled the Riesling to develop the desired noble rot.

Ribera del Duero There was some mildew in parts of the region but the main problem was spring frosts, which reduced the crop to two-thirds. After these bouts, the weather was particularly good throughout the ripening season and in mid-September, and producers were optimistic about a quality harvest. It is, however, thought that many of the vineyards in this region are still too young to produce their finest grapes. Despite the potentially great harvest, Vega Sicilia did not produce their "flagship", Unico, because of the severe spring frosts and abnormal ripening in the very hot summer.

A highly satisfactory year for both whites, drinking well now, and for the well-established, well-managed reds. Most red Spanish wines, no matter their name, tend to be taken for granted and consumed as soon as they come onto the market. 2001 is a vintage which will repay seeking and keeping the top reds.

2000★★★

A problematic year; first drought and heat affected the harvest, but even more worrying for the producers was the significant collapse in grape prices. In Rioja and Ribera del Duero prices fell by eighty per cent leaving cellars with stocks of unsold wines, yet the best results this year came from these two regions.

Rioja The vines were very healthy and the bunches of optimal quality. The dry conditions did have one positive effect – the total absence of disease. A cool September and drought-induced vine stress delayed ripening and picking started later than usual.

Penedès The harvest was interrupted by flooding that left vineyards under several inches of water and drought reduced volumes by between ten to fifteen per cent on the previous year. Isolated storms in July and August resulted in the loss of 50,000 kilograms (49.2 tons) of Chardonnay from one vineyard. The harvest period looked more promising with warm and sunny weather, and the grapes were ripe and healthy.

Ribera del Duero Summer heat gave way to cool, cloudy conditions as the harvest approached in early October. Growers that waited were able to pick grapes that had reached the desired level of ripeness, with good concentration and colour. Fortunately, the heavy storms reached Spain in late October just after much of the quality areas were in.

The whites all need drinking but, apart from the lower quality and commercial brands which are being consumed now, the better producers' reds are of considerable interest and will make extremely good mid-term drinking at very fair prices.

1999★★★★

Spain is not all sunshine, nor is it true that "the rain in Spain stays mainly in the plains"! In fact there was a heavy frost in April which affected all but a small number of vineyards, and the rest of the growing season was irregular with some varieties affected by botrytis owing to intermittent rains in August and September.

Rioja Spring frosts reduced the crop by nearly twenty-five per cent. It would have been more but for some 800 vineyards coming into production for the first time. Good weather thereafter resulted in a good quality crop. In Navarra conditions were similar.

Ribero del Duero After a cold spring, benefited from warm and dry weather from May until the harvest at the end of September.

Penedès The summer was hot and dry though there was a very stormy period in early September with severe hailstorms destroying Cabernet Sauvignon, Merlot, and Tempranillo grapes in the higher vineyards. The result of this, and high winds, reduced the crop by fifteen per cent though the surviving grapes were of very high quality.

Whites drink up. In all the major districts the reds are of high quality, with good colour and ripe fruit and tannins, though most will be drinking well now.

1998 ★ ★ ▷ ★ ★ ★

Variable growing conditions in the north half of Spain – Penedès on the Mediterranean side, Rioja and Navarra to the northwest, and Duero to the east – make generalizations difficult.

Rioja The area (including Navarra on its northern border) enjoyed mild weather from January to March which encouraged vegetation though there were localized frosts in April and May. Flowering was fine and by August conditions were ideal. The picking of the early ripening varieties on September 15, however, was hampered by rain and low temperatures. By October 12 the main harvest was in full swing and continued in excellent conditions until November 3.

Variable but many good reds probably at best – on average – between 2002 and 2008.

Penedès A well-nigh faultless year climatically. Good growing conditions, good grapes, and good wine. A pleasant spring with welcome showers led to a hot summer with a bout of well-timed rain just before *véraison* to complete the growth cycle. August – unsurprisingly in Spain – was hot and dry, September warm and sunny in the day, cool at night. Because of these immaculate conditions very little in the way of sprays and other preventative treatments were necessary, even at what are normally the most crucial periods. The net results: healthy, ripe grapes with high levels of sugar, deep-coloured reds, and aromatic intensity.

Most reds for drinking soon, though the best Reservas will develop and keep well.

Ribera del Duero This raw upland district, not far from the Portuguese border, had a fairly normal cold, wet winter but an unusually cold April, with severe frost damage on April 11–15. Serious damage was caused by hailstorms on June 24 and 30, and again though less serious on August 15 and 18. Late September was cool and wet but, happily, warm and dry from October 9, providing good harvest conditions for the reds.

The now very fashionable reds should prove their worth now to 2010; the unique Unico of Vega Sicilia will not emerge until well after the first decade of this century.

1997 ★ ★ ▷ ★ ★ ★ ★

This year saw a split between the north and south of the country. In the south results were very good, with both quantity and quality high. Rain at the end of 1996 and start of 1997 replenished the previously starved water-tables. In parts of the north the rain did not do as many favours. Wine companies using their own grape production and not buying in grapes were in a better position – especially those who have turned to new technologies for disease control, such as *strobilurina*, a natural toxin to control mildew.

Rioja Unfortunately this was not such a successful vintage as the previous three. Heavy summer rain caused rot problems and a drop in yields, and overall quality was reduced.

Penedès Yields were also marginally down, five per cent against 1996. The region's microclimates were dramatically revealed in spring as coastal areas experienced high temperatures and then rain in July, which shortened maturation. Conversely the central and higher inland areas had very smooth and even development. The conditions were ideal everywhere during September and October allowing uniform ripening and great results – very good whites and excellent reds.

Ribera del Duero Frost in spring caused yields to fall. But fine weather before and during the harvest produced a later ripening crop of high quality. The red wines had good extract and longevity.

Riojas drink up; Duero and Penedès drink soon.

1996 ★ ★ ★

After the previous three drought-affected years, 1996 was one of the wettest on record. Quality varied from region to region.

Rioja A cold and wet December prepared the vineyards for bud-burst at the beginning of April. Certain areas were affected by frost at this time, but flowering was on schedule and quick at the start of June. Summer continued favourably with storms occurring intermittently. August and September experienced rain, but by late September it had cleared up and harvest ran from October to November. Yields were good, as was quality, especially the Reservas.

Penedès Consistent rain during the summer, with hail in June and August, tempered by cooler temperatures which kept rot in check. In mid-September an anticyclone brought ideal ripening conditions, and a delayed harvest at the end of September gave significant yields. The whites were good and the reds even better.

Ribera del Duero The largest vintage since 1990, up forty per cent on 1995. This was attributable to frosts in late spring and during the harvest, plus rain in the second week of September. Picking began on September 26 and the grapes were found to be at optimum ripeness and maturity levels. Quality was high with significant levels of fruit.

Despite the rain, the reds from the northern half of Spain showing well, though best drunk soon.

1995 ★ ★ ▷ ★ ★ ★ ★

Throughout Spain frost, drought, and ill-timed rain plagued many regions. However, although this was not good for white wines, some spectacular reds were produced, with intense colour, high alcohol and acidity levels, and firm structure.

Rioja Declared "excellent" by the Consejo Regulador, this area claimed its largest harvest of all time. Autumn and winter were mild with bud-burst twenty to thirty days early in March. Late frosts in April were followed by even flowering during May and June. The summer was perfect for ripening, with heat and adequate rain, resulting in perfectly healthy grapes. Harvest began in Baja in late August and continued until late October in Alavesa, yields varying by sub-region in this super-ripe vintage.

Penedès Spring frosts, then heavy rain and hail pre-harvest reduced yields by fifteen to twenty per cent. The producers of Cava and still white wines suffered in particular though the surviving whites are very aromatic. Red wines show great character.

Ribero del Duero Severe frost before flowering caused some apprehension, but with the following hot summer and perfect ripening conditions the vines recovered, achieving high quality.

Most reds fully mature, top Riojas will benefit from a further three to five years.

1994★★★

Spain's hottest summer since 1982, with July and August temperatures reaching 40°C (104°F). As a result the vines suffered so much stress that many simply stopped growing altogether, thus quantities were down in many cases.

Rioja A significant amount of rain had fallen during the previous autumn and winter which prepared the vines for the drought that was to follow. Frost struck the region on April 16, but the health of the vines remained excellent. The overall results of the vintage were good, with many age-worthy wines. Volumes were down by only ten per cent.

Penedés Results ranged from good to very good, but with greater reduction in yields – losses of around twenty per cent.

Ribero del Duero The vines suffered even more ripening problems in this region and volumes were reduced by thirty to fifty per cent. The resultant wines, though, were of excellent quality.

Many reds worthy of, indeed needing, ageing. The quality of wines now made by the top producers is such that in a year like 1994 they vary only between good fruity reds for early consumption and those with firmness and balance warranting eight to twelve years' cellaring.

1993★★

Rain throughout northern Spain was the spoiler in this vintage. Downpours during the spring delayed flowering and, after a warm summer, even heavier rain from the middle of September had a further effect on the final size and quality of the harvest. Nevertheless, although the quantities were down, wines of useful commercial quality were made.

Drink up.

1992★★▷★★★

After a dry winter, what began as normal spring rain became unusually heavy during May and June; by the autumn it had escalated into a serious threat to the vintage. There were a few problems with frost, but the major initial complication in the north and east was that of delayed ripening provoked by the continuation of the rainfall into the summer.

Rioja Uneven ripening resulted in reduced Tempranillo yields; no bad thing, but after a warm, fairly dry summer, hopes for the vintage had risen. The harvest began on September 24 under perfect conditions but on October 10 excessive rainfall set in. Only the Baja sub-region went relatively unscathed, being warmer and able to harvest earlier. Elsewhere, the harvest was considerably delayed, with some growers picking until early November. Unfortunately, those who did wait saw their grapes rot on the vine. There were some exceptional results from earlier-picked grapes and the yields were of average proportions.

Penedès The pattern here was similar to other parts of northern Spain. Fortunately, most of the grapes had been harvested before the onset of the rains. Some of the results were very good.

Ribero del Duero Again, harvest rain was the problem in this region.
The better properties gambled and waited for the weather to clear and,
consequently, produced wine of reasonable quality.
Agreeable reds for early consumption. Drink up.

1991 ★★★★

Variable but mainly very good quality results. Production in general down
twenty per cent from 1990, but of approximately the five-year average level.
Rioja Autumn rain, wind, and cold weather delayed the picking of fully ripe
grapes by a week or so.
Penedès Severe spring frosts caused worrying losses but from then on weather
conditions were well-nigh perfect. The final crop was greatly reduced, but of
extremely high quality.
Ribero del Duero The quality was good but quantity down.
Good reds, but drink soon.

1990 ★★★★

After two years of troublesome weather conditions, Spain enjoyed a dry but
relatively normal year and produced some excellent wines.
Rioja A very dry winter was followed by an exceptionally hot summer and a
harvest which began two weeks early. The sizzling heat affected mainly the lower
areas, while Tempranillo grapes from the higher slopes were of excellent quality,
benefiting from the cooler, moister summer nights. Late refreshing rains were
an advantage but the extreme heat proved a problem.
Penedès The summer here was not excessively hot, and cool nights and rains
during June and July were beneficial. The main harvest began mid-September.
Ribero del Duero Despite a very dry summer, yields here were up by more
than thirty-five per cent: good news after the two previous years. A high
quality year.
*All reds now fully mature. However, Vega Sicilia, as mentioned in the introduction,
will have a longer life span, reaching its zenith around 2020.*

1989 ★★

After the appalling difficulties in 1988, the main problem for growers this
year was drought, cutting total yield by eleven per cent.
Rioja Despite drought conditions, the harvest was reasonably bountiful.
The reds are well-structured, the best being the Crianzas and Reservas.
Penedès Good conditions throughout the summer were spoiled by two
hailstorms, in late August and early September, which reduced the size of
the harvest considerably.
Ribero del Duero Dry weather reduced yields here by around twenty per
cent. The quality, however, was excellent.
All fully mature.

1988 at best ★★

Spain experienced more than its fair share of disastrous weather this year. The
wettest spring on record was followed by a poor summer. This was made worse
by the development of rot on the vines, a rare situation which left Spanish
growers unprepared. Widespread, heavy hailstorms then followed. To an extent,
the quality wine regions of Spain escaped the worst effects of the weather, partly
thanks to better management.

Rioja The wet start to the year resulted in a late flowering and uneven fruit set, but this was compensated for by excellent picking conditions. A fair size crop, quality was satisfactory.

Penedès The growers who best controlled the spread of mildew produced the best wines. With some rainfall during picking, cool temperatures and dry soil prevented the spread of botrytis. Some very good wines.

Ribero del Duero Rain, hail, and mildew reduced the crop by fifty per cent; some desperate growers requested that the area be declared a disaster zone.
Rioja and Penedès reds can still be drinking well.

1987 ★★★▷★★★★★

Rioja A very good year. The mild winter and hot, dry spring resulted in an early flowering. A cool period followed, with some slight frost in May, but summer arrived rapidly and held out for the harvest which lasted from October 14 to 23.

Penedès Favourable weather conditions made this an excellent year. After an exceptionally hot summer the harvest began during the third week of August for the Muscat and continued until the end of October for the Parellada grapes. Here, heavy rains during the late harvest resulted in the development of botrytis on the broken grape skins. Damage, however, was minimal and the grapes produced pleasant, if light, wines.

Torres declared that this was their best vintage in fifteen years for red wines, especially those from Cabernet Sauvignon, with deep colour, excellent tannin, and good ageing potential.

Ribero del Duero A mild winter and wet spring was followed by exceptionally hot weather from May until August, which caused the vines to overripen in some areas. September rain caused rot and diluted the level of acidity in the grapes. The quantity was high for this vintage but the quality was variable, ranging from average to no more than good.
The Cabernet Sauvignon from Penedès perfect now; all other reds drink up.

1986 ★▷★★★

A successful year throughout much of Spain, although weather conditions caused problems in Penedès.

Rioja Spring was late after a cold, dry winter, delaying bud-break and flowering. Warm, dry weather continued throughout the summer, broken only by rain in April and October. Harvest took place from October 20 to 28 in good conditions though the crop was below average. The wines had good ageing potential.

Penedès The initial problem in this region was the drought which ran from May until August. When the rain did eventually fall it swelled the sun-dried grapes, causing the skins to split, and the rapid spread of botrytis. Growers were therefore forced to pick quickly and selectively. Cabernet Sauvignon and Tempranillo had been severely affected by the rot, but where the grapes had been picked early, the wines were of decent quality.
Drink up.

1985 ★★★★

One of the driest years for some time in Spain.

Rioja The drought in this region started during a cold, dry winter and continued throughout a good flowering, an extremely hot summer and held through the harvest which started October 20. Fortunately, the soil had retained much of the moisture from the previous wet autumn and so the region harvested a huge crop and made many very good, tannic, long-lasting wines. The best came from the high areas.

Penedès Conversely, the drought did reduce yields in this region. The growing season was cooler with warm days and cool nights, resulting in a small vintage of healthy grapes with good sugar levels which produced very good wines.

Ribero del Duero Classified as a "good" year.

Even the most tannic reds have softened and are fully mature now.

1984★★▷★★★

The end of a four-year drought in Spain.

Rioja A mild, humid winter, frost in May, hail in September, and the appearance of hurricane Hortensia in October, all made this a problematic year. The yield was consequently small and the wines of average quality – not for long keeping.

Penedès Growth was retarded by the mild, damp conditions which prevailed throughout the summer and the harvest started late in October. A good vintage.

Ribero del Duero Classified as an "average" year.

All should have been consumed by now.

1983★★

Despite weather problems a passably good year, though standing very much in the shadow of its two predecessors.

Rioja Cold winter; heavy frost in early spring; localized hail in May; and very hot weather during the harvest – all conspired to damage crops. Uneven quality.

Penedès A cold, snowy winter was followed by a hot spring. A summer-long drought – the worst for 150 years – broke in September. Thereafter the grapes ripened perfectly and the harvest began during the first week of October producing good, fruity wines.

Drink up.

1982★★★★★

An outstanding year which many felt would rank alongside the classic vintages of the century.

Rioja A warm, dry winter and a hot, dry spring. Drought conditions prevailed, causing a loss of around twenty per cent of the yield, but some much-needed rain arrived in August. The harvest ran from October 22 until November 3. Wines with great ageing potential, especially the Gran Reservas.

Penedès A wet spring was followed by a very hot summer – July was the hottest for one hundred years – caused by warm winds blowing off the Sahara. The heat-wave eventually broke and harvesting began during the first week of October. Impressive wines, with good potential.

Ribero del Duero Classified as "excellent".

One of the rare vintages producing red Spanish wines which not only keep but which will benefit from long cellaring – well into the present century.

1981 ★★▷★★★★

Rioja A long, cold, frosty winter, with snow in April, eventually gave way to warmer weather. Flowering was early and thereafter hot, dry weather held throughout the summer until the abundant harvest at the end of October. The wines were officially classified as "good" and thought by some to be excellent. For the wines of Navarra, this was undoubtedly the vintage of the decade.

Penedès Flowering was delayed by a cold, showery spring. Conditions improved later with a warm, dry summer during which gentle, beneficial rain fell in mid-June and late July. An early, small harvest of good wines – some were classified as excellent – but they are mainly past their best.

Ribero del Duero With the exception of Vega Sicilia, this year predates the new-style Dueros.

Drink up.

1980★★★

Rioja A mild, wet, frostless spring was followed by a cool but humid summer. The harvest, which ran from October 5 to November 12, took place during very cold but sunny weather and yielded a large crop. This was an elegant vintage, but the wines tended to lack body and were not for long-keeping.

Penedès A long, wet spring delayed flowering which, despite heavy rain, was successful. The temperatures were moderate throughout the dry summer, but rose in August and the weather remained fine for the harvest. A successful year.

Drink up.

1979★

Rioja A large crop of average quality wines.

Penedès Average sized crop of average quality.

Few to be seen. Drink up.

1978★★★

Rioja Well-balanced, fruity wines which aged excellently.

Penedès A below average crop of good wines.

The very best are still drinking well.

1977★▷★★

Rioja Mediocre wines.

Penedès Very satisfactory wines; the best made very exciting drinking.

Now well past best.

1976★★

Rioja Variable.

Penedès Some good wines.

Drink up.

1975★★★★

Rioja On the whole a very good vintage for reds with good ageing potential.

Penedès The weather conditions proved ideal. Very good wines.

Fully mature though the very best still drinking well.

1974★

Rioja Mediocre.

Penedès Moderately good.

Avoid.

1973★★★

Rioja Generally good.

Penedès Also good.

Pleasant wines now well past their best except for the rare Vega Sicilia, which is drinking beautifully.

1972
Rioja The second of two poor years.
Penedès Not good.
Avoid.

1971~▷★★★★
Rioja A poor year.
Penedès Excellent.
Rioja avoid. Penedès drink up.

1970★★★★▷★★★★★
Rioja Very good wines.
Penedès A legendary year for this region, which provided ideal conditions for the red wines. The crop was small but the quality excellent. (The Torres Gran Coronas Black Label 1970 came top in the Cabernet Sauvignon class at the 1979 *Gault Millau* "Wine Olympics", beating even Châteaux Latour and La Mission-Haut-Brion.)
Best, particularly Torres Gran Coronas Black Label, still lovely.

EARLIER SPANISH VINTAGES

Rioja The following were all regarded as excellent years: **1968**, **1964**, **1962**, **1959**, **1955**, **1952**, **1948**, **1947**, **1942**, **1924**, **1922**, **1920**, **1906**, **1898**, **1897**, and **1894**.
Penedès Excellent years: **1964**, **1958**, **1955**, **1952**, **1934**, **1924**, **1922**. Very good years: **1968**, **1963**, **1959**, **1954**, **1949**, **1948**, **1947**, **1942**, **1935**, **1931**, **1928**, **1925**.
Vega Sicilia (from recent tasting notes) Excellent: **1966**, **1964**, **1960**, **1957**, **1953**. Good years: **1969**, **1965**, **1962**, **1948**, **1942**.

Portuguese Table Wine

Vintages matter in Portugal more than most people seem to realize. There are few catastrophic years but, in spite of the warm climate, there are considerable variations between different harvests. This is especially true in the north of the country where the best years for table wine often correspond closely to "declared" port vintages. In the newer wine-producing regions of southern Portugal, excessive heat and drought is often a problem. But, with modern equipment in their *adegas*, winemakers are now learning to make the best use of these extreme conditions.

Most of the Portuguese table wines currently on sale in shops and restaurants come from recent vintages. However, two principal exceptions are Barca Velha from port producers Ferreira, and Buçaco from the unique Palace Hotel deep in the heart of the country, both of which reward long keeping. The cellars at the Buçaco Palace house wines dating back to the 1940s and even older bottles occasionally turn up for auction.

There are other well-made reds which keep reasonably well, notably those from Bucelas and the Dão and Bairrada districts: some of the best can be found dating back to the 1960s. On the other hand, matured (*maduro*) white wines are something of an acquired taste, but with improvements in vinification a number are becoming more acceptably international in style. Most Vinho Verde is labelled without a vintage date. These wines should always be drunk while young and fresh. Varietal Vinhos Verdes, however, made exclusively from the Alvarinho grape, are usually from a specified year and may benefit from maturation in bottle.

What all Portugal's wines have in common is good value. Most Portuguese white wines are best drunk young and fresh, in short when they first appear on the market. The 1995 and older vintage notes refer only to red wines.

2002~▷★★

A bleak year for Portugal. In addition to an early flowering due to an unusually cool summer, as with the rest of Europe this year, rain played havoc with the Portuguese harvest. It was the wettest September in Portugal, particularly in Alentejo, for the last sixty years, and the humidity, combined with high temperatures, created the perfect breeding ground for the spread of rot and fungus. Growers were forced to squeeze a seven- to eight-week harvest into three to four weeks and carry out a rigorous selection, which lost sixty per cent of the harvest. Overall, production was fifteen to twenty per cent down on 2001. Further north, in Dão, Bairrada, and Vinhos Verdes, many growers simply left their grapes to rot on the vine. The late ripening red varieties were decimated by the rains. Luckily the earlier varieties such as Tinta Roriz, which were harvested before the rain, made surprisingly well-balanced wines, full of colour and concentration, and good levels of alcohol and acidity. Successes this year were generally the result of increasingly sophisticated vineyard techniques, and the high quality of the pre-rain grapes.

Apart from a few good Douro reds, avoid.

2001 up to★★★

Quantity high, quality variable. The winter was the wettest on record, causing several landslides in the vertiginous Douro vineyards and the tragic collapse of the bridge over the River Douro at Entre-os-Rios. The up side was that ground water supplies returned to normal levels following the severe drought of the late 1990s. The weather during the crucial flowering period was fine and dry, and although the summer was both variable and much cooler than normal in places, the white grapes were ripe and in perfect health by harvest time. The harvest began by mid-August in the south and by mid-September in the north where, because of three weeks of wet weather from September 21, picking lasted until the end of October.

Some good white wines from Dão, the Douro, Alentejo, and elsewhere, all for early drinking. The heavy September rains made life difficult for the reds except for the relatively few producers who practise green pruning. Drink soon.

2000★★★★

Quantity was down this year throughout Portugal due to a rainy April and May, which caused delayed and uneven flowering. Quality was, however, excellent. The weather conditions in late spring and summer were the best in the last five years, yielding the best quality in ten years.

There was heavy rain in September in the coastal regions of Bairrada and Estremadura. In Quinta do Carmo, the lack of rain after mid-May was good for quality, but two localized hailstorms reduced quantity. In Alentejo, an important region for table wines, the weather remained cooperative during the harvest. The result was exceptionally high quality grapes, showing good maturity and concentration. It was a particularly good year for reds. The whites were not as good as in previous years.

Drink up whites and enjoy some spectacularly good reds from now on.

1999 ★ ★

The climatic differences between Spain and Portugal cannot be over-emphasized. Together, they comprise the Iberian Peninsular but Portugal has a maritime climate and acts as a sort of bulwark against the Atlantic fronts. Moreover, in certain years – as in 1999 – the weather conditions can be totally different from north to south. Everything was more than well throughout Portugal in the spring and summer. Perfect ripening conditions from July to early September were interrupted only by a brief period of rain in August. Then came the rains, torrential and continuous.

In Alentejo, with its continental climate, and the early ripening white varieties of Barraida, the grapes were picked before the rains. Those with well tended vineyards, and who held off until the drier weather of early October, fared better. Dão was not too badly affected by the rain, but the Douro suffered, Touriga Nacional and the smaller, thicker-skinned grapes withstanding the damp conditions better than the rest.

Drink up all whites; reds variable, not for long keeping.

1998 ★ ★ ★

Small quantity, fairly high quality. Except for the south, conditions were not dissimilar to the Port wine region. The summer was relatively favourable enabling some regions, notably the Alentejo and Setúbal, to start the harvest early. From mid-August to mid-September the major part of the production was already harvested. Then it started to rain. Worst hit were the Minho and Douro Valley to the north, to a slightly lesser extent Dão and Bairrada, though it must be stressed that early harvesting saved the day.

Moderately good quality reds for early to mid-term drinking, say now to 2006.

1997 ★ ★ ▷ ★ ★ ★

Unfavourable growing conditions at the start of the year gave way to perfect harvesting weather. Temperatures were above average during February and March, accelerating the growing cycle. Then, humidity caused irregular ripening which was not helped by a damp June and July. The progress made earlier in the year was lost. Yields fell on average by thirty per cent and rot problems caused losses of up to fifty per cent in Vinho Verde and the Dão.

Under clear blue skies harvesting ran smoothly all over Portugal. Some producers reported extended growing seasons of up to 150 days between flowering and harvest (the average is usually around 110 days). Excellent results were recorded in Alentejo and Douro. Unfortunately, the coastal areas did not fare quite so well. The red wines were of the highest quality, with above-average pH levels and good extract, yielding age-worthy wines.

Reds are ready though the best will keep.

1996 ★ ★ ▷ ★ ★ ★

After four years of drought the weather broke during the winter. Heavy rainfall replenished thirsty water tables, especially in the south. By the time flowering started it was evident that the crop would be very large. Careful producers decided at this point to thin their crop to enhance quality. Autumn was cool causing the vintage to be delayed by two weeks. Alentejo producers started picking at the beginning of September; those in the north did not start until the final week of the month.

Many growers were picking for two months or longer because of the sheer quantity of grapes. Crops were enormous, two to three times larger than 1995, so much so that some cooperatives could not keep up with the volumes. Diligent producers made red wines of very good quality, less carefully made wines have suffered from dilution. White wines fared even better.

Drink up.

1995★★★★

A very successful vintage throughout Portugal, most regions produced excellent wines. On the whole, spring was mild; the beginning of July became overcast and some rain fell during the summer. However, this was to be a saviour to the vines, as a heat-wave struck in August, sending temperatures rocketing for four weeks. The south was hit hardest as drought caused problems, especially in Alentejo where yields were significantly reduced. Further north, Dão yields were also small. In contrast, Bairrada on the west coast produced some of the finest wines, especially reds, from well-ripened grapes.

The better reds are delicious now, but the best will benefit from a further two or three years bottle-age.

1994★★★★

Wet conditions were a problem during winter and spring. In May, some places experienced highly localized frost which almost completely destroyed the crop. The ripening season progressed well without excessive summer heat. A couple of short bursts of rain in the Douro in August and early September helped re-establish a healthy and even ripening, resulting in good sugar levels. In this region, production was down by about forty-five per cent, dramatically affecting the availability of grapes for table wine.

Throughout Portugal a successful harvest. Volumes were drastically down, but the quality high. In the south, growers were very happy with their results.

Most reds drinking well, but top Alentejo reds are still tannic and need a year or two of extra bottle-ageing.

1993★

An extremely unsettled vintage. Drought affected the country during the winter and early spring, followed by rains from late April until June. By the end of this dismal period, flowering was just beginning and clearly not in ideal conditions. The summer was warm, but rarely sufficiently hot to enable healthy ripening.

As September approached, the weather became increasingly unsettled, the only respite being a dry but cool week at the end of the month. The weather barely improved and the harvest started alarmingly late. The rains returned on October 2, causing even more difficulties than already existed.

Avoid.

1992★▷★★

Portugal experienced one of its driest winters on record, followed by an intensely hot summer. Fortunately, heavy rains fell at the end of August, saving

the vintage as the grapes were now able to ripen. By the time of the harvest, conditions had turned cold and wet. The general lack of rain resulted in crops being frequently reduced by at least twenty-five per cent. In the south these conditions delayed the ripening process and many wines were unbalanced, green, and hard. The weather was less extreme in the north and the wines are, consequently, of a higher quality.
Drink soon.

1991 ★★▷★★★★

After a wet winter, warm weather in April and May encouraged early growth. June was unusually cool and wet but this was more than compensated for by hot weather which lasted uninterrupted until the end of August. In the north, a large crop looked likely; however, rain in early September led to rot. Some Vinho Verde growers lost fifteen per cent of their crop. In the south, three weeks of extreme heat undoubtedly caused a setback and, for the third successive year, a lack of water kept yields down below average.

Financial help from the EU aided wineries all over Portugal to become even better equipped to cope with climatic extremes. Although most producers seemed pleased with the quality of their wine, some southern reds (especially those made in the old-fashioned *adegas* where temperature control was lacking) tended to be unbalanced and over-alcoholic.
Middle-quality reds drink up, high quality well into the present decade.

1990★★★

Heavy winter rains around Christmas 1989 replenished the water-table in much of the country, but a prolonged period of dry summer weather, combined with searing heat, quickly brought on a drought in some regions.

Yields were down by about ten per cent in Alentejo and on the Setúbal peninsula, though this was more than compensated for by some high quality wines. In the north, two short bursts of rain in August and September helped to swell the grapes. Growers in Bairrada, Dão, and the Douro harvested an average-sized crop of well-ripened grapes.
Lighter reds drink up; sturdiest reds soon.

1989★★★

July and August were blisteringly hot throughout Portugal. After the previous year's extremely low yield, a large crop was badly needed. In the event, drought in some parts of Portugal retarded development of the grapes and reduced average yields by as much as twenty per cent. The early harvest produced ripe fruit, though some wines suffered from a lack of acidity. In Bairrada they tended to lack colour and depth.
Many still drinking well. Fully mature.

1988★★★★

Disasters are not frequent in Portugal's mild Atlantic climate, but in 1988 vineyards in much of the country came close to catastrophe.

An uneven flowering was followed by rain which continued until the end of June. Many small growers in the north had never experienced such conditions and mildew set in before anything could be done to prevent it. The Minho was particularly badly hit; yields were in some cases eighty per cent below the average. However, low yields often mean high quality and the 1988 vintage was saved by a warm, dry summer lasting until the end of the harvest. Outstanding wines were made in the Dão, Bairrada, and Alentejo regions. In the Douro, which suffered the effects of the poor spring, most of the production was used to make port.

The better reds still drinking well.

1987 ★▷★★

An uneven year. In the north, a drought which slowed down the maturation of the grapes. Consequently, many wines from Bairrada, Dão, and Setúbal were light, astringent, and somewhat lacking in colour. The best wines were produced further south in the Alentejo.

Avoid.

1986 ★★

For many winemakers in the north this was a year to forget. A warm summer was followed by torrential rain at the time of the harvest. Rot set in quickly, badly affecting vineyards in Bairrada, Dão, and parts of the Douro. The south fared better; some excellent, well-structured wines were produced in the Alentejo and on the Setúbal peninsula.

Mainly drink up. Well-structured Alentejo reds still drinking quite well.

1985 ★★★★

In many ways, the reverse of 1986. After a wet spring, the late, hot summer and warm, sunny autumn ripened the grapes and provided perfect harvesting conditions. Dão, Bairrada, and the Douro in the north of the country produced intense, concentrated wines which had the potential to mature well.

In the south, however, the piercing sun shrivelled grapes in many of the vineyards before they were picked. These high temperatures also caused problems during fermentation in the less well-equipped *adegas*, and many of the resulting wines suffered from excess acidity.

Top reds have excellent depth of fruit and are well-balanced; they are lovely now and might well keep longer.

1984 ★▷★★★

Rain in early October followed a cool summer and many growers were caught out waiting for their grapes to ripen. As a result Dão, and Bairrada made thin, astringent red wines. The best came from the Douro. Further south, vines benefited from a relatively cool vintage and good, well-balanced reds were made in the Alentejo and Setúbal regions.

All now fully mature. Drink up.

1983 ★★★★★

The second of two excellent vintages. Overall, the north produced classic, firm-flavoured reds. To the south, where the use of modern equipment was less common, the wines were somewhat less balanced, many having stewed aromas and flavours.

Drink up all but the top quality reds, such as Barca Velha.

1982 ★★★★★

After hot summer conditions growers harvested early. The Douro, Dão, and Bairrada regions made robust wines with plenty of ripe fruit. Ferreira's Barca

Velha has a chocolatey intensity and Buçaco produced some intensely ripe, full-flavoured reds.

Further south, this year was seen to have the edge on the 1983s, particularly in the Ribatejo, where some excellent, ripe, and flavoursome *garrafeiras* were made.

Drink up.

1981 ★

A year which many growers would prefer to forget. The wines were often thin and astringent, lacking fruit and depth. The eastern Douro escaped the worst of the rain and produced a good, spicy Barca Velha – the high note of the year. *Apart from Barca Velha, avoid.*

1980 ★ ★ ★ ★

For many winemakers throughout Portugal this was the best vintage of the decade. A late flowering was followed by a warm summer and a dry autumn, and the grapes were harvested in perfect condition. The Dão and Bairrada regions made fruity, well-balanced wines and further south in the Ribatejo some excellent *garrafeiras* were produced. Curiously, Ferreira did not market their Barca Velha, instead classifying it as Reserva Especial. *Fully mature now but the best reds can still be very agreeable.*

EARLIER PORTUGUESE VINTAGES

Notable earlier vintages include: **1978**, **1975**, **1974**, **1971**, **1970**, **1966**. Barca Velha: **1978**, **1966**, **1965**, **1964**. Buçaco: **1978**, **1977**, **1975**, **1970**, **1966**, **1965**, **1962,** and, particularly, **1959**.

New World

California

It is roughly 1,126.5 km (700 m) from the most southerly vineyards of California, near San Diego, to Mendocino in the north; and in terms of average temperature the range varies considerably between those districts closer to the coast and the broad, hot Central Valley. It is therefore difficult to include weather reports and quality assessments for such widely differing areas. Similarly it is no reflection on the quality of wine made in and around Santa Barbara, Monterey, or Santa Clara that the following vintage notes concentrate almost solely on two major wine districts: the Napa Valley, with its almost continuous string of premium quality vineyards and wineries, and the broader, but equally vine-clad, Sonoma County.

If we take into account the vines planted by Spanish missionaries, the history of wine in what is now California, though not as ancient as that of the Cape, pre-dates all other "New World" wine cultures. The business of vine growing was revived in the second half of the nineteenth century. After the blight of Prohibition, it took off again seriously in the 1940s, gaining momentum in the 1950s, making tremendous strides in the 1970s, and coming of age in the 1980s.

Virtually every variety of *Vitis vinifera* has been cultivated in California, but, by process of elimination, Cabernet Sauvignon and Chardonnay stand supreme. Merlot has fully emerged; Zinfandel ploughs its individual furrow; Sauvignon Blanc (Fumé Blanc) fills an important niche; Pinot Noir is achieving distinction; and the once dull Rieslings have found their apotheosis in late-harvest dessert wines. Perhaps even more encouraging, "new" (old world) varietals such as Syrah and Viognier – rather a cult grape – are being supremely well-handled by a small number of brilliant winemakers.

Like most dry white wine, Sauvignon Blanc, or its synonym Fumé Blanc, is best drunk young – indeed it does not age at all well. The best Chardonnay, pleasant drinking at three years of age, can be consumed with equal enjoyment some eight years after the vintage. The best reds, like Bordeaux and burgundy, need bottle-age though California Cabernets and "Zins" have an innate fleshy character and fruitiness which enables them to be drunk when "released" (put on the market) by the producer. Those of high quality, with a track record and from a good vintage, can develop well for twenty years or longer.

2002★★★ (early to tell)

Was this the vintage of the century or the harvest plagued by a September heat so intense that everything ripened all at once? Perhaps a little of both.

The winter, spring, and summer provided ideal weather conditions for the vines. Frost affected several areas in April, and in May rain at flowering reduced yields, especially for Merlot. But from late July throughout August, cool yet pleasant weather prevailed, allowing ripening to take place at a slow but steady pace. Some growers even started to thin their crops in June and July to concentrate the flavours in the ripe berries. Then on September 4, an intense statewide heat-wave began and was followed by another heat-wave on September 20. Sugar levels rose by as much as three degrees in a single day, sending vintners into a panic as they tried to find enough fermenters for grapes that needed picking all at once. The harvest was compressed, lasting six to eight weeks in comparison to the normal eight to ten weeks. Many growers refused to take a risk and green harvested, reducing their total harvest, and denying their grapes the chance to gain in complexity and intensity. In the Sierra Foothills, the accelerated ripening, after a cool summer, during which nothing had ripened, caused the grapes to become soft and dehydrated. There was, however, a lack of mould and rot throughout the state and late ripening varieties were spared from the sun's most harmful effects, though picking at the right moment was crucial to avoid sunburned berries. The challenge, with the Zinfandels, was to strike a balance between acid and sugar. In the Central Valley and Santa Barbara, the heat-waves were a welcome jump-start to the harvest. The Pinot Noir and Chardonnay were of a very high quality, although yields were low. In the Santa Lucia Highlands in Monterey these varieties were "picture perfect" due to the less intense heat and significant breezes from Monterey Bay.

Good or great? Not a year for some whites which, because of the heat and subsequent high alcoholic content can be too hefty, even blowsy. A much more interesting year for the reds, the best-made "Cabs" and "Zins". Like cream rising to the top of the milk, the top reds will soon be proving themselves. Better to follow the producers than the vintage.

2001 ★ ★ ★ ★ ★

This year's harvest was early, high in quality, and smaller than the previous year's record harvest.

The beginning of the year looked bleak. An extremely dry winter was followed by a severe yield-reducing frost in April, and May and June were the warmest ever, causing vintners to worry about a premature harvest. But cold and fog in July and temperatures in Napa-Sonoma around 20°C (70°F) slowed down ripening. On August 17, one of the earliest harvests began and continued through ideal Indian summer conditions in September and October. Rainless days prevailed after a brief and harmless storm on September 24 until October 30, but by then most of the grapes were in. In the Napa Valley, the harvest was reportedly "near perfect". The whites were "precociously aromatic and intense", the reds "concentrated in colour, tannin, and flavour". Cabernet Sauvignon in particular benefited from the hang time provided by the Indian summer. In Sonoma County, the Pinot Noir and Chardonnay were in excellent condition, but overall yields were ten per cent below average and, due to the cool conditions, acids were a little higher than usual. Zinfandel and Cabernet grapes were also smaller than normal, resulting in excellent colours and flavours. In Mendocino and Lake Counties the lack of harvest rain and the warm, then cool late summer resulted in red wines rich in colour, flavour, body, and alcohol. In Santa Barbara, an early September heat-wave accelerated sugar accumulation, but then the weather levelled off again, allowing even ripening. The warm, offshore conditions along the Santa Barbara Coast bode well for Pinot Noirs and Chardonnays, and ideal for Syrahs and Merlots.

Clearly a highly satisfactory vintage for both whites and reds, no matter which varietal or varietal mix. Apart from Sauvignon Blanc (or Blanc Fumé), always best drunk whilst young, both styles of Chardonnay – the old style buttery and the lighter – should fare well. The reds, with their fresh and soft tannins will be the classics of the future. Drinkable early – compared to their counterparts in Bordeaux – yet with all the component parts in balance to ensure a long life. The real star of the vintage, to quote Joel Butler MW, is the Syrah, a varietal that I have been following and enjoying for some years now.

2000 ★ ★ ★ ▷ ★ ★ ★ ★

After years of El Niño and La Niña California's weather had ostensibly returned to normal. Spring was cool and moist, followed by a massive heat-wave from mid-June to July. Perfect weather in August became cooler towards the end and continued into early September, slowing down ripening and assuring longer hang time. A brief rainstorm swept the state on September 1, but caused no real damage. A second heat-wave, September 17–19, sent growers scurrying to get the grapes in, while heavy rains over October 9–10 caused fears of rot and mildew, but the weather quickly turned sunny and warm again, drying out the grapes. Luckily, seventy per cent of the state's grapes (mostly early ripening varieties) were picked by the final week of October, but late ripeners, including Cabernet Sauvignon, were still on the vines. Then again, floods were predicted for the end of October but by early November, skies cleared again. The quality, however, of Cabernet Sauvignon and related varietals had been compromised. In the Napa Valley, grapes picked before the October rains like the Pinot Noir were in exceptional quality. In Sonoma the warm, dry weather after the September 1 storm produced great quality white grapes, but the late rains had diluted and reduced fruit density of late ripening varieties, including Cabernet Sauvignon and Zinfandel. In Monterey, overall quality was excellent and most of the varieties were rescued before the heavy rains in late October; the cool-climate Syrah was not too badly affected by rot due to its thick skin. In the Sierra Foothills, a May freeze reduced yields in many vineyards, while the early September rains made for a stressful harvest. The cold rains (and, at higher elevations, snow) on October 26 threatened late-picked varieties, including Zinfandel, Barbera, and Mourvèdre. The vintage was generally successful.

The "hallmark" of this vintage is normality; normality does not bean uniformity. Indeed it is a vintage to explore, to seek out the occasional star and, if red, give it bottle-age. The whites are, on the whole, exciting and already drinking well. Pinot Noir, which over the past decade or so, has proved such a successful varietal, is showing particularly well in 2000.

1999 ★ ★ ★ ★

An abnormally cool spring and cool summer slowed vine development and ripening, resulting in one of the longest, coolest, and latest-ever harvests. Vintage continued, abnormally, into November though a nearly week-long heat-wave at the end of September caused grapes in the Napa Valley to ripen quickly.

The overall results: quantity down, as much as fifty per cent below average in places, but quality generally high. Much depends on when wineries picked. Alcohol levels tend to be higher though there is good acidity. In Napa and Sonoma, the Bordeaux varieties, Cabernet Sauvignon, Merlot, and Cabernet Franc have good, ripe fleshy fruit; Pinot Noir is excellent.

High malic acid in the Chardonnay allowed winemakers to go through "the malo", malolactic fermentation, which aids complexity and depth. Sauvignon Blanc grapes were harvested before the very hot period in late September, some being kept back as late as early November to make sweet wines affected by botrytis. The Central Coast area was cooler than the rest of the State, delaying *véraison*. The harvest has been described as "late and light", the smaller crop, with its concentrated clusters, producing vibrant, outstanding wines.

Sauvignon Blanc drink soon; Chardonnays, with good fruit, are generally more robust than their counterparts in Burgundy, drink perhaps now to 2005. All the reds will probably have what it takes for good mid-term drinking.

1998 ★★▷★★★★ very variable

El Niño, the bane of the Americas in 1998, certainly hit California hard, particularly the coastal regions. Unquestionably a difficult year, vine growers having to cope with highly unsuitable weather conditions, a surfeit of pests and diseases, including the phylloxera, and the latest harvest in recent memory.

A winter of severe storms, with February the worst on record, led to a cool and sodden April and May. June was little better with unfavourable weather during flowering. *Véraison* – colour change – was late, around mid-August. Yet there were short, erratic periods of intense heat. Poor weather continued and by mid-September hardly a grape was picked. The harvest ended mid-November, the latest since records began. Yet, despite all this, and a much reduced crop, some good wines were made thanks to the technical expertise of well-established wineries.

Frankly, hard to sum up. Go for the best producers. Cabernet and Zinfandel in the hands of the skilled will probably turn out well. Weather conditions were not kind to Merlot but, given strict selection, it has produced some delicious wine.

1997 ★★★★★

After the run of small vintages this year produced a bumper crop. Yields were up by twenty-four per cent compared to 1996 and the proportion of premium wines was also high. This has helped to relieve price inflation.

January was unusually warm and damp. Spring came early and the weather continued favourably, providing a long, dry, and not overly hot ripening period. The harvest started extremely early with grapes for sparkling wines ready for picking by the end of July. At this point things changed. Sonoma and Napa both suffered tropical storms in August and September which triggered rot problems. These were intensified due to the preponderance of tight bunches on the vines. Chardonnay, Sauvignon Blanc, Pinot Noir, and Zinfandel were most affected as were the lower-situated vineyards. Rigorous vineyard management commenced and, as a consequence, some producers suffered stuck fermentations due to residual fungicides in the grapes. Ripening schedules were also disrupted, causing problems at the wineries during crushing. Monterey County was spared the late storms and was rewarded with a perfect harvest, and with finely balanced wines. Further south, Santa Barbara experienced a certain amount of rain, but is more influenced by microclimates. Nevertheless, the overall quality and quantity was excellent everywhere.

Impossible to generalize. Whites and commercial reds drink up. The top wineries are a different matter: the standard of Pinot Noir is now astonishingly high, yet most are normally best drunk quite young; Cabernet Sauvignon, Merlot, and Zinfandel, though attractively fruity when first released, usually benefit from a further two to five years' bottle-age.

1996 ★★★

Another variable year for the west coast, with some unfavourable growing conditions. This was unfortunate for the consumer as prices continued to rise due to depleted stocks.

Winter was warmer than usual which shortened the dormancy period, reducing the amount of fruit setting on the vine. By spring time the temperatures had cooled slightly and rain brought bud-break two or three weeks early. Further rain in May caused the vines to "shatter" while flowering, compounding the decreased fruiting problem. A heat-wave struck during July and August, advancing the harvest.

In the Napa, a dramatic cooling in late August slowed down the ripening process, allowing more "hang time" for the grapes. A stop/start harvest followed, which some say has added complexity to the wines. The concentration and balance of the grapes benefited most, but quantities were still down: Sauvignon Blanc and Chardonnay anywhere between twenty and fifty per cent; Pinot Noir varied according to area, and Cabernet Sauvignon and Merlot the least affected.

Going south, the weather was more consistent, giving better results. Santa Barbara saw an increase of around fifteen to twenty per cent and yields of very high quality.

Drink up most if not all whites. Pinot Noirs drinking well now, Cabernets and Zinfandels, say now to 2008.

1995 ★ ★ ▷ ★ ★ ★ ★

This year experienced similar misfortunes to the 1994 vintage. Torrential January rain, March floods, and cold weather during flowering resulted in the eventual harvest being delayed by between two and four weeks, and with reduced yields.

The coastal vineyards were hit hardest with Monterey and Santa Barbara experiencing losses of up to twenty-three per cent of total production. Yields of early ripening varieties such as Pinot Noir and Chardonnay fell eighty and fifty per cent respectively. Central Valley was not hit so hard and the extended growing season gave wines with added concentration as a result of good sugar levels and retained acidity. Napa and Sonoma took a hard knock after flooding, and continuing phylloxera problems reduced yields by around ten per cent. Mendocino was spared most of the unfavourable conditions, enjoying a rise in yields of between twenty-four and twenty-nine per cent, plus inflated prices.

White wines suffered most losses with Chardonnay yields falling six per cent. However, red varietals triumphed as Zinfandel jumped forty-six per cent and Merlot thirty-three per cent.

Some really lovely reds, Cabernet and blends, Syrah and the rare "cult" wines, some up to five star quality with further ageing potential. Recommended.

1994 ★ ★ ▷ ★ ★ ★ ★

From mediocre to surprisingly good, the result of somewhat un-Californian weather – rain and unusually cool temperatures at crucial points during the growing season.

Initial problems were caused by spring rains, resulting in uneven flowering and budding. For most varieties the bunches and the grapes themselves were unusually small. The harvest was drastically reduced and yields were markedly varied from site to site. The ripening process had progressed uneventfully until cool autumnal weather arrived which, in some areas, was accompanied by heavy rains. Napa Valley and Sonoma County were fortunately not affected by the rains as much as the more southerly districts, most notably the Central Coast.

The main concerns at the time were the reduced yields of Chardonnay and Zinfandel. The former was down by fifteen to twenty per cent, with many examples suffering ripening deficiencies, and the latter by as much as fifty per cent. Pinot Noir was reduced by about twenty per cent, but with excellent results as it was generally harvested before the rains arrived. Fortunately, Sauvignon Blanc, Cabernet Sauvignon, and Merlot all had healthily proportioned yields with good to excellent quality levels.

A roller-coaster of a year. High-quality Pinot Noir at best now, and some excellent Bordeaux-varietal reds from now to, say, 2010.

1993 ★ ★ ▷ ★ ★ ★ ★

If there are those who still think that "the Sunshine State" makes life easy for grape growers, 1993 must surely correct this inaccurate impression. The weather, from spring to harvest time, was bizarre, erratic, and unpredictable.

The early summer had unusually cold and rainy periods interspersed with strong winds. Summer ripening was alternately advanced and retarded by heat-waves and cold spells right through into October. Crops were reduced by the poor flowering, amounting to an overall loss of around ten per cent; Merlot, Pinot Noir, and Chardonnay were the worst hit. All the white varieties suffered from burned and frequently "raisined" grapes because of the severity of the heatwaves. In southern California yields were closer to normal. The results were very uneven – not even lower yields implied an increase in quality.

Forget the whites; the reds are enormously variable, most for early drinking. But the best delicious now.

1992 ★ ★ ★

The growing season started well. For the first time in six years there was adequate winter rainfall to ease drought conditions. Flowering was successful, two weeks ahead of usual. Much sun and mild temperatures were the rule. Early summer was a little unsettled but by mid-July normal warmth resumed, heating up rather alarmingly in August. But the pattern of warm days and cool nights returned, leading to an early and perfect harvest.

The main problem affecting growers in the Napa area at this time was phylloxera. Of the 13,500 hectares of vines in the valley, nearly 2000 were already affected by this year. Uprooting and replanting is a costly business: from $40,000 to over $60,000 per hectare.

Overall a very satisfactory vintage. All the varieties behaved well: classic Cabernets with good fruit; well-structured wines should keep for considerably longer. Several top estate Cabernets in the five star class.

1991 ★ ★ ★ ★ ★

A worrying year which ended satisfactorily. Weather conditions were similar in the Napa Valley and Sonoma County: record low temperatures in the winter and an ominously dry New Year and early spring. Happily, before bud-break in March, there was exceptionally heavy rain. The spring was cool but the flowering successful, promising an abundant crop. However, the summer was also cool, by Californian standards, and extended. Leaves were removed to enable the sun to penetrate and crops thinned to encourage concentration and maturation – the latter finally brought to a conclusion by an excellent unbroken Indian summer.

Ripe, well-balanced grapes were picked before late October rains and the long, cool growing season resulted in good natural levels of acidity, vital for life and development. Levels of alcohol were conducive to finesse rather than massive structure, yet with enhanced concentration and flavour for all varietals, and intensity of colour for the reds. The only cloud on the horizon at this stage, particularly in the Napa, was the spread of phylloxera (Type B) which was devastating whole blocks of vines on the valley floor, necessitating extensive and expensive replanting.

Pinot Noirs, Syrah, and Merlot drinking well now; top Cabernets and related blends drinking well with further development possible.

1990★★★★

A smaller crop than 1989, but one which was harvested in near-perfect conditions, particularly in the Napa Valley. A dry winter in the Napa, with temperatures below average, led to a late bud-break. However, a long heat-wave in mid-May speeded up growth. Flowering and berry set were affected by heavy rains in late May, resulting in a smaller than average crop. Picking began relatively early in mid-August. Cool mornings and evenings, with gradual warming during the days characterized the harvest, making it, some said, one of the most ideal harvests in recent history. Normal bud-break in Sonoma, followed by moderate weather, led to a good set in the Chardonnay grapes, but not in the Cabernet Sauvignon and Sauvignon Blanc, owing to heavy rain in June. Thereafter the summer was fine, interrupted by short two-day heatwaves. As in the Napa, harvesting proceeded normally in near-perfect conditions, resulting in similarly small yields of high quality, intense, deep-coloured wines.

Classic reds ready and drinking well.

1989★★▷★★★★

A year which will be remembered for the devastating earthquake which struck in mid-October, causing thousands of bottles of the previous vintage to be shattered. After several drought years, rain in March was much welcomed by growers in California. The vines flowered in ideal conditions which held throughout the summer, encouraging high expectations. However, towards the end of September, with forty per cent of the grapes picked in the Napa, the harvest was interrupted by widespread, torrential rain. The weather thereafter was cold, foggy, and stormy, encouraging the spread of rot. Those who picked quickly and selectively produced good wine. Yields were considerably larger than those of the previous dry years but quality was low.

Similar conditions prevailed in Sonoma; however, near-perfect harvesting conditions produced some fine wines. Cabernet Sauvignon had deep colour and good tannic structure.

The best reds drinking well now.

1988★★

Described as one of the weirdest years on record because of the unusual weather conditions. Winter was dry; February and March were hot, and encouraged early bud-break. In the Napa, cold, rainy weather in April then continued through the flowering, accompanied by heavy winds. The summer was very hot and harvesting began on August 24. The drought and erratic weather conditions affected berry and bunch size, massively reducing the crop. Growers reported that the tonnage of Pinot Noir was down by as much as sixty per cent and the Sauvignon Blanc by fifty per cent. Quality, however, was high and grapes picked early and selectively, made the best wines – concentrated in style.

Conditions in Sonoma were slightly different. Bud-break was delayed by a dry winter but growth caught up during a warm spring. Summer was initially cool and wet and thereafter the growing season was alternately very hot and very cool. The vintage was early: picking began in late August and yields were low, quality high.

Pinot Noirs fully mature; Cabernet and Cabernet blends drinking well.

1987 ★ ★ ★

A small, healthy crop. Soils, made dry by low rainfall at the end of the previous season, produced vines with small berry and cluster size – factors which promised an excellent vintage. The growing season enjoyed fine, warm weather, and the arrival of coastal fog cooled the grapes and protected acidity levels.

Picking was early and the harvest was fully under way for all grapes by mid-August. A fine Cabernet Sauvignon vintage.

Cabernet Sauvignon, drink soon.

1986 ★ ★ ▷ ★ ★ ★

A cold, dry winter ended with torrential storms in mid-February. Flowering was early but protracted. The summer was dry and one of the coolest on record, but was followed by hot weather in August and September. The main harvest began early, around the beginning of September, but continued into October. Yields were high and the grapes had good tannin levels. Some excellent Cabernets.

Pinot Noir and Merlot drink up, the better Cabernet Sauvignons drink soon.

1985 ★ ★ ★ ★ ★

Undoubtedly an excellent vintage – one of the best ever in the Napa. Apart from some stormy weather in February, the weather was fine throughout the early spring and the summer. September saw some heavy rains which interrupted the main harvest, but good weather returned at the end of the month to ripen the remaining grapes. The outcome was a broad range of superbly balanced, supple, well-knit wines which had excellent ageing potential. In Sonoma the Cabernet Sauvignon harvest was interrupted in some areas by heavy rains. A small crop of good quality wines – particularly Cabernets – was achieved nonetheless.

Drink up Pinot Noirs, but the superb and beautifully balanced Cabernet Sauvignons are drinking well, the "stars" sublime.

1984 ★ ★ ★

A very wet winter was followed by hot weather throughout the growing season. The summer was exceptionally hot – temperatures, sometimes well above 38°C (100°F), caused some berry shatter and consequently a reduction in crop size.

The harvest was the earliest ever in the Napa and Sonoma, all the major varietals ripening together, making picking extremely busy from as early as the first week of August. Clean grapes made well-balanced, good quality wines with potential for ageing, although not quite up to the standard of the 1985s. Overall, these were attractive wines for early drinking.

All fully mature.

1983 ★ ▷ ★ ★ ★

This year endured the wettest winter on record, and a summer which, apart from one heat-wave in mid-July, was damp and cool. These conditions caused considerable problems, including a lack of soil aeration and visibly "tired", soggy vines, as well as the inevitable rot. The best-drained sites experienced the least problems and everywhere picking was very selective. The harvest yielded a small crop of very variable wines which ranged from poor to excellent in quality. The most successful were the Cabernet Sauvignons.

In Sonoma botrytis was widespread and helped to produce some excellent Rieslings plus some equally good Gewurztraminers and late-harvest Sauvignon Blancs.

A distinctly uneven vintage, some reds very tannic, some soft. Hard to generalize. Drink up or avoid – except for the few good late-harvest wines at their peak now.

1982 at best★★★★

California suffered one of its wettest winters ever, followed by a frostless spring and good weather during flowering. An exceptionally long harvest, held back by rain in mid-September, produced a bumper crop. Some white grapes were lost to rot, although some very good botrytized sweet wines were made. An Indian summer saved the Cabernet Sauvignons, producing ripe, fruity wines.

Though initially tannic, the Cabernets developed well; most are at or beyond their peak now. Some excellent Zinfandels.

1981 at best★★★

The earliest harvest on record in almost all areas of California followed a summer of extreme heat. Budding and flowering were both early and healthy, but Cabernet Sauvignon grapes suffered during the hottest June throughout the United States. Large crop quantities were lost as a result.

The main harvest was well underway by mid-August. The weather cooled in September, though it was followed by an Indian summer, during which some botrytis-affected grapes were picked to make fine late-harvest whites. This was a fairly good year; the white wines were generally better than the reds which tended to be rather light. This was Sonoma's shortest growing season on record. As a result, because of the rapid sugar accumulation, the Chardonnays lacked fruit, while the same leanness proved to be rather more attractive in the Cabernets, though some of the latter can be delightful.

Drink soon.

1980★★★★

A wet winter was followed by one of the coolest growing seasons on record in Napa. Growers feared that sugar levels might be too low but hopes were revived with warm pre-harvest weather. Acidity levels were surprisingly high, even after a week of very hot October weather, and balanced well against sugar levels. The Cabernet Sauvignon grapes became dehydrated in the high temperatures, producing concentrated, powerful wines.

Good results despite difficult conditions. Tannic, long-lasting reds, but all the best should have been consumed by now.

1970s Napa Valley

1979 ★★★ started hot but the cool growing season and September rain necessitated early picking. The best wines were no more than good.

1978★★★★ started with heavy rains which benefited the vines and developed into a warm growing season. A big crop; the wines were ripe and well-balanced, some were excellent. The best are still drinking well. **1977★★** was the second of two years of drought but growers were better prepared for the associated problems. Some good wines were made. High sugar and low acidity characterized the wines of **1976★★★** which ranged from poor to very good. **1975★★★** had a good growing season with some light harvest rains; these were fine, well-balanced, elegant wines.

The star of the decade was undoubtedly **1974★★★★★** arguably the best-ever vintage for California. Growing conditions were ideal: a cool, slightly frosty spring, a long, cool summer, and perfect harvesting weather. These were excellent, well-balanced wines; but some now starting to tire. **1973★★★★** also enjoyed good growing conditions and a record crop of healthy, perfectly mature grapes produced some very good wines.

The first three vintages of the decade were not of the same calibre as those of the middle years. **1972★▷★★★★** was very variable with some very good reds. **1971★★★** was better, the fruit was healthy but the wines were never more than good. Severe spring frosts destroyed half of the **1970★★★★** crop. What was left was generally sound – the best wines were the Cabernets, some very good. Overall, though, a very mixed year.

EARLIER CALIFORNIA VINTAGES (CAB. SAUV.)

1969★★★★ 1968★★★★★ 1966★★★★ 1965★★★★★ 1964★★★★ 1963★★★★
1959★★★★ 1958★★★★★ 1956★★★★ 1951★★★★★ 1946★★★★★

Pacific Northwest

WASHINGTON & OREGON

Although conveniently twinned under the Pacific Northwest heading, the local climate and geography of the vineyard areas of these two neighbouring states could not be more contrasting. The valleys of western Oregon enjoy a mild climate, but weather conditions vary considerably over the growing season, not unlike the maritime climate of Bordeaux. The inland vineyards of eastern Washington State are in a broad, arid, semi-desert valley, irrigated by the waters of the Columbia River.

In Oregon, more northerly, more temperate than California, Pinot Noir has found a natural home, as have the more characteristically acidic Sauvignon Blanc and Riesling. However, Chardonnay, Merlot, and Cabernet Sauvignon are also planted in what are relatively new wine areas. The pioneers of the early 1960s have been augmented by a host of mainly small, highly individual wineries, quality equally variable. It is well worth keeping track of the wines from these two states.

2002

Washington★★★★ A difficult but successful harvest for the fifth consecutive year.

Severely cold weather in early May caused anxiety but passed with no damage done. In mid-July a heat-wave struck, stressing vines and halting growth. The cool start to spring had produced a poor fruit set and the heat-wave further shrank the grapes and reduced yield. However, in some areas, ripening was accelerated and the harvest began as early as September 9. Winemakers welcomed the arrival of cool temperatures in late September as activity slowed down, allowing fruit to mature and intensify flavours. On

October 31, thanks to the freeze, winemakers made Ice Wine. The wines are paradoxically powerful and soft, the reds well-balanced, with extraordinary colour and aromas.

Attractive whites, particularly Rieslings, for early drinking and sound reds probably at their best 2006 to 2009.

Oregon★★★ variable Oregon's string of rainless harvests stopped at four. A cold, wet spring and some frosts were followed by heavy rains in early October. In warmer southern Oregon, a summer heat-wave affected some vineyards, with temperatures reaching 46°C (115°F) causing heat stress and shrivelled grapes. There were even isolated hailstorms. For others the hot days and cool nights throughout October provided perfect ripening conditions. There were two different harvests this year: those with young vines in warm sites who were forced to pick early, sacrificing flavour intensity for reasonable alcohol levels, and those with older vines in cooler sites who could allow the fruit to hang and develop more slowly. All in all, there was considerable variation, yet it was very good for those who escaped the rain, heat-waves, and hailstones. Syrah is the star this vintage.

Some delicious whites for early drinking and reds, particularly Pinot Noir (the success story of Oregon) and Syrah, which will make good mid-term drinking, say 2006 to 2009.

2001

Washington★★★★ The fourth consecutive good-to-excellent vintage. But things got off to a rough start with a cool, wet, and windy spring resulting in smaller cluster size and uneven fruit set. A very dry, hot summer then followed. Surprisingly, the final crush was eight per cent higher than last year's and a record harvest, a reflection of new vineyard plantings. The harvest began on September 1 and extended well into November. Extreme summer temperatures and the cooler weather which ensued combined to make this one of the earliest and longest harvests on record. The whites are soft, with forward, floral aromas, ripe tropical fruit, and high alcohol. Overall the red wines are dark and tannic, especially those earlier harvested grapes that underwent hot fermentation. Syrah is the star.

Some delicious whites, intensely flavoured Chardonnays, and, in particular, some Rieslings made with the expertise of some German producers. The track record of reds is not fully established but some impressive wines, notably Cabernet Sauvignon, Merlot, and Syrah, in this vintage which have staying power though most will be drunk relatively early.

Oregon★★★ variable Overall, a good vintage, but, for the first time since 1997, there were substantial differences in quality from winery to winery. The season began with warm spring weather, an early bud-break, and a mild but sunny summer. Then in early August a heat-wave caused west-facing berries to desiccate from the late afternoon sun exposure. Severe thinning in the vineyard and exhaustive sorting in the winery were vital. In addition to the severe heat, growers were faced with the challenges of very large grapes and clusters, and moderately high disease pressure. White wine grapes were less affected and delivered dense, concentrated wines with ripe tropical flavours. In some areas, heavy rains caused problems for wineries that waited too long to pick. But elsewhere, those who stuck it out were rewarded with additional days of sunny weather.

Impossible to generalize but this appears to be a vintage best for relatively early consumption, both red and white.

2000

Washington★★★★ Despite a wildfire in June and rain, a record harvest in volume and the third high quality vintage in a row. For the first time, fifty-two per cent of the crop was of red wine grapes as new red wine plantings are replacing inexpensive whites.

Optimum summer growing conditions were followed, in some parts, by unusually wet, cool weather in late September and early October, extending what had been a perfect growing season. Frost on September 24 caused a little damage, affecting mainly younger vines, and rain in October protracted the harvest. Patience was rewarded as the prolonged hang time resulted in full-bodied wine with ripe fruit flavours and well-balanced acidity. The reds had good sugar levels and full phenolic maturity. In Walla Walla, the Merlot fruit was big and very dark, the best seen to come out of the valley.

Interesting to see the swing away from minor to more serious whites, but in particular the healthy development of reds, in 2000 mainly for mid-term (2005 to 2008) drinking.

Oregon★★★★★ Another exceptional year in terms of quality and quantity. The spring and summer were warm and drier than normal, with mild temperatures and little or no rain through September. Apart from a couple of spring frosts, perfect spring and summer weather produced an unusually large crop and those wineries that reduced their crop size fared better. *Véraison* in the second week of August was two weeks earlier than in 1999, allowing for uniform development and ripening. Weather for the harvest was also dry, giving plentiful hang time. An early harvest yielded Pinot Gris, Pinot Blanc, and Sauvignon Blanc with high sugar levels, good levels of acidity, and a balance of fruit concentration and firm tannins. Pinot Noir was reportedly the best-tasting fruit ever.

Wonderful dry whites for drinking now, and the now fully established Pinot Noirs can also be enjoyed now but might well be more deliciously evolved around 2006 to 2009.

1999

Washington★★★★★ Some growers reported the best ever vintage in Washington State, most agreeing that it will turn out even greater than 1998 in terms of flavour and acid balance. It was also a record harvest in terms of volume.

Bud-break took place early to mid-March after a relatively warm period, but cooler weather arrived mid-April and lasted through the flowering giving rise to concerns about unusually cold and cloudy spring weather. By mid-August it became warmer, one report stating that the summer was exceptionally mild (which in Washington State means temperatures in the 90s rather than the 100s!). Harvest conditions were much better and drier than usual, with very cold nights, resulting in very ripe, very healthy grapes with concentrated flavours and good acid levels.

Good quality, crisp whites for early enjoyment, Cabernets and Merlots with ageing potential, say 2004 to 2010 – hard to say how much longer as the State's track record, with newer wineries, is not fully established.

Oregon★★★★★ The wineries of Oregon State reported an excellent vintage, with some of the ripest fruit seen in twenty-five years (not that there are many wineries or winemakers who go back that far) combined with good acidity, comparable to 1998. Volume also satisfactory.

A wet spring (a reminder that Oregon is on the Pacific seaboard and Seattle is one of the wettest cities in the United States) led to early bud-break. Summer hung back though and the requisite sun and warmth did not really get going until September when there was virtually no rain. An Indian Summer provided perfect harvest conditions with picking continuing to the end of October.

Oregon is blessed with conditions eminently suitable for the tricky Pinot Noir and this would appear to be an excellent year for Oregon's "burgundies". Try now!

1998

Washington★★★★★ This was the best-ever vintage for the wineries of Washington State both in terms of quantity and quality. A mild winter was followed by a pleasantly warm and reasonably rainy spring, with no frosts. Summer consisted of very hot daytime temperatures, the hottest of the decade, and very cold nights. The harvest began early, on September 1, and finished October 19. Pleasant temperatures and no rain throughout resulted in evenly ripe grapes with good sugar levels, colour, and flavour.

Whites drink up, reds say now to 2008.

Oregon★★★★ Despite their totally different geographical situations on the northwest Pacific seaboard, notorious for its rain, weather conditions in Oregon were not dissimilar to Washington State, with mild winter and early bud-break. However, poor weather seriously affected the flowering which severely reduced the eventual yield by forty to fifty per cent. Happily, summer was warm and harvest conditions were good. The quality of the remaining grapes and subsequent wines was high.

Whites drink up. Reds ready now.

1997

Washington★★▷★★★ Escaping the more ruthless conditions further south, yields were high and of similar quality. There were light showers during September, very unusual in this area, which caused some rot in the tight bunches. This affected Riesling and Chardonnay, but the Cabernet, Merlot, and Syrah were excellent.

Avoid whites. The reds all drinking quite well.

Oregon★★★ The growing season started well and developed into a warm summer. Then multiple storms, compounded by the region's proximity to the coast, brought cold and wet weather just before the harvest. This resulted in some rot, drying winds restored health to the vines and by the time picking started ripeness had been enhanced. The harvest started in mid-September and was finished by the end of October. Yields were up by sixteen per cent compared to 1996, producing light and delicately balanced wines, but many lacked fruit and concentration.

A vintage to give the reds a chance to show their paces.

1996

Washington★★ February was pleasant, then severe frost hit, obliterating all hopes for a large crop. Essential bud development was lost, which reduced the potential harvest between thity-five and fifty per cent, but this diminished crop did have greater concentration as a result. Merlot was the most affected variety – many producers resorted to buying grapes from California to boost stocks.

Oregon★★ Also a challenging vintage. Rain hampered development and flowering fell behind. Despite warmer weather in July ripening was still slow. More rain fell in September and unfortunately many grapes were harvested

while underripe. The later ripening varieties such as Riesling and Chardonnay were also affected by rot when rain continued throughout October.
Not a year to show either region at its best.

1995

Washington★★ A very wet and dismal vintage. The summer was consistently wet, which dramatically slowed down the development of the vines. Autumn brought a slight improvement in conditions and this assisted ripening. Producers then picked at different times as rain threatened again during the harvest. One benefit of the cool weather was to enhance the aromatic qualities of Riesling and Gewurztraminer.

Oregon★★ The season developed similarly, with rain causing problems with rot. Surprisingly the results were not as bad as expected, but the Pinot Noir grapes in the Willamette Valley did suffer significant damage from botrytis.
A somewhat depressing year for the producers. Most wines need drinking.

1994

Washington★★★ The warm weather that started in June and continued through the summer produced small grapes and bunches and intensified flavours. The harvest was of normal proportions, producing good Merlot and Cabernet Sauvignon.

Oregon★★★ The light rains that fell during flowering and budding resulted in the crop being reduced by a third compared with 1993. A fairly uneventful harvest was completed by the end of October. Results were exciting, especially for Oregon's speciality grape, Pinot Noir, which performed particularly well.
The Pinot Noirs have really come into their own and the best of these 1994s are lovely now, some tiring.

1993

Washington★★★ An extraordinarily cool spring initiated one of the most drawn-out growing seasons in the region's short history. Warm weather rescued the crop in September and October to such an extent that it was of record-breaking dimensions. The quality is similar to that of the 1983 vintage – soft reds and excellent whites with good acidity levels.

Oregon★★ A much more varied growing season, frequently dominated by overcast skies and short periods of rain. These occurred particularly during June and July and again towards the end of the harvest. The quality of the vintage was varied but the overall crop size is considerable due to many recently planted vineyards now coming into full operation.
Drink soon.

1992

Washington★★★ A record-sized harvest came as an enormous relief after 1991's reduced crop. Flowering and budding took place two weeks earlier than usual, with the rest of the season warm and dry, refreshed by just the right amount of rain. The wines had slightly lower than usual tannins, full fruit levels, and good, balancing acidity.

Oregon★★★ Dry, warm conditions resulted in the largest crop on record. Production was up by about twenty-five per cent, much of this the result of new Pinot Noir plantings coming into production.
An attractive vintage. A mass of pleasing, full-of-fruit reds all now fully mature.

1991

Washington★★★ An extremely severe winter killed some and damaged many other vines, reducing the potential crop by up to fifty per cent. However, the growing season was satisfactory, the harvest taking place in balmy autumn weather, resulting in fruit with good sugar and acid levels.

Oregon★★★★ A cold, wet spring and late flowering made up for by a virtually perfect summer and early autumn. A large, ripe harvest brought in under hot sun before heavy late October rains.

Merlot, Cabernet Sauvignon and Pinot Noir fully mature, needing drinking.

1990

Washington★★★ Cool weather during flowering cut the crop. Very high temperatures during July and August actually slowed down the ripening of the grapes yet the harvest took place early, starting on September 7 and running through to October 10. September was unusually warm and those who picked quickly and promptly when the fruit hit optimum maturity produced excellent and balanced wines. The smallest yield per acre since 1985.

Oregon★★★ The yield per acre was also very low although quantities were higher than in 1989 as a result of new plantations. Here too, the spring was cool, but the small crop of unusually small berries yielded some wines of great intensity and depth. Picking began in late September. This was a better year for Chardonnay than Pinot Noir, which is usually the most important grape in Oregon.

Drink up.

1989

Washington★★★★ The cool spring and early summer resulted in a moderate-sized crop. Initially the grapes developed slowly but steadily until late August. Thereafter growers enjoyed an extraordinary period of hot, sunny days and cool nights, which provided ideal ripening conditions. The harvest began in mid-September and lasted until late October.

The wines had exceptional concentration and acidity, the reds showing all the potential of a great vintage.

Oregon★★★ A warm, late May and early June brought the vines into early flowering. Mid-June was wet; most vines had set by then but those on higher land set during the rain and consequently the yields were low and variable. Picking began slightly earlier than usual and took place in perfect conditions. Most Pinot Noirs were brought in at perfect maturity; those picked too late tended to lack finesse and delicacy. Overall, the wines were of very high quality.

Top Pinot Noirs, drink soon.

1988

Washington★★★★ An excellent combination of quantity and quality. Very favourable growing conditions resulted in a large vintage of remarkably even quality. The harvest began on September 8 and ended on October 20. The wines had excellent fruit and good balance.

Oregon★★★ A cool, wet spring and summer, but with warmer weather during flowering in May. Temperatures rose in mid-July and remained warm through to the middle of September. The yield was down by fifty per cent.

Merlot, Cabernet, and Pinot Noir drink soon.

1987

Washington★★★★ The hottest summer in twenty years. The grapes were beautifully ripe and in perfect health when the harvest began on August 28. The better reds were attractive and fruity but have aged more rapidly than usual.

Oregon★★▷★★★ With the exception of some cooler weather during July and August, temperatures were high throughout the growing season. Picking took place in hot, dry weather and yields were high throughout the region. Quality varied. The best wines were made by those who picked early, thereby retaining good levels of acidity in their grapes.

Drink up.

1986

Washington★★ A warm summer. The harvest of fully ripe grapes, which began on September 5, was briefly interrupted by rain. Overall the grapes were healthy but the wet weather increased yields in some areas with the result that the wines lacked intensity of flavour. Those grapes unaffected by the rain produced some very good wines.

Oregon★★▷★★★★ A wet but sunny start to the year was followed by warm, dry weather through to the harvest. Heavy rain caused some growers to panic, but conditions improved in October. Yields were of average proportions; those who were prepared to take the risk and postponed the harvest until after the rains, picked mature, ripe grapes and produced the best wines.

Some of the top Pinot Noirs have survived. Otherwise, drink up.

1985

Washington★★★★ The second of two small crops resulting from unusual spring frosts. The vintage was warm enough for an early harvest, interrupted for a very short while by a cool spell in early September. The reds were big and tannic; the best wines came from grapes picked early with high acidity levels.

Oregon★★★★ After a cool, dry start to the year temperatures rose in late May. Early June saw some rain but thereafter the weather was warm and dry, providing excellent conditions for flowering. The growing season and harvest enjoyed the same good conditions and the vintage was mainly completed by mid-October. Quantity was average and the wines showed real ageing potential. This was a vintage which increased international recognition of Oregon wines.

Drink up.

1984

Washington★★ A very uneven year: winter frost, cool spring, warm summer but autumn dry and cooler than usual. Quality varied, but some good wines.

Oregon★ A variable year. The first five months were exceptionally wet; temperatures rose in May but this encouraged mildew. Fruit set was not completed until well into July. Thereafter temperatures were low and the harvest was held back until November in the hope that conditions would improve. They did not and a large crop of light wines were the result.

Few to be seen. Drink up.

1983

Washington★★★★ A cool year, but late summer/autumn was warm and sunny. Picking began on September 19. Very good reds with charming fruit, excellent structure and ageing potential.

Oregon★★★ Perfect flowering in June; thereafter the season was warm and dry with some benign rainfall in late August. Picking took place during the first fortnight of October. A larger than average crop.
Drink up.

1982

Washington★★ Satisfactory flowering, a warm summer, and a cool and extended harvest, with some rain. Charming but lightish wines. Many of the better reds lasted well, but lacked intensity.

Oregon★★★ After a cool, wet spring the weather was perfect for flowering in June. Thereafter trouble-free conditions prevailed and picking was complete by early October. Some very good wines.
Drink up.

1981

Washington★★★ Cool, damp spring, but warm summer weather helped advance development. Cool autumn nights and warm days fully ripened the grapes and picking began September 21. These were fruity, substantial wines; the reds showed great depth and potential longevity.

Oregon★★★ After a cool, wet start warm, sunny weather advanced development until late September when the rain returned. Picking began in early October and the yield was very low. These were wines which would reveal their worth with long keeping.
Drink up.

1980

Washington★★★ The eruption of Mount St Helens blanketed many vineyards in ash throughout this region. Fortunately this occurred prior to flowering.

This was the coolest growing season of the 1980s and the vineyards had not entirely recovered from the severe freeze of 1978 and 1979. Consequently the crop was small and the wines were light. Many, though, were well-balanced, with moderate body. The best reds promised longevity.

Oregon★★★★ Cold, wet weather prevailed throughout the spring until June. Here, too, vineyards were covered with deposits of ash from the volcano, but vines were left undamaged. A late flowering finished in July. Picking began in early October producing a very small crop of excellent, concentrated, dry wines. *Pinot Noirs showed their true varietal character: attractive, rich, root-like, and earthy. Now well past their best.*

EARLIER PACIFIC NORTHWEST VINTAGES

Earlier vintages of these wines are hard to find, but the 1979 Amity and Knudson-Erath Pinot Noirs were showing well in the mid-1980s. On the whole, the few wines that were made in the 1960s, if any exist at all, will be no more than curiosities. Times, and winemaking, have moved on.

New York State

It will come as a surprise to most Europeans that New York is a wine-producing state. Wines have in fact been made in the Finger Lake District, just south of Ontario, for well over a century. However, until the early 1960s only native American varieties and hybrids were grown, not *Vitis vinifera*. Virtually the sole pioneer of classic European grape varieties was the late Dr Konstantin Frank. He was followed in the 1970s by one or two small wineries such as Glenora and Heron Hill, which planted first Riesling, then Chardonnay. In the mid-1970s there was a revival of winemaking in the less northerly, less exposed Hudson Valley, and, even more recently, with classic whites and reds planted on sea-girt Long Island. New pioneers, enthusiasts, and state-of-the-art winemaking, particularly on Long Island, have successfully changed the New York State wine scene: Pinot Noir, Cabernet Sauvignon, Sauvignon Blanc, and Chardonnay are now produced. The reds, though well made, have as yet no track record.

Wines made from native varieties such as Catawba and Concord – very much an acquired taste – and hybrids like Seibel, are not covered in these brief vintage notes that follow. The lighter dry whites, as always, should be drunk while they are young and fresh, although some of the Finger Lake Chardonnays and late-harvest whites will keep for up to five years and sometimes even longer.

2002★★★

Growers were at the mercy of changeable weather patterns. Surprisingly it turned out to be a good vintage. Winter was mild and relatively dry, and developed into a promising spring. Bud-break occurred around April 19, a record early date for both regions, Finger Lakes and Long Island. An ideal spring turned wet and cold, then teasingly shifted again into a hot, dry summer. Autumn saw the return of wet and cold conditions, which later gave way to a warm and dry period, until rainy, cold weather stormed back for the final days of the harvest. Despite the erratic year, the harvest was down only 4.000 tons from 2001, though it lacks the excellent potential of 2001. On Long Island, it was a good year, particularly for the reds, with strikingly dark colours and good fruit, but some growers said that two late autumn storms ruined hopes for an exceptional year. Also, the late frosts wiped out crops in some vineyards.

Finger Lake whites for early drinking, some Long Island reds really coming into their own and worth cellaring.

2001★★★★★

A mild winter followed by a cool spring, then a long, dry summer with just enough rain before harvest, provided ideal growing conditions. In the Finger Lakes dry conditions extended the harvest and allowed winemakers to wait for maximum ripeness in late ripening varieties but also led to lower than average yields: Riesling was down by as much as twenty-five per cent, and Cabernet Sauvignon and Pinot Noir were down fifteen per cent. Some rain showers in late September – followed by dry, sunny weather to avoid rot – gave the clusters an extra burst toward maturity. The reds had excellent ripeness levels, with deep tannins, dense mouth-feel, and very soft acidity.

Long Island vintners reported a near-perfect growing season with early *véraison*, an ideal balance of rainfall and sunshine, and prolonged hang time, enabling optimal levels of ripeness, even for Pinot Noir. Whites displayed strong aromatics, while reds had deep colours and intensity of flavours with softer-than-usual tannins.

Some very appealing whites for early consumption and a "new breed" of well-made, well-ripened reds for mid-term drinking.

2000 ★ ★ ★

Spring was warm and wet throughout the region, encouraging the spread of disease. Growers who neglected to use early, preemptive sprays in May had problems with mildew later in the season. The growing season proved challenging for vintners in the northeast, but those who were up to the challenge made solid wines. Mid-summer brought cooler than normal temperatures that hampered ripening considerably. The chilly summer necessitated rigorous canopy management this year; producers who have yet to adopt modern trellising systems experienced difficulties in getting their grapes to fully ripen. Marginal sites in the Finger Lakes were affected by frost on September 29. Fortunately, October provided ideal Indian summer conditions allowing the region's top producers to ripen their grapes.
Whites drink soon. Reds drinking well now and will develop further.

1999 ★ ★

Summer drought led to an early harvest. A satisfactory vintage in the Finger Lakes area, also on Long Island despite Hurricane Floyd's best efforts.
Whites drink up. Reds still lack a track record though quality is high.

1998 ★ ★ ★ ★

Small quantity, superb quality. A mild winter set the stage for one of the earliest harvests in the State's history, two to three weeks ahead of normal and about a month in advance of California! The uneven flowering of several varieties seriously reduced the potential crop. Ripening was hastened by a dry August, good conditions contined for the harvest and resulted in ripe fruit.
Delighful whites, drink soon but reds with great potential.

1997 ★ ★ ★

A good year, better than 1996, but not as fine as 1995. The ripening period was warm, dry, and sunny, resulting in the grapes ripening consistently up until the harvest in September. Luckily the majority of producers on Long Island had picked all of their grapes before the rains came in November and quality was good. The Finger Lakes produced some fine Rieslings and lighter-style Gewurztraminers, both varietals eminently suitable to survive the cold and rigorous winters of the Finger Lakes area. Long Island is developing well and the reds are worth watching.
Whites need drinking. Reds developing well.

1996 ★ ★ ▷ ★ ★ ★

A break in the run of perfect vintages came this year as a cold and wet season prevailed. Frost in May affected some northern areas, reducing yields and resulting in winemakers buting-in juice. Damp conditions throughout the summer encouraged problems of rot and further reduced the size of the crop. The weather improved during the harvest and those producers who selected well made some good wines.

Yields on Long Island were significantly lower and in general styles were leaner and lighter than usual. In the Finger Lakes production was more substantial, but large berries produced less concentrated juice and the level of quality was not as good as that of 1995. Sugar levels were down in the Chardonnay and Riesling leaving some producers contemplating chaptalization.
Drink up.

1995 ★ ★ ★ ★ ★

The third successful vintage in a row was the result of a prolonged and warm summer which provided ideal ripening conditions. The grapes reached full maturity and sugar levels which resulted in the red wines having great extract, colour, and depth and the white wines achieving near perfect balance of fruit and acidity. The ideal weather continued throughout the harvest and no rot problems were experienced – rot is often a danger in this region during the harvest due to climatic conditions. It is worth noting that as the vines age, yield and quality are improving year by year.

The best reds have developed well.

1994 ★ ★ ★ ★

A good vintage with higher than expected yields after a harsh winter. Although the harvest was larger than the previous year's by about sixty-five per cent, the quality varieties had only average-sized yields at best.

Growing conditions were favourable throughout the state. Spring and summer were warm and dry with beneficial rainfall. Unfortunately, frosts hit the region in the spring. The Hudson Valley experienced the worst of this and many young shoots were damaged, causing as much as forty per cent losses. Overall, results were good to excellent and the wines have good balance. Sugar levels were high, notably on Long Island, where the reds have deep colour and soft tannins. Wines from the Finger Lakes showed a great aromatic quality.

Whites long since consumed. Reds drink soon.

1993 ★ ★ ★ ★

A very good quality vintage throughout the state but with greatly reduced yields. The previous year's cool, wet summer left the vines with a reduced number of buds, and in a vulnerable physical state. Grape clusters were then small but very intense. The growing season was dry, warm, and long, providing ideal ripening conditions. Although the crop was on average twenty-two per cent smaller than the previous year's, the results were exciting. The levels of sugar and acidity were frequently ideal. Most notable were the sweeter wines from the Finger Lakes area, and very good Chardonnay and Merlot from Long Island. Many "reserve wines" with significant ageing potential were produced.

The reds still do not have sufficient track record. They were probably at their best when young.

1992 ~

A very poor vintage: cold and wet for the entire growing season.

1991 ★ ★ ★ ★

A well-above-average vintage. A mild winter; early spring and flowering; warm summer; and early harvest. The northerly Finger Lakes had the earliest ever start of harvest, August 27: a large crop of good Riesling and Gewurztraminer. On Long Island the warm dry year produced wines to equal the 1988s – best vintage of the decade; also echoed in the Hudson River Valley.

Drink soon.

1990 ★ ★ ★ ★

A very good vintage with the exception of the Finger Lakes where yields were good, but crop size was slightly below average. Well-timed rainfall was above

average, but evenly distributed, which contributed to good berry size. Ideal ripening weather in September led to premature harvests for some grape varieties, yet with the same sugar levels as the previous year. Overall, grapes were clean and healthy, promising wines of very good quality.
Drink soon.

1989★★▷★★★

Following the 1988 drought, groundwater levels were low until late spring rains. Disease threatened but stopped before it was too late. This, coupled with the effects of Hurricane Hugo on Long Island, made this a difficult year for many. Improved techniques and careful timing helped winemakers overcome problems. Overall, the early ripening varieties fared best. Those from the Lake Erie region had very good varietal character, and Hudson Valley growers considered the quality of their grapes to be excellent having fought against such difficult weather conditions.
Drink up.

1988★★★★

Deemed "a winemaker's dream" – the best year since 1980 for the reds and the whites alike. Dry weather and a perfect summer and autumn: warm days and cool nights. A vintage of powerful, distinctive wines.
Best reds still drinking well.

1987★★▷★★★★

A year which ranged from average to very good. Occasional adverse weather conditions occurred, including strong winds in mid-September on Long Island which dampened hopes for a trouble-free harvest, and wet weather throughout that month in many areas. Grapes had, however, ripened well until then and the harvest was already two weeks ahead of schedule. The Long Island wineries reported better success with reds than whites, while in the Finger Lakes winemakers reported the reverse. In the end, the hybrid Seyval Blanc and red *Vitis vinifera* varieties were considered to be the most consistent.
Drink up.

1986★▷★★★

A poor year for many growers whose crops were spoilt by a wet harvest. There were, however, some exceptions. Long Island growers considered this to be a very good vintage. Their whites were typically aromatic; their reds showed good ageing potential. It was a good year also for Lake Erie: a Chardonnay from this district ranked second among 223 Chardonnays from around the world in the 1987 Intervin International Competition.
Drink up.

1985★★★

Generally very good, except for Long Island where vines were devastated by Hurricane Gloria which struck on September 27.
Drink up.

1984★★★

The second of two unusually large vintages. Quality varied depending on the grape variety and the region. In the Finger Lakes most early varieties had a problem-free harvest but a severe frost on October 6 virtually stopped the later grapes from ripening further. However, in the Hudson River, later varieties did well. This year also marked a transition in New York State away from the native American species in favour of *Vitis vinifera*.

Drink up.

EARLIER NEW YORK STATE VINTAGES

Long Island enjoyed an Indian summer in **1983**★★★ and produced deeply coloured wines which were exceptionally soft when young. **1982**★★★★★ was excellent and **1981**★ a small crop of indifferent quality, but much better in **1980**★★★★. Some pre-1980 vintages of above average quality include: **1979** (Riesling), **1978** (Riesling, Chardonnay, and late-harvest Gewurztraminer), **1976** (Cabernet Sauvignon), and **1975** (Chardonnay and late-harvest Riesling). All past their best.

Eastern Canada

I am adding Canada in this edition, for the simple reason that some seriously good wines are being made. The shores of Lake Ontario have long been a major vine growing area and its climate is not too dissimilar from upper New York State. Admittedly the former shores are relatively flat compared to the hilly Finger Lake district, but comparisons can be made. Though Ontario is best known for its Ice Wines, good varietals are made.

How things have changed! Less than ten years ago I recall some truly undrinkable wines made on the shores of Lake Ontario, curiously flavoured Chardonnays, and so on. Now, thanks to more efficient vine growing and wine making, producers have mainly to contend with the weather. The market tends to be local for it is hard to persuade an already oversated world to beleive that Canada can produce other than the excellent Ice Wines.

2002★★★★

Another exciting journey that ended well. Two weeks with above seasonal temperatures in mid-April were followed by severe frost on April 23 and 27, and on May 20, with temperatures dipping as low as -2.9°C (29°F). Normally that would not cause a problem, but the warm weather in April had stripped the buds of hardiness. Fears vanished a little as the season progressed and the damage was not as severe as originally thought, in fact all varieties produced a near normal or normal crop, except in Niagara, where the buds were more advanced. Many growers here had a small crop. Summer came in the last days of May with thirty-five days over 30°C (86°F) by the end of the season. A number of wines topped fourteen degrees with no chaptalizing. The season's rainfall varied significantly from one area to another but there was adequate moisture for mature vineyards over the critical months. All the areas were drier than average, as they have been in the past several years, the result being that the vines have developed deeper root systems. This has been good for flavour, concentration, and wine quality. The quality of delicate varietals like Riesling, Pinot Blanc, and sparkling wines was in doubt, but turned out to good, with correct aromatics and flavours. Vintners were delighted with the high quality of the Ice Wine.

A surprising range of refreshing dry whites for mainly Canadian consumers and, of course, the richly appealing Ice Wines which now have a considerable international reputation.

2001 ★ ★ ★ ★ ★

Probably the best vintage yet. The success of this and the preceding four years
have been largely attributable to the fact that Eastern Canada growers now
grow several diverse varieties well-suited to the variable continental climate.
The growing season started well with adequate moisture but by mid-summer,
temperatures were above average. By the end of August the drought was
intense. Irrigation was used in some larger operations near the shores of Lake
Ontario and the Niagara River. While some chose to capitalize on the intensity
of the summer in order to maintain concentration and physiological fruit
maturity, others suffered stressed vines and wilted leaves. Thankfully the rains
did arrive toward the end of September, and continued into October, which
brought the vineyards back to health without diluting quality. The fruit ripeness
was superb with high sugars and low acids including less malic acid than usual.
Merlot and Cabernet Sauvignon did best, but varieties like Riesling were also
good. Unsurprisingly, the quality of the Ice Wine harvest was excellent too.
Some useful dry whites, particularly Rieslings, drinking well but it is the reds which
have impressed. With growing conditions like this, producers have a good opportunity
to demonstrate their skills, and in 2001 many have succeeded. Nevertheless the
classic Bordeaux varietals do not yet have a significant track record and even the best
reds will probably be drunk too young though this is one year to give them a bit of
bottle-ageing.

2000 ★ ★

The success of the vintage was not ensured; yet, paradoxically, it was also never
seriously in doubt, though it was distinctly more challenging than the previous
two years. Early bud-break and bloom were followed by occasional rainfall in
June, which increased by the month's end. A cooler summer, heavy rains in July
and August, and high pressure from fungal diseases did not bode well for the
harvest. In addition, the early end to the growing season resulted in very green
and herbaceous flavours, weak colours, and searing acidity. The vintage's saving
grace was a warm, extended autumn, which enhanced ripening and quality.
Vintners also kept in mind the fact that grapes from early to mid-season-
ripening varieties (Baco, Foch, Pinot Noir, Chardonnay, Zweigelt, Sauvignon
Blanc) had not been affected by frost and would hang on to reach sufficient
ripeness. The difference in hang time translated into some striking wine quality.
The remainder of the autumn remained comfortably warm and very dry,
producing well-matured Merlot, Cabernet Sauvignon, and Cabernet Franc.
Riesling, Gewurztraminer, and Gamay, some later varieties that depend on
delicacy and finesse, also did well.
A useful vintage, mainly – particularly the dry whites – for early drinking, the Cabernets
probably best around 2004 to 2007.

1999 ★ ★

Clearly a good vintage. One of Canada's problems is her extremely severe
winters when, despite lying dormant, vines can be damaged, causing losses.
However, several recent winters have been relatively mild though in early March
1999, temperatures dropped to -21°C (-5°F) in some vineyard areas. Happily,
vineyards close to the lake were protected by mists which kept temperatures
to a "more reasonable" -10° to -11°C (13°–14°F). Sap was not rising and so little
damage resulted. March was mild and unusually dry, April moderately rainy,
ending with a frost of -2°C (28°F) which slightly affected the emerging buds.

Flowering in June was one to two weeks ahead of normal. The dry, warm trend continued, being particularly hot up to the middle of July after which there were intervals of substantial rain. The harvest began as early as September 4 in temperatures higher than normal. Pinot Noir was picked first, followed by the hybrids, then Chardonnay and Gamay. Rieslings, however, were held back until cooler weather arrived in mid-October, as were the Cabernets, Sauvignons, and Francs. Ice Wines were early.

Chardonnay and red Bordeaux varieties were exceptional, the former for drinking relatively early, not beyond 2005. The reds, which do not have a lengthy track record in Canada, are nevertheless worth giving some bottle-ageing.

1998★★★★

Canada's table wines, even the Chardonnays – which deserve a wide showing, are still mainly the province of the solid domestic market. A good year thanks to a very warm summer and autumn with no rain problems. Because of the dryness, yields were down but quality high, with good levels of alcohol and, happily, adequate acidity.

Whites drink up, Ice Wines at any time.

South America

Whereas the wines of Chile are now firmly established internationally, those of Argentina – John Avery's "slumbering giant" – are making a serious appearance beyond their own homeland, whilst Uruguay and even Brazil are starting to get in on the act. For its size of production alone, South America is important, and quality is catching up. However only Chile and Argentina have any track record which is why only these countries – in this edition – will make an appearance in my vintage notes.

CHILE

Chile is an exceptionally long and narrow country. No part of it is out of sight of the high, snow-capped Andes which form the eastern border, whilst to the west the climate is tempered by the breezes of the extensive Pacific coastline. Though vines do not thrive anywhere near the northern and southern extremities, there are distinctive and quite widely spaced vineyard areas radiating from the capital city, Santiago. It is worth reminding readers that here we are in the Southern Hemisphere, the harvesting taking place from mid-March to mid-April, even into May, depending on the growing season and district.

2002★★★★

Despite a wet and problematic year, 2002 turned out some great wines. Volume was, however, twenty per cent down on 2001. Warm, dry conditions in late winter resulted in an early bud-break and continued throughout summer, which allowed growers to control vine stress and intensify concentration. Rains on March 16 compromised parts of the Maule and Curicó Valleys and the southern part of Rapel Valley. The berries had already accumulated good sugar levels and the grape skins had softened as the fruit neared ripeness, resulting in fungus growth. Growers had to either wait for ideal flavour ripeness (adopting ruthless canopy management and the removal of mouldy clusters) or pick with high sugars but unripe tannins and slightly green characters to eliminate the further spread of rot. Winemakers also had to use sorting tables and modify winemaking procedures. Following the rains, a rise in daily temperatures throughout Chile toward the end of harvest accelerated ripening, which shortened the usually long ripening time by seven to twenty days, depending on the variety. In Casablanca the days were sunnier than usual, with less of the morning fog that softens ripening. This more continental growing season produced wines with more mineral and spicy flavours than in previous vintages. *Elegant wines with complex, ripe flavours and expressive, soft, sweet tannins. The Chardonnays will inevitably be shipped, sold, and consumed too young – nevertheless they have great flavour. The standard of production of the reds is nowadays uniformly high and though these will start to be consumed the minute they appear on the market, the best Cabernets and Merlots will benefit from a modicum of bottle-age.*

2001 ★★★ variable

The growing season alternated between very cool and very hot days. Early summer weather in November through to January was warm with hot spells. In February a heat-wave stopped berry growth but March provided very good ripening conditions. Fortunately the storms in March and April had no real effect on the harvest. Despite optimum ripening weather from February to April and a small-to-medium size crop, there was very slow sugar accumulation in most varieties. An extended hang time produced reds with very soft tannins and ripe flavours, and the whites had lower alcohol levels than previous vintages. In the Aconcagua Valley it was a small but excellent vintage, Merlot and Syrah fared very well. In Casablanca ripening was slow, especially in the valley. There was one per cent of botrytis-infected clusters in some sections of late ripening Chardonnay, but the fruit had lower alcohol potential than previous years. *Great Pinot Noir was made. The Rapel Cabernets have concentrated red-berry and cherry flavours with good acidity, the Merlots beautiful blackberry and coffee notes. White wines, Chardonnay in particular, are drinking well now, the Cabernets very successful in 2001 will show their paces around 2005 to 2008.*

2000 ★★★▷★★★★

After a challenging year, healthy yields combined with new plantings to produce a harvest high in quantity and quality. A cool, moist spring was followed by a late spring frost that hit the Casablanca Valley on December 6. Unusual rain on February 12 ensued: the Rapel and Curicó valleys received 30 mm (1.2 in), Casablanca (25 mm/1 in), and Maipo (15 mm/0.6 in); Aconcagua was spared. The rain in Curicó coincided with the ripening of Sauvignon Blanc, necessitating selective picking for clean fruit. Bright and sunny weather took over and remained ideal for ripening until mid-April, but the cool spring had set back the vines considerably, causing late ripening. Another storm on April 13 delayed ripening of the Cabernet Sauvignon in the Maipo Valley. High fruit set and the wet, cloudy spring necessitated rigorous vineyard and canopy management, as well as intensive leaf stripping to prevent the spread of botrytis and encourage ripening. Fortunately, the vineyards had high vigour due to the previous wet winter and late spring showers. Some striking Pinot Noirs in Casablanca, and Merlots and Cabernet Sauvignons in the Aconcagua Valley were produced. It was a difficult year for Syrah because of slow ripening. *Better reds than whites though the latter are seldom disappointing and, in any case, tend to be sold and consumed on arrival, whether in the UK or the USA! The success with Pinot Noir is relatively recent, Chile's reputation being built on their dependable and good value Cabernets and Merlots – all, in 2000, drinkable soon.*

1999★★★★

The cool, wet El Niño spring of 1997, compounded by the very dry winter and spring of 1998, had a cumulatively adverse effect on grape production in 1999, yields of most varieties and in most regions being thirty to fifty per cent lower than the 1998 records. In Curico, to the south, and Maule, the Sauvignon Blanc harvest began in February. Levels of alcohol were slightly lower and acidity improved, resulting in pleasant, stylish wines. The reds, Merlot in particular, have excellent colour and fruit, those in Colchagua being superb. The relatively new and successful Casablanca Valley whites had a naturally high sugar and acid content, the reds being somewhat variable. Drought conditions in the Aconcagua Valley necessitated a late harvest, resulting in very ripe grapes with high alcohol, reds having concentrated tannins and good fruit. Yields in Maipo were down but levels of ripeness and overall balance were similar to the equally impressive 1996 vintage.

White wines mainly consumed by now; the best reds will benefit from three to five years' bottle-age.

1998★★

Not an easy vintage, certainly not straightforward. Heavy rains in the winter, two to three times more than normal, were followed by a cool, wet spring and untypically cool summer with some rain. The subsequent harvest was up to three weeks late and more drawn out than in 1997, with worrying humidity. However, the well-established Chilean wineries are well able to cope with difficult conditions. Crop size was satisfactory, and the wines had high degrees of sugar and alcohol, the whites with a higher level of acidity, reds with good colour.

The agreeably acidic white wines are still refreshing to drink. The reds, so well established in the world's marketplace, offer pleasure and value for money; Merlots and Cabernets more tannic than usual and needing time to soften, ideally say 2004 to 2008.

ARGENTINA

For long a major wine producer – the fifth biggest in the world – yet only relatively recently making wines to a recognized international standard, the Argentine is fast catching up Chile in terms of quality and acceptability. Quite unlike Chile, however, its principal vineyard areas are inland, to the west, and far from the influence of the Atlantic Ocean. Ninety per cent of the vineyards are in Mendoza which lies close to the Andes, on the same latitude as Santiago "just over the hill" – some hill! Two smaller areas are Salta to the north and Rio Negro in Patagonia, way to the south. Again unlike Chile, which has a relatively small number of major producers, the Argentine wine lands have spawned thousands of *bodegas*, though important firms are now moving in and rationalizing production and trade. Historically, the principal major grape variety has been Malbec, but efforts are being made, with some success, to introduce better known, more marketable, varieties.

2002★★★★★

Growers are calling this the most exciting vintage in the last fifteen years, the star being Argentina's signature grape, Malbec, although all varieties did better than expected. Moderate temperatures in spring allowed for good bud-break and even shoot growth. Some rain in November hampered the earlier flowering varieties, such as Criolla, but the remainder of spring and the summer were dry and moderately warm. One thunderstorm in February set back the harvest of the white varieties Sauvignon Blanc and Chardonnay. But a long stretch of cool, dry weather through March and early April slowed down ripening and allowed acidity levels to increase. In Mendoza the destructive hail than usually occurs at harvest time did not arrive this year, resulting in a larger crop than average. Rain began again during the second week of April but by then, most growers reported that their Malbec, Bonarda, Syrah, and Tempranillo grapes had been harvested with superb quality. It was an extraordinary vintage for reds.

In 2002, the wines of Argentina came of age, in time to partner a new outlook in regard to production and marketing. The whites are not as well known as the reds and in any case have to compete in an oversupplied world market but in 2002 they are refreshing and will make agreeable, less serious drinking than the reds which will make importers sit up and take notice.

2001 ★★★▷★★★★

A variable harvest in Mendoza, although sub-regions which picked early or late produced superb wines. Unusually cool weather and rain during the last week of March and early April dampened prime harvest time. Luckily the rain was not torrential and had little effect on the harvest. Chardonnay, Sauvignon Blanc, and the small amounts of Pinot Noir were spared as they were harvested in the first half of March, at optimum quality. The country's prized late ripening reds – Malbec and Cabernet Sauvignon – were not as fortunate. Growers in fear of severe damage to their crops harvested amid the rains, producing underripe, diluted wines. Patience of those who delayed was rewarded on April 5 when sunshine returned and lasted to the end of the harvest, allowing for good ripening in the red varieties for both sugar and polyphenols. Overall 2001 is a year of moderate-to-good quality with top quality producers making good wine. Vying with 1999 as the best vintage since 1997.

The whites largely successful and drinking well now – the same cannot be said for the reds which vary from weak and lacklustre to hearteningly good.

2000 ★★ variable

Some successes this year, despite fewer sunny days and more rain than usual. In late February and March, Argentina was hit with heavy rains that damaged the whites and set back the reds, and March and April were both cool and overcast, depriving the Cabernets of valuable ripening time. Only the best vineyards with low crops and well-supervised vines with timely pruning and adequate rot- or disease-preventing treatment could make good wine. Luckily the rain in Mendoza fell hard and drained fast and the usual dry weather returned, helping the grapes to recover. Grapes harvested in late March and early April – the harvest was delayed a few days – were of a good quality. The lower temperatures kept sugar levels lower than usual (thirteen to fourteen degrees), but also resulted in more mature tannins and polyphenols, without high degrees of alcohol, especially for Syrah. Merlot and Malbec from Maipo and San Rafael did well. *All for early drinking.*

1999 ★★★★★

All are agreed that the 1999 grape harvest was one of the best of recent years. Dealing just with the major region, Mendoza, excellent weather conditions in the spring, with no hard frosts, followed a normal winter (June and July in the southern hemisphere). There was a good bud-break, with vigorous shoots.

Summer was warm, with high temperatures in December and January, but drought conditions slowed growth. Daytime temperatures rose to 35°C (95°F), even 38°C (100°F), but nights were cool. February was dry but warm, allowing good sugar concentration and low acidity, and the harvest began ten days earlier than usual. Grapes were in an excellent state of health, and where there was no rain there was no rot. Those who held out picked grapes in superb condition, resulting in some of the most complete and elegant reds, ever. A vintage to take note of.

The whites have very good concentration of fruit, with balanced alcohol levels and low acidity. Most successful: the new Chardonnays and Chenin Blanc. Reds, from perfectly mature grapes, have good colour, high alcohol, and low acidity. If you were to start taking an interest in Argentinian reds, this is definitely the vintage with which to begin. The better wines will be drinking enjoyably when they appear in select shops and will probably be at their best between, say, 2003 and 2006.

1998★▷★★

El Niño wreaked havoc on the Argentine side of the Andes. Mendoza, by far and away the most important district, suffered its wettest and worst summer, some said, for a century, its harvest down thirty per cent. However, roughly 1,000 km (621,4 m) to the south, the Rio Negro region managed to avoid the hailstorms, heavy rain, and humidity suffered by Mendoza and produced some good wines. Overall, it was a disastrous year for a country whose wines are just beginning to make an impressive international showing.

Not a complete washout everywhere, but take care.

Australia

Australia is a continent, albeit a sparsely populated one. The wine areas are far apart, the oldest classic district, the Hunter Valley in New South Wales, being some 1,287 km (800 m) from the newest vineyard areas of Western Australia. The cooler regions such as Coonawarra and Tasmania, are in the south. Confusingly, it is quite normal practice to produce good red wine blended from different grape varieties grown in different regions.

Though vine-growing and winemaking dates back to the penal colony days of the early nineteenth century, the demand was for fortified and, frankly, undistinguished table wines. Thanks to new attitudes and techniques, to brilliant pioneers, imaginative wine education, and publicity, the past thirty years or so has witnessed a quality revolution. The results: instantly appealing Chardonnays; impressive Cabernets, Shirazes, and well-constructed blends; fruity Rieslings and idiosyncratic Semillons (no é), not to mention luscious liqueur Muscats and very good sparkling wines.

However, unlike the more temperate and stable regions of Northern Europe, the weather in Australia can fluctuate between extremes of heat and drought and excessive torrential rain. Vintage variations can be correspondingly dramatic.

Not only vintage variations; the once highly successful marketing of Australian wine – to the extent that it began to overtake French exports to the Unted Kingdom – has backfired "due to a confusion of mammoth amalgamations and over-competitive over-promotion affecting many major brands". Excellent wine is being made nonetheless and will continue to offer relatively good value.

2002 ★ ★ ★

This year one of the coolest summers and driest harvest periods in the past one hundred years enhanced flavour development and acid levels with no disease pressure. Warm autumn weather extended the ripening period, resulting in good sugar levels and well-balanced wines of great finesse. Inconsistent quality proves again the fact that generalizations cannot be made about a country as vast as Australia. While undeniably exquisite red wine emerged from Coonawarra, the Hunter experienced a much more typical vintage, with fierce heat during the summer, then a rain-plagued harvest. In some extreme southerly and very cool areas, such as Victoria's Mornington Peninsula, some vineyards suffered underripe berries. The Yarra Valley, meanwhile, endured frosts, hail, and a cool summer, yet produced amazing wines.

New South Wales In the Hunter Valley Semillon and Chardonnay escaped the heat and rain, producing elegant, built-to-age wines. The reds were a little bedraggled, although some have good colour and acid balance.

South Australia Wet spring weather caused poor fruit set, and though yields were down in the Barossa Valley and in McLaren Vale, the unusually moderate summer temperatures created high quality wines with stylish finesse. The Clare Valley produced Rieslings with good flavour concentration, and great structure. Coonawarra's wines had great depth of flavour and good acid balance.

Victoria Yields in the Yarra Valley were down by fifty per cent. Thinner fruit loads ripened effectively during the cool summer producing excellent quality for all varieties.

Western Australia The Chardonnay harvest in the Margaret River was between ten and fifty per cent lower than 2001 due to uneven bud-burst, although the cool summer weather contributed to flavour concentration and finesse. The quality of the reds depended largely on whether they were picked before or after the rain started. Early ripening varieties Chardonnay and Pinot Noir were exceptional.

Ever popular Chardonnays will be consumed as soon as shipped, the branded reds also tend to be ready when released. The serious Coonawarra Cabernets and Victoria's Pinot Noir will benefit from bottle-ageing.

2001 ★ ★ ★ ★

Unfortunately space does not permit detailed descriptions of the amazing range of weather conditions in the different states and regions. The 2001 harvest was up almost fourteen per cent from last year, as a result of new plantings, and good winter and spring rains, which encouraged excellent canopy coverage and enabled the vines to withstand the dry summer heat stress. The overall quality is far superior to the 2000 vintage, especially for the red varieties.

New South Wales A classic vintage in the Hunter Valley with a warm and sunny growing season. The Sémillon, which was picked before the mid-harvest rain, was exemplary. Although hail wreaked havoc in some vineyards in Mudgee, it experienced its best vintage in three years. Semillon and Chardonnay both good, Shiraz uneven.

South Australia After a disappointing 2000 vintage, success this year was welcome. The hot, dry summer in the Barossa Valley, McLaren Vale, Clare Valley, and Coonawarra (a ten-day period of over 38°C/100°F was recorded in Adelaide) placed vines and winemakers under considerable stress. But once the early arriving harvest was under way, the temperatures cooled down with rain in March, extending the picking to make it one of the longest harvests in recent memory. The reds had intense colour, good concentration, and rich ripeness. Riesling and Shiraz were the highlights of the Clare Valley, showing good fruit intensity, fine structure, and excellent varietal character. In McLaren Vale Sauvignon Blanc suffered from intense heat.

Victoria A more difficult vintage in the Yarra Valley, largely due to rain in late March and late April, during the harvest. Quality was, however, very good. Where the Chardonnay and Cabernet Sauvignon were picked before the rain, quality was exceptional.

Western Australia This region had the most favorable weather for winegrowing in the country, producing excellent quality wines. The Margaret River region had winter rain, a dry growing season and none of the cyclonic activity that has caused anxiety in the past. As a result, fruit quality was very good with excellent flavours and acid balance. This year's Cabernet Sauvignon, Merlot, Chardonnay, and Riesling are easily some of the best in the country. Birds were a problem this year and vineyards without nets lost a lot of fruit.

All in all, some exciting wines at most ends of the vinous spectrum. Rieslings, though successful in past vintages, have become "respectable" and, at last, better appreciated. Also well established and deservedly popular are the Chardonnays which, in 2001, can be enjoyed relatively young. Shiraz for mid-term drinking and Cabernet blends for drinking not long after release though the classic Grange will have a long future.

2000★★★ variable

Generally, challenging weather kept this from being the vintage hoped for in this millennium. Fortunately the weather turned warm just before the harvest, saving many regions from total disaster, and prompting an early harvest in most parts.

New South Wales The Hunter Valley had one of the driest, hottest seasons, resulting in "one of the best vintages on record", with Shiraz faring even better than in 1998.

South Australia In the Barossa Valley and McLaren Vale a winter drought followed by unseasonable rains and temperatures during flowering led to poor fruit set and reduced crops. The rain benefited late ripening Shiraz and Cabernet Sauvignon but overpowered soft-skinned white varieties. Those who picked their whites before the rain and waited to bring in the reds had good quality grapes. One of the hottest mid-summer periods in over a century followed, hindering growth and further shrinking yields by forty to sixty per cent. Sugar levels also rose unprecedently ahead of flavour development. Coonawarra escaped the February rains, and although quantities were down, quality was exceptional, particularly for Cabernet Sauvignon and Shiraz, which enjoyed the warmer-than-usual summer temperatures. The reds had dense colour, great flavour, and firmer tannins.

Victoria A warm to hot February and March was followed by a mild, dry April and some rain in early May. There was some sunburn, especially in the Pinot, and some vineyards experienced water stress, but generally the warm conditions were ideal for ripening and the prevention of disease. The wines are excellent, with rich colours, and fine, focused flavours for the reds. Of the whites, Semillon and Sauvignon Blanc are the highlights.

Western Australia The weather between October and December swung dramatically between extremes, before settling down to mild weather for the rest of the growing season. An early March storm created a little fear amongst growers, but had little impact on quality. Margaret River's Cabernet vineyards did especially well.

Virtually all the whites are being marketed and consumed now. The reds tend to be drunk early whilst young and fruity; the finest benefit from four to six years bottle-age.

1999 ★★★▷★★★★★

Thanks mainly to increased plantings and higher yields, Australia's grape harvest was over twenty per cent bigger than the record 1998. Australia is, of course, a vast continent, and the wine districts are spread and diverse, the vineyards of the Swan River of Western Australia being literally "a continent apart" from the Hunter Valley in New South Wales.

In most regions the winter was dry and an early spring resulted in rapid growth, though frosts in New South Wales and inland Victoria severely reduced some crops. Unsettled weather during flowering and fruit set resulted in widespread *coulure* and *millerandage*. December and January, Australia's summer, were mild and cloudy, interrupted by stormy conditions which went through to February. However, Western Australia recorded an excellent vintage and the relatively narrow strip of vines in Coonawarra, South Australia, enjoyed a highly successful vintage, particularly for the Cabernet Sauvignon on which this "cool" southerly district's "Bordeaux of the antipodes" reputation rests. North East Victoria suffered from heavy rainfall around harvest time, as did South Australia and the Hunter Valley, delaying picking.

Interestingly, Chardonnay was the most prolific with twenty per cent of total national production, Shiraz next with 17.6 per cent, Cabernet Sauvignon 11.5 per cent. Merlot production increased considerably, comfortably ahead of Sauvignon Blanc, in turn exceeded by Riesling though the latter was reduced, as was Pinot Noir – mainly due to frosts.

The quality of Chardonnays and Sauvignon Blancs has benefited from the cooler ripening conditions, Rieslings are crisply acidic, Cabernet Sauvignon and Shiraz generally have good colour and ripe fruit character, with supple tannins. On the whole a satisfactory outcome. The whites for early drinking and, as always, the better reds warrant a modicum of bottle-age.

1998 ★★★

Overall good results, particularly for the reds, with a record crop due to increased plantings, roughly ten per cent up on 1997. The vintage was reportedly strongly influenced by El Niño, particularly in Tasmania.

It is hard to generalize about weather conditions on such a large continent whose wine-producing areas lie so far apart, but on the whole a very dry winter left moisture levels dangerously low. Spring temperatures were also lower than average, and several areas, for example the Yarra Valley, suffered frost damage which reduced the crop. Summer rainfall was below average in most places, and it was cool in South Australia. However, vintage time was another matter. Many districts had to endure extreme heat, up to 40ºC (104ºF) in the Hunter Valley which was painful for the pickers – but the net result there was "the best vintage for fifteen years", particularly for the reds, notably Shiraz. There was rain in the Adelaide Hills and, towards the end of the harvest, in Coonawarra, though it caused no problems; indeed some reported quality on a par with 1990. Western Australia had an early harvest, though rain caused some problems.

Virtually all regions were more than happy: full-coloured reds; Chardonnay good, Rieslings in Clare excellent, and the right sort of botrytis

in Milawa where quantities were down but quality best for a decade.
Sauvignon Blanc was the most variable, good in Victoria, some problems
due to the heat, elsewhere.

By and large the excellent Sauvignon Blancs and Rieslings should have been drunk by now but the Chardonnays are still showing well. Clearly the top class reds are worth cellaring though most, I am pretty certain, will be consumed – and give pleasure sooner than later.

1997 ★★★▷★★★★

One of the best of recent years and a definite success for premium wine
production, up six per cent on 1996 (red wines by nearly two per cent and white
wines by nearly ten per cent). A cool spring and early summer, with some frost
problems during flowering, diminished true crop potential. Excessive heat in
February caused vines to shut down and delayed the vintage by two weeks.
A long Indian summer followed with warm, still days and cool nights ripening
the grapes to a rich concentration.

New South Wales A few first-time harvests in Cowra this year, however
yields were still fifteen per cent down. The Hunter Valley suffered rot after
rain in February, whereas Mudgee saw increased yields after a very dry year.
Some excellent Semillon and Chardonnay, but not a year for red wines.

South Australia Adelaide Hills, McLaren Vale, and the Barossa Valley
harvested super-concentrated late ripening reds, but uneven fruit set cut
yields. Clare Valley made excellent Riesling due to welcome pre-harvest rain.
Eden Valley produced excellent reds despite frost and storms; Padthaway
harvested the ripest Chardonnay in years. Coonawarra lost thirty per cent
in volume, but gained in quality, especially Sauvignon Blanc.

Victoria The Yarra Valley had its driest ripening in one hundred years,
and yields fell by up to fifty per cent. Pinot Noir and sparkling wines were
especially good. In contrast the Great Western region had a bumper crop
of high quality grapes.

Western Australia A long and challenging late vintage yielded exceptional
Semillon and Shiraz. Some had problems with bird damage in the Perth Hills,
yet yields were still up twenty-five per cent.

Drink up whites. The best reds still evolving in bottle but can be drunk with pleasure now.

1996 ★★★★▷★★★★★

The heavens looked favourably on this vintage. Winter rains replenished
reserves and a warm spring triggered bud-burst three weeks early.
Consequently picking started in early February in the Riverlands and finished
in May with the botrytis-affected grapes of the Eden Valley. This produced
high quality wines and in sufficient quantity to satisfy the market. Yields were
approximately ten per cent higher than in 1995, providing a welcome break in
the trend of rising prices for Australian wines. The largest increase was in non-
premium white wines; premium red wines fell slightly below average.

New South Wales A very dry winter caused worry, but spring rain provided
a good, clean vintage. Unfortunately, storms in October reduced the expected
yield. In Mudgee and Cowra, later ripening Cabernet Sauvignon and Merlot
had great results.

South Australia The Barossa Valley and McLaren Vale achieved outstanding
quality in their Cabernet and Shiraz – some of which was sourced for Penfolds

Grange and Bin 707 wines. Padthaway also enjoyed excellent quality in all
its varietals.

Victoria After a touch of frost in Great Western, results were very good for
Chardonnay, Riesling, Sauvignon Blanc, Cabernet, and Shiraz. Rutherglen
also made some outstanding fortified wines.

Western Australia Definitely a year for the reds, especially the Cabernets.
In the Margaret River region conditions were perfect, allowing the grapes a
slow and even development, and providing fully ripe and balanced wines.
Drink soon.

1995 ★★★★★

This was a very difficult vintage as severe drought gripped the whole of eastern
and southeastern coastal areas. Water stocks for irrigation were seriously
depleted which resulted in highly stressed vines, consequently reducing
the final size of the yields. Overall, the crop appears to have been reduced by
twenty to twenty-five per cent. Nevertheless, the quality is good to excellent.

New South Wales Yields were severely reduced in this region this vintage;
with grapes used for bulk wine production being the most badly affected.

South Australia Losses, sometimes as high as thirty per cent of the crop,
were considerable throughout. Late rains salvaged the crop in many areas,
and quality was high, particularly for the reds.

Victoria Much less affected by drought than its neighbouring states and the
results are excellent, although slightly reduced in quantity.

Western Australia An ideal growing season resulted in a fine crop throughout
the region. Some yields were reduced in the Margaret River area due to dry
summer conditions causing the vines to become stressed, but the main – and
common – problem faced by this region was damage by birds at harvest time.
*Reds from mid- to long-term depending on district, type, and quality, most fully
mature now.*

1994 ★★★★

After the disastrous 1993 vintage, 1994 turned out to be a godsend. The response
was almost euphoric, many regarded it as one of the best Australian vintages ever.
Dry, warm conditions offered prolonged ripening. Overall, the crop was large, with
high levels of good quality, intense fruit, balancing acidity, and soft, ripe tannins.

New South Wales Unrepresentative of this vintage, this region was beset by
more problems than other parts of Australia. In the Hunter Valley the dryness
and heat resulted in bush fires. In other areas heavy rains were a problem in the
run up to, and during, the harvest. Overall, the results varied from disappointing
to good and the volumes were reduced by ten to thirty per cent.

South Australia Mild, warm weather resulted in a long ripening season and
exceptionally dry vintage. For many growers the harvest started two weeks later
than usual. Fortunately all varieties had great intensity of flavour, and the best
reds have good ageing potential.

Victoria Flowering and ripening were delayed by cold spells, the most
worrying occurring half way through the summer. The weather improved and
many areas experienced an Indian summer, but the harvest was generally about
a fortnight late. Results were of considerable quality, but overall quantities
were down, often by as much as thirty per cent.

Western Australia Extremely dry conditions: the period from September
to April was the driest ever recorded in the region. All grape varieties ripened

in optimum conditions and the lack of rot and disease was remarkable. Exciting results.

An attractive and challenging vintage. Good dry whites delightfully mature. Reds were of very acceptable commercial quality but some Pinot Noirs and Shirazes well worth cellaring.

1993★▷★★★

It never fails to surprise me that weather conditions in the southern hemisphere frequently mimic those in the north, despite the converse calendar (their spring coinciding with Europe and California's autumn). Having said this, it is always dangerous to generalize about conditions across as widespread a continent as Australia. With the exception of the Hunter Valley the Australian summer was marred by incessant rain, which not only hampered ripening but caused severe mildew problems. Those grapes that survived benefited from the late burst of hot weather. However, there was a twelve per cent shortfall of red grapes, Cabernet Sauvignon being worst affected.

New South Wales The Hunter Valley was the only region not affected by the rains. Consequently, the results were good, with healthy levels of production.

South Australia Cabernet Sauvignon and Shiraz production were dramatically down in Coonawarra, whereas the neighbouring Padthaway's crop was of more regular proportions. In the latter area, the white varieties posed more of a loss problem, Chardonnay suffering the most.

Victoria This generally cooler region suffers particularly from damp conditions. A cool, wet summer resulted in reduced yields and many disappointing wines due to widespread rot.

Western Australia The Margaret River region was severely hit by hail in some areas which damaged the vines considerably. The region underwent further heavy losses during harvest, due to birds. Meanwhile, the Swan Valley had one of its most successful vintages for years.

A roller-coaster vintage. The reds vary enormously, many are still drinking well, and some of the best will continue well into the present decade.

1992★▷★★★

This was one of the most difficult vintages in the past twenty years, making generalizations even more than usually hazardous.

New South Wales A region which experiences very different weather patterns to those of southern Australia – the harvest in the Hunter Valley is one to two months earlier. This year was one to forget. A severe winter and spring drought sharply reduced potential yields and was followed by heavy rain throughout the harvest. The odd Semillon, a few Chardonnays and occasional Cabernet Sauvignon succeeded.

South Australia The coolest summer since records began well over a century ago. Powdery mildew appeared on a scale not seen since 1974. Three periods of rain in early March, the end of March, and late April turned vintage time into a game of Russian Roulette. Those producers who guessed correctly made some wonderfully intense and aromatic wines; those who got caught by mildew and/or rain fared poorly.

Victoria Similar summer weather, the coolest this century, but missing the rain. From northeast Victoria (superb Muscat and "Tokaji") through to the Yarra Valley in the south (great Pinot Noir), the state's 200 vignerons have a smile broadened further by the good though not excessive yields.

Western Australia Yields and expectations were high, but rain during the vintage caused headaches for many winemakers. The white wines suffered most; some good Cabernets made in the south.
Drink soon.

1991 ★★★

A generally warm and dry vintage produced smaller than usual crops and wines of power and concentration. For some regions a better year than 1990, but not for all.

New South Wales For once the Hunter Valley had a good growing season followed by a dry vintage, resulting in fleshy, rich wines giving tremendous pleasure early in their lives, but not particularly long-lived – especially the white wines.

South Australia A wet spring followed by a dry, warm summer and autumn. Yields were down on 1990 by ten to thirty per cent, with red wines most affected. The compensation was great depth of colour and extract, although time will show whether they have the vinous heart of the best of the 1990s.

Victoria Much the same conditions as South Australia, with yields down by fifteen to thirty-three per cent. All regions – of which there are a dozen – had a relatively early start in March and moved through to the end of April in benign conditions, making lush, concentrated wines which provided a great contrast to the more elegant but lighter wines of 1990.

Western Australia This year the Swan Valley had a mild (relatively speaking) vintage of high quality. Ironically, the southern regions experienced a Swan Valley-like heat-wave in early February. Most damage was done in the lower Great Southern region but this did not prevent some of the top vineyards making lovely wines from yields down by fifteen to forty per cent. Much less impact was felt in Margaret River.
Reds are rich and concentrated and have matured well.

1990 ★★★

A good growing season for most regions in Australia and a mild summer suggested that this would be a vintage with relatively high natural acid levels and therefore one suitable for ageing.

New South Wales A wet winter was followed by excellent conditions during the spring and summer. Bud-break, flowering, and fruit set all took place in ideal conditions. However, around harvest time rainfall was heavy, diluting the Chardonnay and Semillon in the Lower Hunter Valley and consequently reducing the yield. The later-harvested reds were less affected, but overall, this was an uneven year.

South Australia A wet spring in most areas, particularly Coonawarra, was followed by a cool summer. Vines then suffered some stress due to exceptionally dry weather throughout the growing season. Picking began early in the Barossa Valley thanks to prompt ripening of Pinot Noir. On the whole, average yields. Winegrowers in the Adelaide Hills judged this to be their best vintage for three years.

Victoria A generally good growing season, experiencing cool temperatures and two wet spells in the western areas. Humidity caused the odd problem, particularly in the Yarra Valley, but disease was kept under control. Growers held out until the end of March for their Cabernet Sauvignon, anticipating a very special vintage. Yields were up by twenty per cent.

Western Australia Mild weather during the summer provided good growing conditions. Picking began around mid-March, later in the Swan Valley. Late February rains caused some bunch rot in the later ripening grapes, particularly Chenin Blanc. Yields were above average in the Margaret River, but lower in Swan Valley. Overall, the quality was good.

Drink up.

1989 ★▷★★★

After five highly successful years, this vintage came as something of a disappointment to Australian winemakers.

New South Wales The Hunter Valley harvested first after a wet spring, dry summer, and further wet weather just before picking. A mediocre year for Chardonnay and Cabernet, better for Shiraz.

South Australia A cool growing season produced healthy vines and a heat-wave in early March reduced the yields. Where irrigation was used, the heat did not affect the wines so much. Overall, a good but not great year. In Coonawarra growing conditions were also very good, except for some rainfall causing minor botrytis in the later ripening grapes.

Victoria A problematic year. High winds during spring in the Yarra Valley resulted in an uneven fruit set which seriously diminished crops. The summer was mild and wet, leading to widespread rot. However, some fine wines were made, in particular deep-coloured, full-flavoured Pinot Noirs.

In Milawa a combination of better conditions and modern technology made this a more successful vintage. There were, sadly, some casualties: bad harvest weather forced early picking and consequently no botrytized Rieslings were produced. The Cabernet Sauvignon grapes were picked earlier than usual and tended to make finer, lighter wines.

Western Australia An easier year generally. A hot, early vintage in the Swan Valley turned cool, resulting in light wines. The reds had good fruit flavours and showed much promise.

Drink soon.

1988 ★★▷★★★★

Overall some exceptional wines produced, despite difficult weather conditions.

New South Wales In the Upper Hunter Valley, a warm, wet winter followed by a mild growing season enabled growers to pick early before the rains came. In the Lower Hunter, however, the harvest was delayed and rain nearly ruined the vintage. Yields were above average and subtle, elegant wines were produced.

South Australia In the Barossa the year followed a similar pattern, but included a hailstorm on October 14 which cost some growers up to fifty per cent of their crop. On the whole, a large yield of good wines was produced. Further south, in Coonawarra, the dry, warm weather meant irrigation was necessary and resulted in the earliest vintage of the decade. Yields had been slashed by September frosts but quality was correspondingly enhanced.

Victoria The perfect weather conditions produced outstanding Shiraz, and the late harvest proved ideal for dessert wines.

Western Australia Hail and high winds in the spring, plus excessive heat in the summer, made this a difficult year in Margaret River. The Rieslings and Cabernet Sauvignons tended to lack acidity but, earlier ripening varieties had better balance.

Mainly all consumed though the top reds can still be delicious.

1987★★★★

An excellent vintage throughout Australia.

New South Wales Apart from heavy rain in October/November in the Upper Hunter Valley, followed by cold weather which disrupted flowering, conditions were good.

South Australia Heavy hailstorms in the Barossa region diminished the potential yield of the earlier ripening varieties, including the Chardonnays and Pinot Noirs. Then high winds here, and in Coonawarra, pruned the crop further. Thereafter conditions were generally good and the harvest began late (mid-May) in Coonawarra. Overall, an elegant vintage.

Victoria Apart from a poor fruit set in the the Yarra Valley, which reduced yields by thirty to fifty per cent, conditions were very good.

Western Australia A cool growing season resulted in a late vintage. High yields and high quality.

Shiraz and Pinot Noir fully developed; the few remaining Cabernet Sauvignons can be kept longer.

1986★★★★★

A consistently good vintage, possibly the best of the decade.

New South Wales An extremely wet winter in the Hunter Valley, followed by a damp, mild spring, resulted in an excellent fruit set and flowering. Dry weather held until early June but mild temperatures allowed the grapes to ripen slowly. Picking began ten days late and conditions were excellent. Long-lived, tannic reds and superb Semillons.

South Australia A mild winter and spring in the Barossa region. Temperatures during the growing season in the hills were the lowest on record, but luckily rose everywhere in time for the harvest. Overall, this area produced some superbly balanced, powerful, and stylish wines.

Victoria A cool growing season. The summer saw the lowest seasonal temperatures on record; grapes in Milawa ripened very late so that some of the normally late varieties were ready for picking before the earlier varieties.

Western Australia Generally, conditions were similar to those in the rest of Australia. There were exceptions, including a tropical cyclone in the Swan Valley, making February here the wettest on record, and yields were down by twenty per cent.

Chardonnays were of the quality and style that put Australia right into the top league. Perfect late-harvest Rieslings are lovely now. Substantial reds, such as Grange Hermitage, are superb, some needing more bottle-age. The best will last well into the present decade.

1985★★★★

Another consistently good year throughout Australia.

New South Wales Good growing conditions in the Hunter Valley, with high temperatures in January, brought the harvest forward to mid-January.

South Australia Heavy rains in Barossa during spring, but a summer drought caused problems for unirrigated estates. Sugar levels were below normal in Coonawarra due to cool weather, but the conditions allowed the later varieties to ripen perfectly. South Australia's largest ever crop, due mainly to the new vineyards.

Victoria The coolest ripening season in Milawa for years was followed by a warm Indian summer. The harvest finished in May, producing grapes with high sugar levels. Heavy rain during the harvest in Yarra Valley reduced yields by as much as fifty per cent, but grapes brought in prior to these rainstorms made good wines.

Western Australia The wines from the Margaret River were the stars of the 1985 vintage. Cool temperatures prevailed until late February. Picking took place in ideal conditions.

A strange coincidence that 1985s in the southern hemisphere were as agreeably fruity and balanced as the classic regions from the northern half of the globe. Attractive, rich, but easy-drinking reds. The late-picked dessert wines and Muscats can still be delicious. All others fully mature, needing drinking.

1984★★▷★★★★

The first of a run of elegant, stylish Australian vintages.

New South Wales Unlike most of Australia, the Hunter Valley did not enjoy a good year. Vines were damaged in the Upper Hunter by Christmas and New Year storms, then hail. Conditions were better in the Lower Hunter Valley. Rain later on, however, caused mildew and rot.

South Australia Despite a wet start to the year the yield was low in Barossa which was still suffering from the effects of the previous year's drought. A cool summer and autumn encouraged good levels of botrytis, making this an excellent year for the late-harvest wines. Outstanding Cabernet Sauvignon and Shiraz.

Victoria Stable conditions in Milawa made for a trouble-free year. In the Yarra Valley cool, wet weather throughout the year delayed the harvest; some very good late-harvest wines were made.

Western Australia Apart from a lack of late rain in the Margaret River region, and a cooler than normal growing season in the Swan Valley, this was a trouble-free year.

The reds are good, but not great. The late-harvest Rieslings are superb. Drink soon.

1983★★

An excellent vintage for some, though most areas were dogged by disastrous weather conditions.

New South Wales The third of four years of drought in the Hunter Valley, but some excellent reds and rich, full-flavoured Semillons and Chardonnays.

South Australia The long drought in the Barossa region ended halfway through the vintage with widespread flooding. In Coonawarra conditions were better, with the exception of late rains around the harvest. Variable quality.

Victoria An early vintage in Milawa followed a cool growing season and a hot spell in February. It was a year of disasters in the Yarra Valley region, with frosts in October, hailstorms in November, a summer-long drought and an invasion of European wasps – all of which caused considerable damage.

Western Australia In contrast to the rest of Australia, this was a near-perfect year in the Margaret River region. Yields were up by ten per cent.

Despite dramatic weather conditions some lovely golden Chardonnays long past their prime and some velvety Pinot Noirs and Cabernets. Most need drinking, many on the downward slope.

1982★★★★★

Near-perfect conditions in most areas produced some well-balanced, stylish wines.

New South Wales Good levels of rainfall throughout the spring and summer in the Hunter Valley brought an end to the drought. Warm to hot weather followed, enabling the fruit to ripen well.

South Australia Good spring rains in Barossa counter-balanced high temperatures in January and February. A late harvest produced some excellent wines. Coonawarra enjoyed a stable year and produced fine Cabernet Sauvignon with exceptional ageing potential.

Victoria A mild growing season was followed by rains which delayed the harvest in Milawa. An average-sized yield. In the Yarra Valley the cool, dry summer enabled fruit to ripen well. Again, a very good year.

Western Australia Margaret River saw its coolest growing season for many years, with much frost damage. In the Swan Valley it was a cool, stable year. *With luck, some superlative reds, both Cabernet Sauvignon and Shiraz still drinking well.*

1981 ★★

A difficult year. The hot, early vintage produced dull wines.

New South Wales A serious drought in the Hunter Valley drastically reduced yields.

South Australia Growers in the Barossa harvested their grapes early. The yield was very small, and, as a result of the drought, the berries were generally small and of uneven quality. Coonawarra, however, missed the worst of the drought, and had a slightly better year.

Victoria Mild, occasionally hot weather in Milawa led to an early harvest taking place in ideal conditions. Some good reds.

Western Australia Poor weather disrupted the flowering in Margaret River, and the potential crop was further reduced by high winds in late spring. But, thereafter, conditions were good. In the Swan Valley the grapes were harvested in excellent condition.
Drink up.

1980 ★★★★

A stunning vintage with an excellent reputation, especially for Cabernet Sauvignon.

New South Wales An exceptionally hot and dry year. Picking began several weeks earlier than usual, beginning January 11 in the Lower Hunter and continuing into early March, but drought resulted in a very low yield.

South Australia In both Barossa and Coonawarra this was a trouble-free year which produced a large crop of grapes. The Cabernet Sauvignon-based wines showed excellent ageing potential.

Victoria Described as a "copybook year" in Milawa for all styles from dry to sweet. In the Yarra Valley a severe year-long drought produced excellent wines from a small crop of good, ripe fruit.

Western Australia A dry year for the Margaret River producers where winemaking was still in its infancy. In the Swan Valley a mild to warm year produced evenly ripened fruit.
Most 1980s are things of the past, but tannic Cabernets have been keeping well.

1970s

Prior to 1980 it is safe to say that all the white wines will be well past their best, but Cabernet Sauvignon, the best Shiraz, and blended reds can still be superb.

Star ratings for top reds: **1979★★★★ 1978★★★★ 1977★★★ 1976★★★★
1975★★★★★ 1974★ 1973★★★★ 1972~ 1971★★★★★**

1960s

The decade of the 1960s was one of development, the market dominated by
the bigger, well-established producers. The best years for Cabernet Sauvignon
and Shiraz: **1967★★★ 1966★★★★★ 1965★★ 1963★★★★ 1962★★★★★
1960★★** – all fully mature.

New Zealand

Of all the so-called "New World" wines, New Zealand's are the youngest and, in
relation to appeal, quality and price, most successful. Prior to 1970 New Zealand
was noted for sheep, butter, and beautiful, uncrowded countryside. Then vines
were planted and, throughout the 1980s, dramatic advances were made.

Several things must be borne in mind. New Zealand is not a "district" but
two large islands, each with its own vineyard areas. The wine zones stretch
roughly 1,207 km (750 m) north to south and vintage variations are often
considerable. In 1988, for example, the Gisborne wine region was devastated
by a subtropical storm while, under 322 km (200.1 m) away in the south,
Marlborough and Martinborough enjoyed well-nigh perfect conditions.
New Zealand's weather is strongly influenced by the surrounding oceans.
These moderate the temperature range – both the diurnal and the seasonal.
However, the country is also exposed to both sub-tropical and sub-polar
climatic influences, which make the weather conditions from year to year
extremely variable. In fact, the climate is marginal for red wines, though in
many years they can be excellent. In addition to Cabernet Sauvignon, some
excellent Pinot Noirs are now produced. In the sense that the well-known
and deservedly popular Sauvignon Blanc and Chardonnay tend to be sold
and consumed as soon as they come on to the market it might be assumed
that vintage notes are irrelevant. Not so!

Over the past few years New Zealand has hardly put a foot wrong,
producing well promoted, attractive, and attractively priced wines. The market
is dominated by Sauvignon Blanc, the planting of which now occupies over a
third of the total vineyard area of New Zealand. The only cloud on the horizon
is over-planting and over-production in an over-supplied world market. The
recent success with Pinot Noir has given New Zealand a new slant and
renewed reputation.

2002★★★★

A return to normal yield levels after a frost-affected 2001, and a large increase
in vineyard area, combined to produce a seventy per cent increase over the
previous year's harvest.

Conditions were similar over all regions, with neither a dominant El Niño
nor La Niña weather phase. Bud-burst and flowering took place in ideal
conditions. Rain in late spring and throughout most of summer resulted in
vigorous growth, while the late, hot, dry summer kept disease at bay. A warm,
dry autumn persisted across most regions during the critical ripening period,
allowing growers to let their grapes hang and ripen fully. The increase in overall
production spread across all grape varieties and most regions, except Nelson,
where wet weather during flowering and fruit set reduced the crop by about

thirty per cent below average. Otago's harvest was also down, but by just two per cent. Nelson did, however, benefit from better conditions later in the season, and the resulting wines are reportedly among the best in the last ten years, and in the vintage. Sauvignon Blanc, Merlot, Malbec, and Cabernet Sauvignon ranged from good to excellent. Riesling is outstanding and both Chardonnay and Syrah excellent. In Hawke's Bay and Martinborough, favourable weather conditions allowed for wines with flavour intensity and weight, but only if crops were restricted to below five tons per acre. The Central Otago region on the South Island had forty days without rain before the Pinot Noir was picked producing the smallest, most flavour-concentrated berries, possibly the best yet.

The ever popular NZ Sauvignon Blancs and Chardonnays tend to be listed and consumed almost the minute they reach their export markets. And why not? They are delicious. Cabernets, both Sauvignon and Franc, are very good in a year like 2002 but like all good Bordeaux lookalikes they are tannic and the best need bottle-ageing. Pinot Noirs are exciting, full of flavour – yet with a tannic bitterness, needing time to soften the edges.

2001 ★ ★ variable

A vintage of two parts. On the North Island Hawkes Bay, Northland, Auckland, Waikato, and Gisborne had a cool November, which affected flowering and fruit set, and cut crops. The upside was that the lower yields helped the grapes to ripen well. A dry December and January was followed by four weeks of tropical humidity and rain during the final ripening phase of the white grapes. Growers in Auckland and Northland had to thin and drop botrytis-affected bunches. Gisborne had persistent wet weather in the growing season, and a localized spring frost in November in Hawkes Bay affected isolated vineyards. In Hawkes Bay Cabernet Sauvignon, Cabernet Franc, and Sauvignon Blanc were good but Merlot and Chardonnay were more seriously affected by the weather.

In the South, Marlborough, Nelson, Canterbury, Otago, and Martinborough had a normal flowering period and good fruit set. After a cool start to the season, a prolonged drought produced favourable conditions for Sauvignon Blanc and Pinot Noir. Water management proved challenging for some, while the long warm days and cool nights helped others to produce exceptional fruit and record yields. This is Marlborough's best vintage ever.

It is perhaps as well that much of the huge production of the ever popular Sauvignon Blanc is of high quality in 2001; the other whites, notably Chardonnay and Riesling, also good. Pinot Noir successful in Central Otago and Martinborough, the Cabernets variable, the best good. All the whites are being shipped and consumed with hardly a pause for breath. Pinot Noirs need more time as do the Bordeaux style reds.

2000 ★ ★ ★ ▷ ★ ★ ★ ★

The growing season was cooler than normal, with lower than average cropping levels. Wine quality was exceptional with great intensity of flavour, particularly in Sauvignon Blanc, where high sugar levels had been reached during the cool weather. In Marlborough, a warm spring led to early bud-burst. But then cool, wet weather during flowering reduced yields, particularly Sauvignon Blanc, by as much as thirty per cent. In the other grape-growing regions, the generally cool weather would have had negative consequences in previous years, when vine canopy management was less stringent. But thanks to vertical shoot positioning, shoot thinning, and leaf-plucking, even the reds of Hawkes Bay avoided the overly herbal character peculiar to cooler years. Martinborough and Central Otago Pinot Noirs fared well. They showed dark, healthy colours, bright fruit aromas and crisp acids.

The whites all drinking well now, the reds variable, but as with the exciting new Pinot Noirs, good flavoury mid-term – for New Zealand – drinking.

1999 ★ ★ ★ ★

No question about it, New Zealand is an outstanding producer of seriously impressive white wines and increasingly impressive reds. All show well in 1999; to date, New Zealand's largest ever vintage. Despite the already stated geographical extremes, it is, however, fairly accurate to say that New Zealand enjoys a beneficial climate, and throughout 1999 the summer was warm, encouraging ripening. The autumn however, was mixed, Hawkes Bay on North Island enduring more rain than the sunny and dry conditions in Marlborough at the top of South Island. Happily, virtually all regions reported ideal growing and ripening conditions, resulting in naturally high sugar levels, excellent fruit flavours, good balance and structure, and the best ever year for reds.

The 1999 Sauvignon Blancs have enticing fruit and zest, the Chardonnays are excellent and the reds well worth cellaring.

1998 ★ ★ ★ ★

One of the biggest and best vintage to date. New vineyards coming into production for the first time were mainly responsible for the extraordinary increase in volume, thirty per cent higher than 1997. As for the quality, this was quite simply due to well-nigh perfect growing and ripening conditions, the hottest and driest on record – attributed to El Niño. In Marlborough for example, Sauvignon Blanc, rapidly becoming the most important crop, was harvested three weeks earlier than normal and, unusually, before the Chardonnay. Some of the spicier varieties like Gewurztraminer suffered from the heat, but the reds, fully ripe, with excellent sugar levels and balance, are developing extremely well.

The fragrant and floral Sauvignon Blancs should now all be consumed though the best Chardonnays are stil drinking well. The reds have come of age. Hitherto suffering from a lack of track record, the 1998s should develop well.

1997 ★ ★ ★ ▷ ★ ★ ★ ★

Below-average rain and a greater number of sunshine hours encouraged development after poor fruit set during flowering. A favourable autumn and continuing Indian summer provided ideal harvesting conditions and allowed for optimum ripeness at picking. Small berry size also permitted greater extraction and enhanced the flavour of the wines. In the north yields were lower than 1996, whereas in the south, Nelson's crop was alone in being ten per cent higher. Marlborough produced elegant and refined styles and some especially good Riesling. Merlot and Pinot Noir were the success stories for the reds.

Definitely wines for those who like good colour, abundant aroma, intensity of fruit, and lots of flavour. Whites drink up. The relatively untried Pinot Noirs, now, Cabernets now to 2006.

1996 ★ ★ ★ ★

The second largest vintage ever in New Zealand and the largest so far with significant increases in the volumes of Chardonnay and Sauvignon Blanc –

around twelve per cent for both. For the reds, Merlot rose seven per cent and Pinot Noir increased by three per cent.

After successful flowering, perfect conditions continued through to vintage time. Some vineyards even experienced the simultaneous flowering of Cabernet Sauvignon and Chardonnay, this being very uncommon. In certain instances, serious producers had to thin crops in order to control the vines and maintain quality.

The reds, whilst still lacking a track record, will probably be drinking well now.

1995 ★ ★ ▷ ★ ★ ★ ★

A vintage of enormous proportions – as much as thirty-nine per cent up on 1994, making it the second largest crop since 1983. Conditions were favourable during the spring and summer – very warm and dry, which resulted in record sugar levels in many areas. Due to the advanced state of the vines, harvesting started in late February, clearly the earliest since 1991.

Unfortunately, after such perfect conditions, the rains fell throughout the country in April. This led to a large variation in quality between grapes picked before and during this period. The later ripening regions experienced a certain degree of dilution.

A popular commercial vintage.

1994 ★ ★ ★ ★

After the low yields of 1992 and 1993, this crop was very generous, as were the quality levels. This can be explained by the favourable conditions throughout the growing season and the increasing number of vines being planted. The general response of the growers was that the overall quality of the fruit was the highest it had been for several years.

Reds still certainly worth looking out for.

1993 ★ ★

The spring was late, poor weather delaying budding and flowering. This resulted in a dramatically reduced crop in many districts. The greatest effect was on certain white varieties used for home consumption. The ever popular exported varieties were not quite as badly affected.

Most reds fully mature.

1992 ★ ★ ★ ★

Good wines, though crops were below average in some districts. A cool, windy spring delayed flowering and caused *millerandage*, so reducing the anticipated harvest. The fallout from the Mount Pinatubo eruptions brought atmospheric disturbances throughout the 1991/2 growing season, reducing sunshine levels and temperatures throughout the summer. Prior to, and during, the harvest there was some fine but cool weather – particularly in the South Island.

The red varietals had good colour and balance and, now fully mature, could be interesting.

1991 ★ ★ ★ ★

A well-above-average, though late, vintage following variable but generally good weather conditions.

Drink up.

1990 ★ ★ ▷ ★ ★ ★ ★

An above-average yield of good wines. Sunny conditions alternated with showers, keeping winemakers on their toes, though, ultimately, most producers appeared fairly satisfied with their wines.
The best reds have matured well.

1989 ★ ★ ★ ★ ★

Declared the "vintage of the century" by several enthusiastic winemakers. This was certainly an excellent harvest throughout the country. Abundant sun and heat, near perfect ripening conditions, and a bountiful harvest produced many top wines from both white and red grapes.
Reds fully mature. Drink up.

1988 ★ ▷ ★ ★ ★ ★

A notoriously variable vintage thanks to a tropical cyclone which devastated Gisborne and severely impaired quality in Auckland and Hawkes Bay. Many Gisborne vineyards were totally submerged by torrential rain and the region was officially declared a disaster area. Nevertheless, some surprisingly palatable wines emerged from even the hardest hit regions. In dramatic contrast, Martinborough and Marlborough both had a good vintage.
Best reds, now hard to find, fully mature.

1987 ★ ▷ ★ ★ ★ ★

Following two abundant harvests, 1987 saw a drop in quantity and quality. Poor fruit set reduced the size of the crop and heavy rain early in the harvest caused further problems.
Some botrytis-affected sweet wines still drinking well; the rest, drink up.

1986 ★ ★ ★ ▷ ★ ★ ★ ★ ★

Wet weather in most areas during January and February got the vintage off to a bad start; early varieties suffered from rot. Thereafter, the weather cleared and 1986 enjoyed mostly outstanding results from the later ripening varieties. Several of the now classic estates achieved new heights in quality, with wines that have been proven to have real ageing potential.
Cabernet Sauvignon came into its own this vintage; all are fully mature, though the best might keep longer.

1985 ★ ★ ▷ ★ ★ ★ ★

A very large vintage which added to a growing wine surplus; as a result the government sponsored a vine culling scheme the following year. Heavy rain during the beginning of the harvest caused outbreaks of rot which encouraged many growers to pick their white grapes before optimum ripeness. Even the usually dry Marlborough suffered because of the wet weather and made few memorable wines. Red grape varieties benefited from better ripening weather late in the season.
Drink up.

1984 ★

Poor fruit set and hail damage in some regions reduced the crop by one-third, despite an increase in the number of vineyards. Due to widespread rain and

humidity all varieties suffered from a lack of ripeness and flavour. Overall, a
below-average year.

Avoid.

1983★★★★★

A top vintage which combined quality and quantity.

Drink up.

1982★▷★★★

Strong variations from region to region, with heavy rain in February and March,
some producers lost heart and picked their grapes too early and, predictably,
made poor wines. Hot, dry conditions towards the end of the growing season
favoured red grape varieties.

Drink up.

1981★★

A poor flowering and fruit set was followed by a fairly dry, but rather
sunless, growing season. The harvest yielded a small crop of clean but
rather unripe grapes.

Drink up.

1980★

Overall, this was a poor year.

Avoid.

pre-1980

Earlier vintages less relevant for this relatively new wine country.

South Africa

Cape wines can hardly be called "New World". Vines were planted and wine
made by the earliest Dutch settlers of this region in the late seventeenth century.
During the eighteenth the wines of Constantia were renowned – fashionable
and highly priced – but fell out of favour as the nineteenth century progressed.
Indifferent table and fortified wines were then made, the principal export until
well into the 1950s being good, inexpensive, sherry-type wines.

The renaissance of fine table wines began in the 1960s and 1970s though it
was largely unnoticed or, for political reasons, ignored. Over the past three
decades, great strides have been made in the selection of cultivars (vine
varieties), winemaking, and effective control systems. Over a dozen red cultivars
are grown in the Cape, of which Pinotage, Cabernet Sauvignon, and Pinot Noir
are the best known, and around fifteen white cultivars, the most widely planted
being the versatile Steen (Chenin Blanc), also Sauvignon Blanc, the increasingly
successful Chardonnay, some Gewurztraminer, and a small amount of high
quality Riesling.

It might be imagined that the Cape enjoys one long, hot season after
another. Not so. Being the southern tip of South Africa winters can be cold and
wet, the Coastal Regions having variable springs and summers. At vertical
tastings in the Cape, I have noted that potentially hefty reds made with cultivars
such as Pinotage are better after a long, cool growing season. The ageing ability
of many South African red wines, even the most commercial brands, is

remarkably good. Moreover, the quality/price ratio is very favourable for the consumer. The wines of the Cape have achieved the reputation that they lost nearly two centuries ago – but the styles of wine are somewhat different! In fact the table wines of all the South African regions have improved out of all recognition. The Pinot Noirs and Chardonnays pioneered in the Walker Bay area, a coastal area east of the Cape, are particularly oustanding.

2002★★★ variable

A harvest of climatic extremes, although conditions and quality varied depending on location. The winter provided growers with ideal conditions: copious rain and cold temperatures. Unfortunately, the rain was endless – the wettest in the last forty years – and more rain through spring and January encouraged outbreaks of downy mildew and rot. Those who held on were rewarded with dry, moderate weather at the end of January, lasting through February, resulting in slow ripening and the build-up of concentrated flavours. Early ripening Sauvignon Blanc and Chenin Blanc grapes were harvested in good condition, even though yields were reduced. Then at the end of February, a heat-wave, which lasted four weeks, stressed the mid-season ripeners, Merlot, Cabernet Franc, and Chardonnay. With ground moisture still high from the wet winter, mildew and rot became a concern for winemakers. Luckily, mild weather returned at the end of March, and the late ripening Cabernet Sauvignon was able to recover. Stellenbosch produced one of the smallest crops on record, but, if harvested before the heat-wave, Shiraz and Merlot were well structured. Shiraz also performed well in warmer parts of Swartland and Paarl. Walker Bay, Elim, and Elgin produced elegant, powerful Pinot Noirs and intense Sauvignon Blancs. In wine regions farther away from Stellenbosch, the weather was more uniform, with no heat-waves at the end of harvest, harvesting good crops, especially in the Orange River district.

The whites, apart from Walker Bay Chardonnays, are destined for early drinking, Shiraz medium-term but the late ripening Cabernet Sauvignon should have a good future.

2001★★★★

This year's harvest was the smallest in fourteen years, despite increased vineyard plantings throughout the country. However, except for Chardonnay, quality was generally higher than in recent years.

There was an abundance of rainfall late in the winter season creating ample water supplies and a cool ripening season. The downside was that the humidity and heavier canopy growth encouraged downy mildew spores at flowering, and this was exacerbated by dew and heavy fog. Later varieties, particularly Cabernet Sauvignon, were affected. Vigilant growers who acted quickly in the timing of fungicides earlier in the season had clear vineyards. In addition, the cool conditions in the summer months of November and December resulted in smaller berries, further decreasing yields. The extended hang time was welcome as it allowed a slow ripening, encouraging a good intensity of colour and flavour. Later ripening varieties such as Cabernet Sauvignon and Chenin Blanc had to be brought in quickly due to a heat-wave during the harvest in late February, but wine quality was not affected. Cabernet Sauvignon, Pinotage, and Shiraz have better structure than in 2000, and denser colour and flavours were extracted from the smaller berries. Although the majority of wine makers agreed that it was not a good vintage for Sauvignon Blanc some excellent examples were produced in Stellenbosch, as was Merlot in the same district.

Overall a notable vintage, though small; happily the proportion of quality wine continues to increase.

Dry whites for immediate drinking. Some good reds, notably Shiraz and Merlot; Cabernet Sauvignon and Pinot Noir from dependable to very good indeed though some minor reds will be best for short term drinking.

2000 ★★▷★★★

This vintage will be remembered for the erratic ripening of the grapes and a disastrous fire on January 16, which scorched sixty per cent of the Chardonnay, Sauvignon Blanc, and Pinot Blanc vines, and ten per cent of Gewürztraminer. The vineyards recovered rapidly but the fruit-bearing cordons were damaged with a knock on effect for 2001.

Growers were optimistic about the promising weather in September and October, which was followed by a perfect spring without the damaging South Easterlies, allowing for optimum flowering conditions. Then an extremely hot, dry December, January, and February resulted in early and uneven ripening in some varieties, necessitating a rigorously selective hand harvest, especially in the dry land, non-irrigated vineyards. New clonal vineyards that had continuous irrigation throughout the dry period performed well with even ripeness and better fruit maturity, while others experienced a severe loss of crops, low acidity levels, diluted sugars, and ruined primary aromas, particularly in their Sauvignon Blanc. Vintners who employed Californian drip irrigation techniques to measure and work out where vines should be to access the soil's moisture were at an advantage. Sauvignon Blanc in cooler areas had good fruity flavours and higher sugar levels, without losing too much aroma. It is a red wine vintage as the red grapes went through *véraison* earlier and showed excellent colour hues and rich fruit. The Pinotage was stunning. Botrytized wines were difficult to make due to the dry conditions.

Not the easiest of vintages and not the easiest wines to assess, the effects of the fire and erratic conditions varying so much between regions and districts. Sauvignon Blanc particularly variable but, on the whole, a red wine year for medium-term drinking.

1999 ★★

It is commonly thought that there are fewer vintage variations in South Africa than in other wine-producing countries, 1999 confounded this perception, for the growing season had confusingly abnormal weather conditions .

An unusually warm and dry winter encouraged early vegetation but the flowering was upset by a cold spell which reduced potential yields. November and December had higher than average rainfall but January to March – the ripening period – was drier than usual. January was also cool, the low temperatures continuing on the south Atlantic coast but becoming exceptionally hot elsewhere in February and March. 1999 and 1998 were the two warmest consecutive vintages this century in Stellenbosch. Red wines are generally hefty and opulent, Pinotage around Stellenbosch being particularly successful. Inland, in Robertson, the Pinot Noir harvest started in January and finished three months later, the grapes being ultra-ripe, with high extract and alcohol, which will take some time to develop. In Paarl, conditions were similar to Stellenbosch, with whites and reds generally for early drinking.

Chardonnays seem more impressive than Sauvignon Blancs and are ready for drinking. Reds are above average in quality, whether they will warrant long keeping remains to be seen.

1998 reds★★★★ whites★★★

A hot and dry year in which the Western Cape was fully under the influence of El Niño and the warm Atlantic. Owing to the exceptionally dry summer, with rainfall well below average, and a heat-wave in January and early February, picking began two to three weeks earlier than usual. Yields were down roughly ten per cent due to heat stress, but the quality of the red varietals was high.

Even in the generally cooler maritime wine areas it was still the warmest summer for several years. Harvesting was early here, too, but good Chardonnays are reported and extremely good Pinot Noirs. Whites tended to be high in alcohol, perhaps lacking zest, but an excellent year for Syrah, Pinotage, and Cabernet Sauvignon.

Whites drink soon. The better reds will benefit from a little bottle-age, particularly the top-class Pinot Noirs and Cabernets.

1997★★★▷★★★★

Still struggling with demand outstripping supply, this year did not do South Africa any favours. In fact grape prices were still rising. Yields were five per cent lower than in 1996.

The season was long and cool, giving low pH and high acidity levels in the grapes. Spring brought early rain, promoting canopy growth, and a wet, humid December, causing downy mildew, caught out some growers. Then the weather dried up for the harvest. Producers had to delay picking, hoping it would not rain. The results were of fine quality, especially the reds. The extended hanging period had allowed tannins to ripen before the sugars developed; top wines will age well. Pinot Noir produced some excellent wines and Sauvignon also benefited from a later harvest.

Whites for early drinking. The reds of this vintage qualify for a moderately extended period in the cellar.

1996★★★

After an uncharacteristically wet December and January, February was hot and listless. Anxieties about disease were high. Conditions changed again, turning cool in early March, and localized frost affected a few producers. Late flowering and a longer ripening period delayed the vintage and a little rain during the harvest caused rot problems. The wines showed more European style due to the long, cool ripening period. The best results came from those who harvested early from virus-free plants. Chardonnay and Chenin Blanc fared well, Sauvignon Blanc less so, while most reds show good, deep colour. Yields were marginally up – by seven per cent, alleviating the ongoing problems of wine shortages.

Whites drink up, reds ready.

1995★★★★

The 1994/5 growing season was dominated by warm and dry conditions, and vine stress became a serious problem. The situation was eased in early February with the arrival of rain, followed by three hot days. The result was that grape sugars suddenly rose, acidity dropped, and harvest took place uneventfully. The fruit quality is remarkable and wines generally have fullness of body and flavour.

The better quality Pinotage ready now; Cabernet Sauvignon, soon. Some excellent Pinot Noirs lovely now, but will keep and develop further.

1994★★★▷★★★★

The smallest and earliest harvest for six years, due to the severe dryness and unseasonal winds. Despite reduced yields, quality was frequently good to excellent. The wines generally have powerful fruit aromas and good balance. The red varieties have intense levels of fruit and soft, ripe tannins. In general the quality was considered comparable to the 1991 vintage which was regarded as South Africa's best ever for red wines.

The best reds agreeably mature.

1993★★★▷★★★★

Good results this year, particularly in the Coastal Region, despite cool, damp conditions and fierce sunshine. The vines were healthy with an ideal level of ripeness by the time of the harvest. The reds were good to excellent, with an impressive depth of colour and intensity, high levels of fruit, and considerable ageing potential. The whites had good acidity and attractive aromatic quality.

The best reds are drinking well now yet will keep well into the present decade.

1992★★★★★

An all-time record crop: over ten million hectolitres. Cool conditions during the harvest produced juice with good acidity, excellent concentration, and good colour in the reds: Cabernet Sauvignon of superb quality, exceptional Merlots.

The best cask-matured reds drinking well now and will keep.

1991★★★★

This year had the wettest winter on record. May and June also wet, but an early spring was followed by a cool, dry summer. High quality reds, particularly Cabernets, deep-coloured, concentrated, and long-living.

Classic reds might benefit from further bottle-ageing. Otherwise drink up.

1990★★▷★★★★

A hot growing season. Moderate whites, better reds.

Pinot Noir and Pinotage at peak. Cabernets might still benefit from further bottle-age.

1989★★▷★★★★

Passable whites, some very good reds.

"Reserve" quality Cabernet Sauvignon now fully mature.

1988★★★★

A hot year, some very good wines.

Some excellent Cabernet Sauvignon, Shiraz and new blended reds, some quite tannic, all with good fruit. Fully developed now.

1987★▷★★★★

Variable weather conditions and wines. Better for reds, but some notably good Rieslings and late-harvest wines.

Cabernet Sauvignon, Pinot Noir, and late-harvest Rieslings drinking well.

1986★★▷★★★★

An unusually hot and dry summer. A small crop of mediocre whites but good to excellent reds. Some good Chardonnays – a relatively new cultivar in the Cape.

Late-harvest whites can still be excellent. Best reds drink soon.

1985★★▷★★★

A cool, wet summer resulted in variable quality, but good sugar/acid ratios. Whites were better than the rather light reds. A year of much experimentation with new blends of classic European grape varieties.

Drink up.

1984★★▷★★★

High temperatures during the harvest resulted in overripe whites with low acidity. A better vintage for red wines.

Botrytized late-harvest wines still superb. Top reds excellent now, but will keep.

1983★★

A large crop, even higher than the 1982 record-breaking harvest, but unfortunately lacking in sugar and acidity. Moderate quality.

Drink up.

1982★★★★

Largest production of quality wines up to that time, resulting from well-nigh perfect climatic conditions. A very good year for reds.

The best Cabernet Sauvignons still drinking well and will probably continue into the present decade.

1981★★▷★★★★

Cool weather from flowering to harvest resulted in white wines of high fruit and acidity. The reds less good, soft, and lacking colour.

Drink up.

1980★▷★★★★

Hot, dry summer. Dry whites lacked acidity: moderate quality. Very good reds and dessert wines.

Reds passing peak. The rare sweet wines magnificent.

1970s

A decade of development. **1979★★** had the driest and warmest winter since the mid-1920s, autumn was warm and wet resulting in much botrytis and some very good late-harvest whites, also some good Pinotage. **1978★★★★** good quantity and quality. **1977★★** wet harvest, high-acid whites, light reds. **1976★★★★** almost ideal conditions, excellent reds, good whites. **1975★★** a large crop of average quality, low-acid whites, rain-spoiled reds.

1974★★★★★ a warm, very dry year; some excellent reds now passing their best. **1973★★★** a cool vintage, small crop. **1972★★▷★★★★** a hot, dry vintage producing high quality reds, the best still holding well. **1971★★★** a large crop, relatively light wines, yet the reds can still be good to drink. **1970★★★**

1960s

Of the 1960s decade, **1969** and **1963** were the top vintages. Reds are now faded but the best, and best kept, retain flavour and charm.

Champagne & Fortified Wines

Champagne

Champagne has something in common with port in that grapes are harvested and wine made every year but only in years producing wines of top quality are they marketed as "vintage".

Champagne is a blended wine, usually, but not always, a blend of three different major grape varieties: Chardonnay, Pinot Noir, and Pinot Meunier, each chosen for its different character. The grapes themselves are grown in different districts, some surprisingly far apart, but all strictly classified by quality. Most Champagne is marketed under a brand name, no vintage stated. These non-vintage (NV) wines may, in turn, be of different years, blended by the master blender to match the house style.

Non-vintage Champagne varies in quality from passable to excellent, the best benefiting from further bottle-ageing. Some of the top wines are finer than many vintage Champagnes.

A vintage Champagne from one of the *grande marque* houses represents a level of quality superior to even its most successful bread-and-butter "NV" brand. The proliferation of smartly dressed and high-priced *de luxe* Champagnes are an up-market ploy, though they should, and mostly do, represent the highest and most refined quality of a major Champagne house.

Straight vintage and *de luxe* vintage Champagnes are not marketed until some five years or so after the vintage and, though most can be – and are – drunk within a couple of years, most benefit quite considerably from further bottle-ageing. Generally speaking, vintage Champagne is best drunk between five and fifteen years after it was made, depending on the weight and style of the wine – and one's personal taste. I aim for an average of twelve years.

Old Champagne has a peculiarly English appeal. After twenty years it gains colour and loses its pristine sparkle. Its bouquet and flavour becomes deeper and richer. If the bottles have been well cellared and the corks are firm, Champagne can be delicious after thirty, even fifty, years. If the wine lacks effervescence, it can be refreshed half and half with a young or non-vintage wine, the young Champagne providing zest and sparkle, the old wine character and flavour. Older-vintage Champagne disgorged in the original cellars shortly before shipment has a different character to bottles which have never been recorked. The date of disgorging/recorking often appears on the back label. In my opinion all should be drunk within a year of so after disgorging. Lastly, do not hang on to, or pay high prices for, old vintages in half bottles, in jeroboams, or in larger sizes. Stick to bottles and magnums, the latter from only the top Champagne houses.

2002 potentially★★★★★

The Champagne region, unlike the rest of France, enjoyed favourable growing conditions, with sunny weather which enabled each of the three grape varieties to achieve good maturity levels. Harvesting began early, the Côte des Blancs from September 12, preceded by unusually high day and night temperatures, whilst northerly winds prevented the development of botrytis. Expectations were high and a great vintage forecast.

Grande Marque Champagnes of this vintage will not appear on the market until around 2008/09 but will be well worth looking out for.

2001★

The growing season began with a warm wet winter. By the end of March, rainfall was well ahead of normal, budding beginning early April for the Chardonnays and around the 20th for the Pinot Noir and Meunier. An outbreak of mildew was cut short by two frosts mid-April but thereafter the weather improved, June being warm and sunny, flowering at its peak around the 21st/22nd. July unsettled with some violent and destructive hailstorms and periods of very high temperature. August was warm but the high hopes were dashed by the onset of cold, wet, and unstable weather which caused outbreaks of botrytis and limited the quality potential. One of the coldest Septembers on record, the lowest sushine for forty-five years and double the monthly rainfall resulted in one of the most dismal harvests since 1873, when records began. *This will not be a vintage year.*

2000★ (early to tell)

The early part of the growing season was variable, weather veering unpredictably between cold spells, rain, some heat, then storms. Happily the flowering period was satisfactory. July again variable, August making a good ripening start. However, September was the wettest on record, twice the average, hampering ripeness and causing rot. The harvest was premature, the grapes better than expected but because of the yield the wines were diluted. *Unlikely to be a vintage year.*

1999★★★

Following the predictably high Millennium celebration sales and stock depredations, champagne producers needed a "top up" vintage. In 1999, their prayers were answered.

Winter and the New Year in this climatically northern wine-growing area were about normal. A pleasant enough spring was rudely interrupted by violent though very localized hailstorms which occurred in April and May. However the flowering took place speedily and in settled conditions from June 10–15 which anticipated a good size crop. Some rainstorms in the summer though they did not interrupt the ripening process, nor did later rain spoil the harvest. *The result, a large healthy crop of good wines which will tempt many Champagne houses to market the 1999 – in due course – as a vintage Champagne.*

1998★★★possibly★★★★

Rated a great success both in terms of quality and quantity, the abundant harvest ensuring that post-millennium stocks would be replenished.

The weather was mixed. The winter was dry with a mild windy January and frosty February. March was also mixed, encouraging early growth. Budding in early April was interrupted by cold and rain, but a mild and sunny May enabled the vines to catch up, flowering taking place in June. The summer started badly, cold and humid, then a complete change to extreme heat in August followed by heavy rain in September. Happily the weather during the harvest was well-nigh ideal, and the large crop was gathered in a reassuringly mature state, grape musts of high quality being reported with good levels of alcohol for such a northerly region and, for the same reason, with customarily good levels of acidity. Much of the wine will be used for non-vintage blends but the likelihood is that in due course it will be launched as "vintage".

Look out for some Champagne houses launching the 1998 around the time of this publication, others probably around 2005 for drinking, at their best, until 2010 or beyond.

1997 ★ ★ ★ ★

A very good vintage, quantity below average.

Late frost in May caused irregular flowering, and as the miserable weather continued into July, producers became extremely worried about rot. August came to the rescue, bringing gloriously warm weather and countless sunshine hours, which promptly relieved rot concerns. These perfect conditions continued throughout the harvest and as a result many grapes were left longer on the vine to ensure a high degree of ripeness. The harvest started on September 12 and, due to the vines being rot-free, minimal sorting was required. This allowed the vintage to progress quickly, and it was finished by the first week of October. In some areas Pinots Noir and Meunier were picked before Chardonnay which is unusual. Together they have produced rich and full wines and another memorable vintage for this region.

A Champagne for well into the new century.

1996 ★ ★ ★ ★ ★

Hailed as "the vintage of the century", producers said that the region had not seen a result like this since 1955, close to, perhaps even better than, 1988.

Heavy rain in August worried producers but September brought the most perfect ripening conditions. Warm and sunny days were followed by cool nights, sweeping the grapes into harvest on September 15. Some rain fell sporadically during October, but by the second week the harvest was complete, the grapes showing an unusually high level of sugar and acidity. Previous years had seen either one or other.

Results were great for all varieties, but Pinot Meunier suffered lower yields after some flowering problems.

There was pressure to put this vintage onto the market prematurely, but clearly a Champagne to buy for future drinking.

1995 ★ ★ ★ ★

Following two less than average years, it was a relief to have a very good vintage. Growing conditions were favourable throughout the summer. A touch of dry rot occurred due to some rain, but, happily, good weather and ideal temperatures returned in time for the harvest which commenced on September 18 for the early ripening grapes, and which continued until October 18. Careful selection and pre-pressing of the hand-harvested grapes produced highly satisfactory results.

Some Champagne houses launched their 1995s as early as 1999, anticipating Millennium celebrations. Certainly a most attractive vintage drinking well now.

1994 ★

The overriding problem this year was the rain at harvest time, dashing all hopes of a great vintage.

Climatic conditions for the growing season began favourably, permitting an even flowering of the three varieties in close succession. July was fairly warm, with slightly higher than average temperatures and a small amount of rainfall. However, August was a little less settled, with cooler temperatures and some rain. By the end of the summer the prospects were good to exciting. The harvest was due to commence around September 15 but rains had struck the region ten days earlier. More than a week of continuous rain caused widespread dilution and rot, with Chardonnay being the worst affected variety. Although the sun re-emerged in time for the second week of the harvest, careful selection was the key to making wines of any quality.

Most used for non-vintage blends.

1993 ★★▷★★★

Winter and early spring were uncharacteristically clement, with a reassuring absence of frost. Spring was very warm, with only the occasional cool, wet spell. In May hail struck parts of the region, generating some losses and providing a natural check on the size of the harvest. The temperatures were remarkably high during May and June, at times almost tropical. Growth was rapid and flowering took place early around June 2, in the course of a mere forty-eight hours. As summer progressed, despite rain in July, prospects for the vintage were good. Unfortunately, rains hit the region just before the harvest and continued virtually incessantly. Some 140 mm (5.5 in) – as opposed to the usual 20 mm (0.8 in) – fell and the effects were most dramatic in the Côte des Blancs. Serious widespread dilution was the obvious problem.

Some Champagne houses managed to produce better-than-average wines this year; one or two grande marque *wines are drinking deliciously.*

1992 ★★★★

This year the growing conditions were highly favourable and all three varieties produced healthy, ripe, and abundant crops. The harvest took place early and was completed quickly. The vintage has been a particularly interesting one to watch in that it was the first to be governed by new self-regulatory measures to control quality. This followed a spate of disappointing quality levels from the region. The industry confirmed the notion that if a wine is to be marketed under the name "Champagne" it must be representative of the superlative quality associated with the region and its traditions. The new measures aimed to control the size of production at every level – limiting the quantity of grapes harvested and the number of pressings, thus improving the quality of the musts. Wines produced from over 9,000 kg of grapes per hectare must now be held in reserve for possible future blending. However, growers can apply to formally extend their yield in certain circumstances. Clearly, it will be fascinating to monitor the effects of these proposals and to taste the difference in the glass.

Frankly variable, not all of the highest quality but the best warranting four stars and drinking well.

1991 ★★

This is described generally as a useful year, in which an abundance of grapes helped stabilize prices and top up depleted non-vintage stocks.

The growing year started with early problems. There were two spring frosts, the first in April destroying many of the buds, particularly in the valley of the Marne and the Côte des Blancs. The *grand cru* vineyards, particularly in the Montagne de Reims, were less affected. There was further frost damage overnight towards the end of May, mainly hitting the outlying districts of Aube and Aisne. However, when the weather improved a second wave of buds appeared. Chardonnay flowering began uneasily around June 25 but the weather brightened up a week later for the Pinot Noir and Meunier whose flowering ended on July 10. The grapes developed perfectly through a hot summer. However, on September 21 the weather suddenly deteriorated, causing rot, though rain did help swell the grapes. The sun returned for a fairly late harvest on September 30. The wines are light, with low acidity levels, not of *grand marque* vintage quality.

1990 ★ ★ ★ ★ ★

An excellent vintage, the third-largest vintage on record and the fifth successive above-average yield.

Frost damage in April affected the crop, sometimes dramatically – as much as forty-fve per cent was lost in some instances. Flowering was abundant but affected by unseasonable weather, resulting in *coulure* and *millerandage* in all three grape varieties. Summer was hot and dry, leading to a second flowering and thereby recouping as much as sixty per cent of the crop, some of which was gathered at a second picking (the second such harvest in two years). The late summer rains and cool winds helped fill out the grapes and had the effect of significantly increasing the potential alcohol. Both alcohol and acidity levels are excellent.

Most of the *grandes marques* declared this a vintage. "For forty-five years I have lived in Champagne, and never have I seen such a year", said Claude Taittinger, president of Champagne Taittinger. Some expressed doubt though: "To say today that it is an exceptional year, that is wrong", said Bollinger's director, Christian Bizot, after the harvest. For others, however, this was undoubtedly a great year. Henri Krug considers 1988, 1989, and 1990 as the outstanding trio of the century.

Superb wines with body, length, and finesse. Delicious to drink now but their firmness and length promises more to come.

1989 ★ ★ ★ ★ ★

A large crop of superb quality. The grapes were grown and the wines made in perfect conditions, producing wines which rivalled 1982 for the title "vintage of the decade".

A warm spring was broken by frosts in late April. Conditions improved rapidly thereafter and flowering took place in late May. The summer was hot and sunny and produced luscious, healthy grapes ready for the harvest which began on September 4 for Chardonnay and September 12 for the Pinots. Quality apart, this was also an exceptional year as there were two harvests, the second taking place in October, a rare event in Champagne. The second crop produced slightly acidic wines, suitable for blending.

Very appealing wines, delicious now.

1988 ★ ★ ★ ★ ★

This year produced some very good Champagne. The quantity was down by ten per cent on the previous year, forcing the Champagne houses to compete for grapes at a time of high world demand for the finished product. A mild, frostless spring was followed by a good flowering in early June under perfect conditions. Progress was hampered by a cloudy July and heavy rainfall before the harvest, which began on September 19.

Firm wines for drinking now, though the best may benefit from further bottle-ageing.

1987★

Not a true vintage year, but one which produced some useful wines to stock up the cellars of the trade. A poor, wet summer resulted in some grey rot, but the crop was saved, in terms of quantity if not quality, by fine weather during the harvest.

1986★★▷★★★

Following a poor spring, flowering took place in late June under ideal conditions. The summer was hot and sunny, but rain during August and early September adversely affected grape quality. This was a moderately good year except where growers did not successfully spray against rot.
Drink soon.

1985★★★★★

Growers predicted a tiny crop this year. They were pleasantly surprised by the small but excellent and stylish wines, the best of the mid-1980s.

The severe winter, during which temperatures dropped as low as -25°C (-13°F), decimated around ten per cent of the region's vines. In some areas as much as twenty-five per cent of the vines were destroyed. Wet, dull weather in spring and early summer eventually gave way to a sunny July. The months of September and October were the deciding factors *vis à vis* the quality of this vintage: delightfully warm, sunny weather swelled and ripened the grapes and the harvest took place late, producing a perfect balance of fruit, character, alcohol, and acidity in the grapes.
Beguiling now, so why wait.

1984

A non-vintage year. A dull, wet spring led to a poor, late flowering. The weather did not improve during the summer, September rains caused rot.

1983★★

Initially hailed as an excellent year throughout Champagne, the wines do not in fact merit such praise, but are mainly pleasant, flavoury, and nicely balanced.

Good weather during spring and summer provided ideal growing conditions for the cultivation of a large crop of healthy grapes. September saw isolated patches of rain but October provided good harvesting conditions. The amount of grapes needed for pressing one hectolitre of must was increased by the CIVC from 150–160 kg, resulting in more concentrated wines.
Some assertive and potentially long-lasting wines, but all now fully mature, some showing a touch of age.

1982★★★★

A substantial vintage in every respect, not least the biggest crop on record.

With the exception of a bout of mildew in June and July, excellent conditions prevailed throughout the year. The grapes were ripe and healthy and rain shortly after the start of the harvest prevented them from over-ripening. This was an elegant, seductive year for vintage Champagne.
All are delicious now but the more substantial blends will continue to drink well into the present decade.

1981 ★ ★ ★

Difficult weather conditions severely reduced the size of this vintage. The smallest crop since 1978, though quality was very good. A mild spring, which encouraged the early development of the buds, was followed by frosts in April and hail in May. The vines flowered during a cold July but the hot weather in August and September ripened the fruit well before rain in late September. Picking began September 28. Most of the wine was used for blending, but many of the vintage Champagnes showed finesse, firmness, and ageing potential. *Few remain.*

1980 ★

Cold, wet weather in June and July led to a poor flowering, which resulted in the vines suffering from *millerandage*. Then, last-minute sun in September saved the vintage from complete disaster though the wines turned out to be acidic and lacked body. A few Champagne houses declared this a vintage year but on the whole very little vintage wine was made, and wisely so. *With one or two exceptions: avoid.*

1979 ★ ★ ★ ★

An exceptionally cold winter which lasted through to April, followed by frosts in May. Favourable conditions then continued throughout the summer and an abundant harvest of fully mature grapes was picked. Stylish wines with acidity to provide longevity. *The best are deliciously mature. Drink soon.*

1978 ★ ★

The weather brought conditions close to disaster for the vines: a very small crop was produced. Untypical wines. *Drink up.*

1977

A dreary summer followed by better weather in September; the vines suffered mildew and grey rot. *Avoid.*

1976 ★ ★ ★ ★

This year was characterized by a summer of great heat and drought. The harvest, which was the earliest since 1893, began on September 1. *This was one of my favourite vintages; except for one or two great wines, drink up.*

1975 ★ ★ ★

After a wet winter, snow fell in March but the weather improved at the end of April. The summer was hot but not sunny and a slightly below-average size crop was picked late. A good year: the wines tended to be a bit acidic but otherwise well-balanced, rounded, and full of fruit and flavour. *Some lovely wines, at or just past their peak. Drink up.*

1974 ★

Difficult weather conditions. Variable wines, best being average, but overall not really up to the standard of vintage Champagne. *Few shipped. Avoid.*

1973★★★

A very wet September followed a hot, dry summer and produced an appealing vintage of fairly reasonable quality. The wines had neither the body and flesh of the 1970 vintage, nor the lean firmness of the 1971, but were nevertheless quite enjoyable.

Despite some agreeable surprises, best to drink up.

1972

Not a vintage year due to a wet, sunless summer.

1971★★★★★

This year experienced all the elements. After spring frosts, June hail, August rain, and even a tornado, September was mercifully hot and dry. A small crop of irregular grapes was picked as a result. But, the wines were refreshing, lean, stylish, and crisp. Champagne with finesse.

The top marques can be perfection now, but drink up.

1970★★★★

After a cold spring and wet June, the growing conditions were favourable through to the harvest. Less shapely than the 1971 wines but good, substantial wines.

All but the biggest of the classic grandes marques are well past their best.

1969★★★

Moderately good. Unstable weather conditions and frequent violent storms during the summer, plus the worst mildew since 1958. Harvest began on October 1 in good conditions, producing fragrant wines with a slightly higher than average acidity.

It is possible that this only moderately good vintage was released for two reasons: to make up for the two previous non-vintage years, and to supply an over-inflated market though by its release in 1974, there was a recession.

The wines were at their prime in the late 1970s to early 1980s, though the top marques are still excellent.

1968

A disastrous year due to bad weather conditions.

1967

Vintage not declared due to disastrous harvest weather which caused widespread rot.

1966★★★★

A very good vintage. Some vines killed by harsh January frosts and then further damage caused by hail from May to August. An early June blossoming, some of which was damaged by a cold spell; August was wet with some mildew. The harvest took place in fine weather. Despite the difficulties, 1966 produced a good quantity of firm, elegant, perfectly balanced, stylish Champagnes.

One of my favourite vintages though, except for well-stored top wines, they are now past their best.

1965

Bad weather damaged crops; a poor year.

1964★★★★★

A first-class year demonstrating the importance of bottle time for a big vintage.

The vines enjoyed perfect weather conditions throughout the year. After a cold winter and early spring they flowered early, then ripened during a hot, dry summer. Gentle rain swelled the grapes during August, ready for an early harvest on September 6. These were full-bodied, ripe, and fruity Champagnes, broader and more rounded than the 1961s and 1962s though without the finesse of the former or the elegance of the latter.

The best, if well kept, still interesting and flavoury despite increasing depth of colour and loss of vigour.

1963

Appalling weather resulted in a poor, non-vintage year.

1962★★★★

These were consistently good, dry, fruity, interesting wines.

Some are excellent but drink up.

1961★★★★

A stormy April and cold May followed a mild, damp winter. Fortunately, the vines flowered in fine, sunny weather during June; after a cold July, good weather continued until the harvest on September 28.

No point in keeping longer, though still delicious if kept well. Expect bottle variation.

1960★★

An abundant crop welcomed by the trade who needed to stock up with non-vintage Champagne.

1959★★★★★

An exceptional and timely vintage. Coming after a run of bad years 1959 was, at the time, thought to be the best for decades. The weather was wonderfully hot from May through to an excellent harvest. Well-constituted, ripe wines which held well for several decades.

The great, full-bodied, classic marques can still offer a lovely mouthful – if you like the mature bottle-age style.

1955★★★★

A first-class but slightly underrated vintage. Apart from a bout of May frost, good weather rallied throughout the year. Picking began on September 29 and reports noted an unusually high quality of juice from the grapes.

Lovely wines if well stored, though past their best; drink up.

1953★★★★

Apart from a prolonged cold spell, the summer was satisfactory. Picking began early on September 14 and finished in fine weather. This was a highly satisfactory year. The wines were perhaps less firm and refined than the 1952s, but overall, well-balanced and appealing.

Charming wines, now long past best.

1952★★★★

This vintage enjoyed good weather conditions throughout the summer, then welcome rain fell in August and swelled the berries, causing only a very limited amount of rot. Extremely healthy grapes were harvested. Despite being somewhat variable, overall the wines produced were firm, well-balanced, and stylish.

A better bet than the 1953s, body and acidity holding them together well. Scarce. Can still be delicious.

1949★★★★

A small crop which prompted cautious optimism after the harvest. After a long and difficult flowering, conditions improved with an exceptionally dry summer interspersed with occasional rain and hail. This was a very good year, producing firm, fruity, elegant wines. Many gained enormously from bottle-age.

Now straw-coloured and lacking effervescence, at best lovely old wines. Depends on storage.

1947★★★★

A classic year. The vines flowered very early in June and then record hours of sunshine during August produced a small crop of wonderfully healthy grapes picked in ideal conditions. Despite their soft fruitiness, the wines lasted well.

Drink up.

1945★★★★★

Bud-break was early, followed by April frosts and a difficult flowering. Picking began in haste on September 6 and yielded a very small crop of exceptionally high quality grapes. A long-lasting, elegant vintage.

If perfectly cellared, can still be delicious, Pommery for example.

1943★★★★

Low temperatures and showers brought flowering problems. Oidium also attacked vines, especially on the Côte des Blancs.

This was, however, a very good year: remarkable for being more successful than any other classic French district and, more importantly, for being the first major vintage to find its way onto export markets after the war. Mainly drunk too young.

Over-the-hill now. Beware of 1943s specially disgorged and shipped in 1953 to celebrate the Coronation of HM Queen Elizabeth II. They should have been drunk at that time.

1942★★★

A good but little known war-time vintage.

Can still be good, but drink up.

1941★★

A moderately good, if rather light, war-time vintage.

1930s

The 1930s saw four vintage years and six undeclared vintages of very poor quality.

1938★★ was the least successful of the declared years. Wines of uneven quality, not shipped because of the war. **1937**★★★★★ was excellent – turned out to be the highlight of the 1930s. These were rich wines with the acidity to give them a long life; still survive. **1934**★★★★ produced healthy grapes and an abundant harvest. **1933**★★★★ also benefited from very good conditions. The wines were reported at the time to be possibly the best of the century. However, the trade was more interested in the 1934s.

1920s

A decade which included many exceptional vintages.

1929★★★★: a large quantity of soft, charming wines. **1928**★★★★★ a great vintage: well-constituted wines which, if well kept, can still be excellent. The next vintage was **1926**★★★ producing a small crop of good wines. Two non-vintage years; then a small crop of good quality wines in **1923**★★★★ the best of which were still excellent in the early 1970s and, if perfectly cellared, can still be lovely – wonderfully golden colour with a hint of sparkle.

1921★★★★★: great vintage, top-class wines, despite the difficult weather conditions. **1920**★★★★ subject to bad weather and mildew, but enjoyed glorious harvesting conditions. A very good vintage.

1910s

1910s witnessed several good and one exceptional vintage.

1919★★★ refined wines, coming after three mediocre years. **1915**★★★ the next good vintage. Grapes were picked early by prisoners of war and soldiers on leave. Much of Champagne was under German occupation in **1914**★★★★ a year which, nevertheless, produced some delightful and lively wines.

The best vintage of the decade was **1911**★★★★★ and probably the best since 1874. The weather was excellent; the harvest early. This year also endured Easter riots in the Champagne industry.

1900s

Apart from three successful years, this was not a great decade.

1906★★★★ a small quantity of very good wines. **1904**★★★★★ outstanding quality: lively, flavoursome wines. **1900**★★★★ an abundance of very good wines, but phylloxera was also progressing through the vineyards. The rest of this decade was menaced by torrential rain and disease, or, as was the case in 1907, a shortage of labour.

1890s

Some good vintages.

They included the excellent **1899**★★★★★ and the good **1898**★★★ but not the poor and uneven period between 1897 and 1894. **1893**★★★★ was harvested in late August – the earliest harvest ever. Much wine of very good quality was made, though the grapes were perhaps a little too ripe. The finest vintage of the decade was **1892**★★★★★, also noted for the advent of phylloxera. Previous two years not declared.

PRE-1890

The best vintages recorded: **1874**, fashionable and high-priced; **1868**, **1865**, **1857**, **1846**, and **1815**.

Sparkling Wine

There is scarcely a wine producing country or wine region which does not produce sparkling wine: in France, its *vin mousseux*, Germany *sekt*, Italy *spumante*, Spain cava, and so forth; much produced on a large industrial scale, some of limited production and high quality, from the closed cuve to *Méthode Traditionelle* (formerly *Méthode Champenoise*) – but none of it can be called "Champagne" unless it is from the strictly regulated Champagne region.

The reason I have not produced detailed vintage notes is not merely because of the huge diversity of regions and names but, from the consumer's point of view, the vintage year on a bottle of sparkling wine, even if it implies quality, is rarely a deciding factor. For instance, I am not aware of any connoisseurs who seek out, to give bottle-ageing, specific vintages of sparkling wine in the way that they will cellar top vintages of Champagne.

Beyond Champagne, France has always been a big producer of sparkling wines, historically from St-Péray in the Rhône, Blanquette de Limoux, and Loire *mousseux*. But good sparkling wines are made in Alsace, and some well-known brands in the Jura, Burgundy, Savoie, and elsewhere. Germany (*sekt*) and Italy (*spumante*) are large producers of varying qualities, Spain is best known for its vast manufacture of inexpensive – and very acceptable – cava; and in Italy, francia corta.

As for the "New World", the best come from California, the Napa Valley in particular, Australia, old-established, and New Zealand more recently. Add to these South Africa, even India, and, back in Europe, Austria, Switzerland, and elsewhere, not forgetting – surprisingly enough – England, and the consumer is spoiled for choice. In the final analysis, you get what you pay for.

Port

Port, the quintessential "Englishman's wine", comes in several guises. In the old days, prior to 1960, there were "wood ports" and "vintage ports". All except for the white ports of the former category were sweet. White port, never popular in the United Kingdom though delicious before lunch in a shippers' lodge or on a hot day up at a *quinta*, is made from white grapes and is generally medium-dry. The other two wood ports took their names from their colour: "ruby" being a lusty young wine, undergoing relatively little maturation in cask or vat, and true "tawny" having lost its colour in cask, at the same time becoming softer, mellower, more nutty-flavoured.

Then there was the "vintage port". Up to 1970 it was customarily shipped to the United Kingdom (and just a few other countries, Denmark for example) in 550-litre (110-gallon) "pipes". It was then bottled two years after the vintage by the importer, by a wine merchant, or even (not uncommon in former times) by the butler of a big house. Since 1970 all vintage port has had to be bottled by the shipper (the producer; the company owning the brand) in Vila Nova de Gaia (commonly referred to as "bottled in Oporto"). The lodges – warehouses where the port is matured – are all across the other side of the river Douro in Gaia. Over the past few years the market has been greatly complicated by "late-bottled" vintage port (LBV) and, even more recently, by a rash of new "single-*quinta*" wines. But the quality end is dominated by fine old tawnies, still under-appreciated, and the classic vintage ports, which represent the *crème de la crème*, the pinnacle of the port market.

The subject of this pocket book is vintages. Happily, despite some of the complications referred to above, port vintages are relatively easy to understand and remember. A vintage is "declared" when the circumstances are right: that is when the year in question has produced wines of the highest quality and, at the time of considering a declaration (normally after the next vintage), the market is likely to be receptive. For example, 1931, a great year, was not declared because of the great depression in 1932/3. Life is made even simpler if the declaration is general, *i.e.* that the majority of the major shipping houses agree together on quality and timing. The only problem with vintage port is that it takes so long to mature and requires capital to be tied up for a considerable length of time, at least ten, often over twenty years. But at its zenith, it is the loveliest of wines. Americans, now the biggest buyers of vintage port, have partially solved this problem by drinking it before it has achieved maturity: they consume it whilst it is lustily fruity.

2002★★★ variable

Mixed results. Unlikely to be a declared vintage but the best will probably make a good LBV (late-bottled vintage), probably a single-*quinta* port.

Spring and summer were dry, but without excessively high temperatures. By early September, yields were low, there was little hydric stress, the grapes were in near perfect condition, and the mild weather conditions had encouraged balanced ripening. Then rain on September 13 interrupted harvesting, which had begun in the quality vineyards of the upper Douro a week before, and ruined hopes of a great year. Those that harvested before the rain set in yielded small quantities of good – possibly outstanding – wine, certainly enough to make a single-*quinta* wine. Lower down the river, lesser quality Port producers found that their berries were either swollen by rains or that they were rotten. Some producers opted to wait for the grapes to dry out before harvesting again.

Early days. The LBVs will start appearing in the second half of the present decade.

2001★★★

A moderately good vintage of satisfactory volume, probably destined to be a single-quinta year.

After four very dry years, one of the wettest winters on record was welcome. An early bud-break in March was followed by a dry and moderately hot spring and summer and rain at the end of August which helped to ripen the grapes. Harvest lasted from mid-September to mid-October, with only two days of rain. A number of good wines were produced this year, those made at the start were particularly fine.

Much of this year's crop will go into rebuilding depleted stocks of rubies, tawnies, and vintage character Ports. Although the wines are not as exuberant in aroma, many of the wines show as much colour as in 2000.

2000★★★★★

Widely declared vintage Weather conditions led to quality admirably timed for the millennium.

A cold, dry winter in the Douro lessened groundwater supplies, limiting bud-burst, and virtually guaranteeing low yields. High temperatures in February and March prompted early growth and rain in April and May rejuvenated the vines but also led to poor fruit set and outbreaks of mildew. Yields throughout the Douro were as much as one-third less than 1999. Then almost ideal weather started in June and lasted through much of September, enabling ripening to take place in hot, dry conditions with a maximum temperature of 40°C (104°F) for four successive days. This, combined with a series of short rain showers in August, produced exceptionally high quality grapes. In fact, quality was so high throughout Portugal that the Instituto do Vinho do Porto confiscated tons of grapes that entered the Douro region which were being sold to Port producers by unscrupulous grape brokers and growers. Harvesting took place in clement conditions with only one rainstorm passing through in late September without affecting the harvest. The grapes were healthy with concentrated juice and good sugar levels.

Tasted prior to and around the bottling (in Oporto in 2002). The wines were uniformly impressive: deeply coloured, fairly powerful, and concentrated. A wine to buy and cellar, the leading shippers' wines destined for a highly satisfactory life, ideally somewhere between 2015 and 2025 though doubtless much will be consumed prematurely, though with appealing fruitiness, prior to 2010.

1999★★

Good vintage, upstaged by 2000. The popular conception of Portugal is that it is a land of perpetual summer. Whereas this might be true in the holiday resorts of the far south it is certainly not so in the more northerly half of that friendly country. Torrential rain and cool temperatures can catch out the unwary, both tourist and vine grower. It was in fact cool weather and rain in late September 1999 which made harvest conditions difficult.

An exceptionally cold and dry winter failed to replenish the water table and led to a late bud-burst in the Douro Valley. April and May were very wet, further delaying vine development. However, flowering in late May took place in perfect weather conditions ensuring a good-sized crop, much needed after the very low 1998 production. June and July were warm, with some intensely hot periods where temperatures reached 40°C (104°F), and virtually no rain. Fruit development was still some two weeks behind. There was rain in early August, mainly beneficial despite some heavy thunderstorms, to refresh and swell the grapes. The remainder of August was fine and not excessively hot, and there was some useful rain in early September followed by good weather. At this stage the conditions were well-nigh perfect for a vintage of exceptional quality. Unfortunately the weather broke on September 23, becoming cool and unsettled with twelve days of rain at a critical period, which made harvesting difficult. However, those *quintas* that started the harvest three days earlier, and those which postponed picking until early October achieved good results, particularly those that still used *lagares* for treading.

Unquestionably good wines, but any hesitations were set aside as soon as the high quality of the vintage 2000 was realized. Nevertheless there will be a good range of LBVs from around 2005 and some very good single-quinta ports have been released (around 2003) en primeur.

1998 variable, but up to★★★

Despite far from ideal weather conditions, the quality overall is good, though the crop was the second smallest of the decade.

The winter of 1997/8 was wet, replenishing the water reserves but eroding old terraces. In February the weather changed dramatically, becoming hot and dry, more like late spring, and advancing vegetation. Rain returned in April and continued for two months which, with cold weather through May, seriously

affected flowering and fruit set. This set the stage for a very small harvest.
Some of the higher vineyards were also hit by frost. On the other hand, at
least one well-known *quinta* enjoyed unusually early bud-burst and flowering
before the rains set in. June was mild and warm, July and August hot and dry
into September. However, the weather broke at the end of September, dashing,
for some, the hopes of an excellent harvest. Overall, production was down, at
some *quintas* as much as fifty per cent.

The Douro runs from east to west – but in anything but a straight line.
It is serpentine, so the steep valley slopes have very different microclimates,
the quality and quantity of wine varying from *quinta* to *quinta*, particularly in
a year like 1998.

*1998 was not generally declared though there are some good single-quinta ports
which will be ready for drinking soon. The bulk of the relatively small production is
being used for standard shippers' blends.*

1997 ★ ★ ★ ★

Widely declared Development progressed in fits and spurts due to
very unusual weather patterns this year. Spring brought unusually high
temperatures, which promoted initial growth, and encouraged flowering
to occur one month early. June and July then became very cool which halted
this progression. Rain and humidity caused further upset during the summer,
bringing problems of mildew and other rots, including botrytis, especially at
higher altitudes. Fortunately the weather then became hot and dry towards the
end of August and this continued into September. This helped ripen the grapes
for the harvest which started on September 15. Yields fell dramatically owing
to this unsettled growth and irregular ripening – by forty per cent compared to
1996. In some of the subzones this loss was as much as sixty per cent. Fortunately
this did not cause worries in terms of overall production, as in 1996 the Douro
experienced some of the highest yields of the century. This year's smaller harvest
has concentrated the wines, producing high quality, and very happy producers.
*A deliberately limited quantity of high quality 1997 vintage port came on to the market
at ever-increasing prices. The best with a twenty-year life-span.*

1996 ★ ★

Not declared Heavy rain in December and January – 533 mm (21 in) was
recorded at Pinhão, in the Douro valley. Consequently, there was some
flooding and damage inflicted in certain areas. Spring was mild, which
promoted good flowering and vine development. Not a drop of rain fell
between June and August and ripening was behind schedule. Most *quintas*
did not start harvesting until late September and the highest quality grapes
were picked right at the end, after a beneficial extension of their ripening
period. Yields were larger than normal. The wines produced this year were
characteristically deep in colour and aroma, with wonderfully ripe fruit.
*A large crop of commercial quality. Some LBVs and single-quinta wines for relatively
early consumption.*

1995 ★ ★ ★

Not generally declared Good wines but not declared as it was hard on the
heels of the much-hyped 1994 vintage.

A wet winter turned at the end of February into seven weeks of fine weather.
A mild spring followed, with an early bud-break in April and vine-growth two

weeks ahead of schedule. A short frost on April 21 caused damage to some of the northern vineyards. A very hot July caused drought and restricted maturation. The heat continued into August and some producers in the Upper Douro brought the vintage date forward to August 23 as they watched their vines become stressed. Vintage started on September 4 with a short burst of rain from September 5–10, to rehydrate the shrivelled vines. From September 11 conditions were ideal and the finest wines were produced from grapes harvested at this time. Having reached their full maturity the grapes had greater depth of flavour and softer skins, which facilitated maximum extraction.

Yields were higher than expected – good news after the deficits of 1992 to 1994. Quality was excellent: deep colour, aroma, and concentrated flavours. However, not a vintage year though some individual *quintas* were marketed. *LBVs drinking well now. Single-*quinta *ports best from now to 2010.*

1994★★★▷★★★★

Widely declared After a relatively dry December, the year started dismally, with rains right through until March. In April and May the weather was poor – it was damp without much warmth and humidity was a problem. The result of this was *desavinho* – an uneven ripening of the grapes. Some storms during the spring caused severe damage, but on a local scale.

Summer was generally satisfactory though rain fell around August 10 and 11 and temperatures rose briefly to 40°C (104°F) the following week. The condition of the grapes was excellent but the crop was relatively small. Picking started on September 8 with some growers completing their harvests quickly to avoid the problems that beset the previous year when rainfall ruined the grapes. An ideal amount of rain fell on September 13 and 14 which softened the skins, swelled the grapes and increased sugar levels. Those who waited benefited enormously. The results were good, although volumes were reduced.
Full-bodied fruity wines, many drinking well now but with cellar life up until around 2015, alas many already consumed.

1993~

Not declared One of the worst years in recent memory.

The weather pattern in Portugal was markedly different from the more northerly European areas. Autumn and winter were extremely wet, with twice the average rainfall recorded in Pinhão. Landslides occurred in some of the terraced parts of the Douro. New Year and spring were dry, but damp weather in May inhibited flowering. Summer, less hot than usual, was followed by unsettled weather. Those who harvested early were fortunate because exceptionally heavy rainfall started on October 2 and continued consistently for two weeks, making picking difficult, uncomfortable, and unsatisfactory. The rainfall was so extreme that the river Douro and its tributaries came very close to flooding. The dramatic drop in production made up for recent years of rampant overproduction and, to some extent, helped stabilize the market. *Drink up.*

1992★★★▷★★★★

Limited declaration Despite a fairly curious growing season, the results were satisfactory – good quality wine was produced. Because of the unsatisfactory 1993 harvest, those shippers who did not declare their 1991 instead declared their 1992, but that was not the only reason: quality was high.

What was curious about the growing season? First of all, the worst winter drought conditions since records began, with almost no rain for six months; a cold, damp spell in the late spring, followed by a very hot and dry early summer. Mercifully, rain at the end of August resuscitated and swelled the berries. Dry weather returned as the harvest approached and it finally took place in relatively cool but showery conditions. Some very good wines were made, the better ones being the result of grapes brought in during October. In comparison with 1991 the yields were down by about twenty per cent.

Some very good wines. Drink from now to 2010, or well beyond.

1991 ★★★★

Widely declared A very good year despite a fairly sodden start. A generally dry winter sadly turned very wet in January and the rainy conditions lasted through to April, though flowering took place in May in warm, dry weather. June through to August was hot and dry and the flower set excellent, but the result of the heat and lack of summer rain was thick skins and reduced flesh. Light showers fell on September 10 and 11, with more rain towards the end of the month, which helped the swelling of the berries. Mostly deep-coloured, ripe wines whose promise has held.

Needs ten to twenty years ageing, though doubtless good single-quinta and LBV port will be – should be – drinking well in the early years of the present decade.

1990 ★★★

Not declared Severe heat in July and August held back the ripening of some varieties; the Tinta Barocca grapes were particularly badly affected by *queima* or burning. Picking began early, on September 3, but the maturity of the grapes was uneven. Instead of the super-ripe fruit that many growers had expected, sugar levels were frequently low and acidity too high; better grapes were, however, picked after overnight rain on September 19–20. A huge quantity of high quality port would have been made but for a shortage of *aguardente*, or brandy, used to fortify the wine. As a result, many reputable growers were forced to make table wine from high quality must that would otherwise have been used for port. However, it has since transpired that the "shortage" of brandy was in fact due to the officially permitted, yet not widely known, overproduction of port wine.

Despite some excellent wines being made, 1990 was not declared, owing to the recession in the UK and the USA – the two largest markets for vintage port. Some good single-quinta wines drinking pleasantly now.

1989 ★★▷★★★

Not declared After a disastrous year, the port trade hoped that 1989 would produce a much-needed abundance of good-quality wines that would be suitable for blending. This was not to be.

A dry winter and a hot, dry spring. Drought conditions prevailed though there was localized rain and even the occasional hailstorm in early summer, recurring later in August. Elsewhere the drought continued throughout summer until the harvest (beginning September 6) when rain swelled the grapes, rewarding growers who picked late. The drought led to a small crop of rather dry grapes and as a result the wines tended to lack sufficient colour and balance. The best came from the central port-making vineyards. Because of the 1988 shortfall of wines for standard blends, 1989 was not declared.

Used mainly for ruby and tawny blends, though some very good single-quinta wines drinking well from now to 2010 and beyond.

1988★★

Not declared A mild winter was followed by a cold, dry spring. The months from April to July were the wettest in thirty years, causing *coulure* during flowering and later mildew, reducing the crop by around thirty to thirty-five per cent. The wines were good but not of vintage quality. Meanwhile, the market was suffering from a severe shortage of wines suitable for blending. *Mainly used for blending, but single-quinta wines drinking well now.*

1987★★▷★★★

Not declared Had it not been so soon after the 1985 declaration, the best 1987s might have qualified for vintage status. A mild, dry winter and warm spring provided good conditions for a prolific and successful flowering. However, hopes for an abundant crop were marred by three months of uninterrupted drought and heat. This gave small, dehydrated berries which consequently reduced the potential yields. The harvest began as early as September 7 in some areas in scorching, arid conditions which broke on September 21 when rain swelled the remaining grapes. The wines made from these grapes were of better quality than those picked earlier, which were overripe and tended to lack acidity. This was a bigger than average vintage of variable quality. *Some good single-quinta wines, but drink soon.*

1986★★ variable

Not declared After a cold, wet winter, a long, cold spring with frosts in April followed and the weather did not warm up until early May. The vines were by now three weeks behind their normal growth pattern but warm weather during the first week of June provided perfect flowering conditions. An uneven summer produced small, shrivelled grapes, then in the second two weeks of September heavy rainfall caused flooding in the Douro (508 mm, 20 in, in one weekend at Pinhão). However, warm weather followed, encouraging a rise in sugar levels and providing better conditions for the harvest. In the Upper Douro a good quantity of grapes was gathered, but in the Lower Douro the wet weather returned in October and the grapes suffered from rot. *Drink up LBVs. Some single-quinta wines drinking well now.*

1985★★★★

26 shippers declared Unquestionably an attractive vintage, almost, but not quite, of the calibre of 1945, 1963, and 1977. An extremely wet winter and late spring retarded the growth of the vines by around two weeks. Some localized areas saw severe thunder and hailstorms during the first days of June, causing the loss of over one-third of the crop. Elsewhere summer was hot and extremely dry and the healthy but too-dry grapes were harvested from mid-September. Some winemakers experienced unwelcome difficulties during the fermentation of their grapes, mainly due to the very high temperatures. Some of the resulting wines lacked freshness and bouquet. Otherwise, this was a first-rate, vibrantly fruity and fairly concentrated vintage. *Lovely wines, tempting to drink now, but the classic shippers' ports will develop beautifully, well into the present century.*

1984★★

Not declared A cold, dry winter was followed by a wet spring. With the exception of very high temperatures in July the summer was cool. Conditions improved with a hot, dry September and harvest began on September 24. Four days later rain came, followed by high winds which dried the grapes and minimized the risk of rot. The harvest was eventually completed under ideal conditions. The wet weather had reduced high sugar levels and a large quantity of grapes made good, sound wines.

*Variable single-*quintas *and LBV wines. Drink up.*

1983★★★★

Approximately 10 major shippers declared The third of a moderately good to very good trio of vintages, declared too close together and by no means generally, which led to confusion.

A dry, very cold winter and a cool, wet, uneven spring which did not warm up until early June resulted in *coulure* which reduced the potential crop by around twenty per cent. Then, after an uneven summer, September temperatures rose to as high as 30°C (86°F) with a few localized rainstorms at the end of the month. The harvest was one of the latest recorded in the Douro, starting on October 3 in the Upper Douro and a week later in the Lower Douro. The best wines came from the Upper Douro: good colour, flavour, and bouquet; some outstanding. They are overshadowed by the 1985s and remain under-valued.

Minor shippers and quintas *drink now; major shippers to 2015 and beyond.*

1982★★★at best★★★★

12 shippers declared Some big names, including Cockburn, Graham, and Warre, were not among those declared, having more faith in the 1983s. After a dry winter and mild spring, flowering took place in May in mainly warm, sunny weather. Hot, drought conditions prompted an early harvest, starting September 8, during which a light sprinkling of much needed rain freshened the grapes. High temperatures during fermentation resulted in uneven quality and perhaps a lack of elegance, making this a distinctly underpriced vintage. The best wines, however, are full, firm, and robust with good underlying fruitiness.

All can be drunk now but the relatively few top shippers' ports, such as Croft, will keep well into the present century.

1981★

Not declared A winter drought and cool spring delayed flowering until early June. Extremely hot weather followed and growth was retarded further by the lack of moisture in the soil, resulting in a reduction of the potential crop size due to stressed vines. Heavy rain, storms, and severe gales affected both the area around Oporto and the Douro, coinciding with the harvest around the middle of September. They did, however, freshen the by now dried-up grapes and cooled temperatures down. Eventually, the sun reappeared. The best wines were made in the Lower Douro where the grapes were picked latest. There were some reasonable LBV ports. The rest were used for blending.

Drink up.

1980★★★

Widely declared A vintage which was thought by many to have come too soon after the excellent 1977s and the originally well-thought-of 1975s.

A wet winter was followed by a cold, wet spring which continued, unchanged, until flowering. The summer was hot with virtually no rainfall until September 20 to 21 when it rained heavily in most of the Douro. Sadly this was too late to improve the grapes, which were picked from September 22 onwards. But in the Lower Douro, where picking started later, grapes did benefit from the rainfall and made good quality wines. Overall this was a small vintage which produced some extremely pleasant wines, considered by some authorities to be much underrated. *Most are delightful now, the top wines will develop further.*

1979★★

3 minor shippers declared A wet, unsettled spring; drought from June onwards; heavy rains mid-September.
Hardly ever seen. Drink up.

1978★★★

8 shippers declared A cold, wet spring was followed by a long drought from June to October. Heavy, somewhat coarse, full-bodied wines. A notable vintage mainly for the large number of single-*quinta* ports marketed.
Most at their peak now and drinking well.

1977★★★★★

20 shippers declared A vintage in the classic mould.

A cold, wet winter ran into a dreary spring and a cool summer, which retarded the development of the vines, but the situation improved radically with a September heat-wave. Grapes were picked from September 28 and were, with the exception of those picked late in wet weather, in perfect condition. Although there was some anxiety that the 1977 vintage had come too soon after the previously declared 1975, this was declared as a vintage unusually early – shippers were impressed by the fresh bouquet of the wines. Martinez, Noval, and Cockburn did not ship the 1977, a decision they later regretted. Generally, these are fairly deep, consistently good quality wines.
Now to 2020, even beyond; well beyond for the top wines. The minor wines and even some major shippers' wines very enjoyable now.

1976★

2 shippers declared So hardly a vintage year.

A drought ran through winter, spring, and summer and ended in late August. Heavy rains fell during the harvest in late September. A small quantity of quite pleasant single-*quinta* and LBVs.
Drink up.

1975★★★

17 shippers declared A vintage welcomed by all (including shippers in Oporto where life was dominated by the serious but bloodless revolution) and consequently somewhat overrated when it was declared. A wet winter, followed by a long, hot summer. Early September rain swelled the grapes, but bad weather at the end of the month caused some damage in the vineyards. Doubtless the wet weather prevented the 1975 vintage from living up to earlier expectations.
Most are, in fact, drinking very pleasantly now, but should be consumed before the 1977s and vintages of the early 1980s.

1974★

Grapes were ruined by heavy rain during the harvest.
Drink up.

1973

A wet spring, hot summer, and a wet, unsettled September.
Rarely seen. Drink up.

1972★

3 shippers declared Heavy rainfall flanked by heat and drought.
Some appealing wines. Rarely seen. Drink up.

1971★

A late flowering and late harvest produced wines suitable for blending.

1970★★★★★

23 shippers declared An underrated year. Also significant as this was the last year in which a port could be shipped in cask for bottling in the UK. After 1970 bottling at the shippers' own lodges was made mandatory. After a cold, dry spring, an ideal summer and some beneficial rain in September, harvest took place in great conditions. Sound, healthy wines resulted, much sturdier than originally considered, and with plenty of life ahead of them. The more I taste and drink the 1970s, the more impressed I am. They are still worth seeking out for laying down, even after thirty years.
Minor shippers drink up; major, well into the present century.

1969

Bad weather conditions led to unripe wines.
Avoid.

1968★★

Some nice wines: LBV and single-*quinta* ports.
Drink up.

1967★★

4 shippers declared Apart from a wet May, the summer was hot and dry. Rain in September swelled the grapes and the harvest took place under favourable conditions. Cockburn, Martinez, Sandeman, and Noval declared this vintage rather than the 1966; I am convinced that they misjudged both the vintage and the market.
Drink soon.

1966★★★★★

20 shippers declared An attractive, elegant vintage. Wet winter, stormy May; July was hot but generous foliage protected the grapes. Some rain. Overall an appealing, well-constituted vintage which was originally underrated and undervalued, but then upgraded in the 1980s. Many will easily outlive the 1963s.
Most drinking beautifully now but have the balance to achieve fuller maturity. The best have a better future than the more fashionable and pricey 1963s.

1965★
Nice, ripe wines.
Drink soon.

1964★
Difficult weather conditions and a labour shortage made this a problematic year.
Drink up.

1963★★★★
25 shippers declared An outstanding vintage which met with great acclaim.
A wet, snowy winter and spring ran right through to April; cold and rain lasted
until mid-June, thereafter the weather was fine and dry. Picking took place in
good conditions, following beneficial September rain. A large quantity of
vintage port was made. Well-constituted, elegant wines.
Though unquestionably good, many are losing colour and developing more quickly
than expected. Drink soon.

1962★★
Some good wines. Disastrous winter floods, but generally good summer. A
great, classic year for Noval Nacional.
Noval Nacional now to 2020, drink up.

1961★★
Some good wines. Undeclared largely due to its proximity to the 1958 and
1960 vintages. Some single-*quinta* wines and good, commercial LBV ports
were made.
Now rarely seen. Drink up.

Prior to 1960, only declared vintage years noted

1960★★★▷★★★★
24 shippers declared A popular and overall satisfactory vintage. Apart from
two months of rain during February and March, the weather conditions were
ideal: fine, hot, and dry. Heat and rain caused fermentation problems. Generally
well-balanced wines.
All are fully mature now but will continue to give pleasure.

1958★★★
12 shippers declared Good, though light wines. Uneven weather conditions
included a hot June with the highest rainfall since 1896.
Drink up.

1955★★★★★
26 shippers declared A very successful year – the best of the post-war
vintages prior to 1963. A heat-wave throughout April and May; a good
flowering; some beneficial rain during late May and June, and a hot August.
Grapes harvested in good conditions. Generally well-balanced and potentially
long-lasting wines. Overall, my favourite vintage for current drinking.
Mainly perfection now but most have the fruit, body, and balance to continue
gloriously well into the present century. Vintage port at its most sublime.

1954★★★

3 shippers declared A good vintage but not widely declared due to the success of the 1955s. Rarely seen. Malvedos very good.

1950★★

13 shippers declared A generally satisfactory year weatherwise, but light, uneven wines.
Drink up.

1948★★★★ ▷ ★★★★★

9 shippers declared A good but partially by-passed year. The budding was early and the flowering healthy. However, intense heat throughout August reduced the size of the crop, thickened the skins of the grapes, and concentrated and raised sugar levels. Deep, powerful, alcoholic port resulted. Fonseca good, Graham excellent, Taylor outstanding, even greater than its 1945.
Perfect now.

1947★★★★

11 shippers declared A good, abundant year. The summer was long, hot, and dry with some welcome September rain. Picking began on September 22 in perfect conditions.
Fully mature; needs drinking.

1945★★★★★

22 shippers declared An outstanding vintage; one of the best of the century and certainly the best since 1935. All the port was bottled in Oporto. A very hot, dry summer was followed by some September rain. Harvesting took place in great heat, prompting anxiety over fermentation. Ultimately, the quality was superb but quantity small – insufficient to fill the war-depleted cellars.
Generally, magnificent, firm, fruity, and powerful wines which at their best can still be superb, but some drying out. (Provenance very important.)

1944★★★★

3 shippers declared Superb quality but shippers concentrated on the 1945s. Rarely seen.

1942★★★

10 shippers declared A very good year which suffered war-time neglect. Not often seen. Generally good weather conditions with the exception of a stormy June.

1930s

Only two vintages declared in this economically dismal decade, but some very good port was also made in other years.

1935★★★★★ (15 shippers) Healthy, top quality grapes harvested in perfect conditions. The best were from Cockburn, Croft, Graham, and Sandeman; the most magnificent of all was, and still is, the Taylor. The quantity, however, was smaller than that of **1934★★★★** (12 shippers), which was the first widely declared vintage after 1927. Once one of my favourites: good, balanced, classic wines. Now rarely seen.

1931★★★★★ though a splendid vintage, was not declared. The demand was low, the British market being in the depth of recession, and cellars were still full of 1927s. There was, however, an abundance of good ports and this vintage was made famous by just one: the magnificent, deep, full-bodied Noval, the Everest of vintage ports.

1920s

This decade produced one classic vintage, two good vintages, and a string of undeclared years of disappointing to good quality.

The classic year was **1927★★★★★** (30 shippers). After a difficult ripening, ten days of fine weather blessed the harvest. This vintage coincided with the height of the port market. Some now thin and "spotty", others still magnificent, multi-dimensional. **1924★★★★** (18 shippers) produced good quality port. The quantity, though, was small due to four months of drought ending with heavy rain in September. Overall, the 1924s are still keeping well.

Prior to this, two other vintages were declared during the 1920s. **1922★★★** (18 shippers) a sorely neglected year that produced a small quantity of lightish wines, similar in style to the 1917s. **1920★★★★** (23 shippers) the first major vintage after 1912, which produced a small crop of good, robust, long-lasting wines, which, if well kept, can still be good.

1910s

A decade which included one classic vintage, one very good vintage, and several mediocre years. A light, elegant vintage was made in **1917★★★** (15 shippers) with smooth, attractive wines, but not substantial and now very rarely seen. The classic vintage of the decade was **1912★★★★★** (25 shippers). Apart from rain in September which delayed the harvest, the summer was hot, and rich – now ethereal – port was made. One of Taylor's greatest vintages, still good. **1911★★★** was a "coronation" vintage, shipped only by Sandeman. Still lovely when last tasted in the 1960s.

1900s

The 1900s produced three of the four great classic vintages prior to World War One, (the fourth being 1912).

1908★★★★★ (26 shippers), was initially darker and fuller-bodied than 1904 and 1900, and maintained its depth throughout its life. Cockburn's famed vintage is still magnificent. **1904★★★★** (25 shippers) was also an excellent vintage, but lighter than 1900, though the wines have kept very well. **1900★★★★★** (22 shippers) was a year of exceptionally fine quality, though rarely seen now.

1890s

Several good vintages and one classic.

1899★ (one shipper) was definitely not among them. And only seven shippers declared the **1897★★★★** (known as "The Royal Diamond Jubilee Year"). Interestingly, it was fortified with Scotch whisky as all the brandy had been used for the 1896s. **1896★★★★** (24 shippers) was the great classic vintage of the decade, but now of variable quality, thinning, and tired. **1894★★** (13 shippers) middling to good, of better quality than **1892★★** (10 shippers) moderate, now rarely seen. **1890★★★** (20 shippers) made tough, tannic wines.

OLDER PORT VINTAGES

1887★★★ Queen Victoria's Golden Jubilee vintage, this can still be good
to drink, as are 1884★★★★★ 1878★★★★ 1875★★★★ 1870★★★★★
1863★★★★★ 1851★★★★ and the greatest of the mid-nineteenth century,
1847★★★★★. Almost unique amongst the major port houses, Ferreira hold
stocks of vintages going back to 1811.

Madeira

At first sight madeira seems an unlikely candidate for a vintage pocket book.
It is a fortified wine; its method of making resembles sherry in some respects,
port in others. Unlike either, however, it undergoes a heat treatment which
gives it its inimitable "tang". Despite the complexity of its production it is both
simple to understand and enjoy. There are four major "noble" grape varieties:
Sercial, Verdelho, Bual, and Malmsey (or Malvoisie); each making dry, medium-
dry, medium-sweet, and sweet wines respectively. Another more prolific grape,
the Tinta Negra Mole, is used to make the less expensive wines as it imitates,
surprisingly effectively, the four basic grape styles just mentioned. Most madeira
is blended and marketed under a brand name. Relatively recently a leaf has been
taken out the port shippers' books, by producing excellent ten-year-old blends
of the major grape varieties. But the glory of madeira lies in its vintage and
solera wines. Happily, both are still made, boding well for the future.

Madeira is a semi-tropical island in the Atlantic, off the coast of West Africa.
Though there are weather variations, the climate is delightful all the year round.
Vintage time is unusually long, from mid- to late August until early October,
depending on the grape variety and, in this spectacularly mountainous island,
on the altitude of the vineyard.

It might be imagined that Madeira's weather is as idyllic as its setting and
that vintage variations would not exist. This is not so. Weather conditions on
this mountainous volcanic island in the Atlantic are extraordinarily variable.
One day I remember driving to a north coast buffeted by rough seas and
strong winds, traversing from west to east across the high spine of the island
with hail lying like snow, and on down to the south coast into warm sun and
clear blue sky.

Happily, the demand for high quality island-bottled wine is increasing; and
it is in high quality blends and, I believe, the small quantities of vintage madeira
that the future lies.

"Vintage" madeira is a wine made from one named grape variety (they are
never mixed) of one vintage, matured in cask. A "*solera*" madeira, also with a
named grape, usually bears on the label the year the *solera* was started: the
original wine is topped up with younger wine of the same grape and quality
as the matured blend is drawn off.

After sufficient maturation in cask the wine can be put into demijohns for
an unspecified storage time until needed for bottling. It is not always clear
from the label, or from a stencilled bottle, whether a dated madeira is straight
(unblended) vintage or *solera*. Although venerable vintage madeira tends
to command a higher price, old *solera* madeira is often the finer drink. The
following are the best known shippers of vintage and *solera* wines: Barbeito,
Blandy, Cossart Gordon, Henriques & Henriques, Justino, Leacock, Pereira
d'Oliveira, and Rutherford & Miles; and amongst the old vintages, Acciaioly
and H. M. Borges.

When to drink? Generally speaking, madeira is ready for drinking as soon as it is put on the market; young vintages are not bottled for "laying down". It can safely be assumed that any vintage or *solera* wine prior to 1970 will be mature and ready for consumption. Also happily, madeira is virtually indestructible and old vintages will, with few exceptions, still be drinkable.

Because most wines are destined for blending, and because a straight vintage cannot be put on the market until it has had a minimum of twenty years in wood and two years in bottle, the following vintage notes serve to give readers an idea of the tremendous variations in growing conditions and quality, the latter not just due to weather but to the skill and conscientiousness of the large number of individual, mainly small, growers and the supervision and skill of the shipping houses, brand owners, and their blenders.

2002★★ variable

A year characterized by high quantity but average quality. Quality was compromised by a late maturation cycle, affecting mostly the late ripening varieties, and rain after September 15, which resulted in a small amount of *desavinho*. But apart from a few hiccups in the S. Jorge area, overall the growing season was healthy.

Quality was generally mediocre this year and increasingly stringent quality requirements compounded the situation. Some very good wines were, however, made. Tinta Negra from from S. Vicente & Estreito de Camera de Lobos unquestionably produced the best wines of the vintage. Sercial was of medium quality with the exception of the harvest from Porto Moniz and Arco de S. Jorge. The quality of Verdelho was excellent but there was a lot of competition for fruit from the table wine producers, which limited the amounts available for production. Bual was the most problematic varietal this year.

Growers still need to make a more concerted move away from volume and towards quality. In many cases this year farmers allowed their vines to produce a second flush of grapes, which hampered the maturation cycle. The growers compensated by stripping the leaves to let in more sunshine, but this had the effect of colouring the grapes and hindering real maturation. The result was greater volume but distinctly lower quality.

It is worth stressing at this stage that though the growing conditions and the eventual quality at the time of harvesting can be stated, the net results, in terms of when to drink, wil be lost in the mists which cap the Maderia highlands: most of the wine will be used for varietal blends (or five-year old madeiras which are not of stated varieties) or, if a wine turns out particularly well – after the statutory twenty years in cask – will be bottled as a "straight vintage".

2001★★★★

January, February, and March were cold but with beneficial showers. In April the weather stabilized, bringing a healthy amount of sun and considerably less rain, which was crucial in preventing rot infestation. The subsequent months brought more sunshine and warmth, allowing for good maturation of the grapes and medium to high alcoholic levels. The weather remained clement during the vintage, which started in the second week of August. Overall, it was a very good year both in quantity and quality, with the exception of Malvasia in São Jorge, where much rot and *desavinho* was recorded, and Sercial and Verdelho in the north, where volumes were low and quality was not what growers had hoped for.

Some high quality wine for varietal blends; even, hopefully a vintage Bual or Malmsey might appear – in inevitably small quantities – in or around 2023. In the meantime take advantage of the old vintages which occasionally come up for sale at auction.

2000★★★▷★★★★

Although overall quantity increased by thirty-five per cent, quality was uneven.

The year was almost identical in the north to the 1999 vintage: a lower white grape yield, which was only just compensated by the new vines which began to produce more this year. Bual production was up this year in Camara de Lobos and Calheta. It is thought that the vintage would have been of a higher quality if the grapes from the north of the island had been delivered in better condition. Growers in the south and west were able to produce superb quality because of the dry conditions. The grapes were picked in peak condition with exceptional maturity levels.

1999★★

High production but moderate quality. The growing season was satisfactory from start to finish, with no rain during the ripening period. The harvest began on August 17 with Tinta Negra Mole grapes grown at the lower elevations in the south at Camara de Lobos. It ended on October 1 with the Sercial at the high altitude vineyards at Jardim da Serra. The grapes were in a very healthy condition though sugar levels were no more than average, the best being Sercial, Verdelho, and Bual. Demand from the shippers was high – surely symptomatic of the growing interest in madeira. However, with the exception of three "noble" varieties just referred to, farmers picked without bunch selection, resulting in very low levels of sugar in some grapes.

1998★★★

The growing season in 1998 started uneasily with an unseasonably warm winter and an early bud-burst soon after pruning, following two weeks of strong winds and extremely high temperatures for that time of year. The weather then broke, with cold and humid conditions unfavourable for flowering and fruit set. The summer, both in the north and the south of the island remained hot and relatively dry, and the ripening period was satisfactory. As always, the length of the harvest was long, starting on August 11 in the lower vineyards of the south and ending on October 2 with the Sercials on the higher slopes.

1997★★★★

Winter rain provided rehydration for the vines before the onset of a hot and dry ripening period. The season was perfect and problem-free, with a very uniform ripening for all varieties.

1996★★★★

Another good year for both quantity and quality. Total production was up by fifty per cent compared to 1995.

Winter rains had provided a good stock of water for the warm, dry ripening period. "Textbook" conditions prevailed throughout the year which provided a uniform, problem-free development until harvest. Harvesting began fairly early, on August 22 and was completed in the north by October 18. Vinification also ran smoothly, producing excellent results – especially for Bual, Verdelho, Sercial, and Tinta Negra Mole.

1995 ★★★★

A very good harvest with yields up by ten per cent. The growing season was hot and favourable with minimal rain. This encouraged rapid and consistent ripening and a very early harvest, which began on August 2 in the lower areas for the Bual, Malmsey, and Tinta Negra Mole. The grapes were picked by September 20 and a week later the harvest of the later ripening varieties began. Verdelho and Sercial were the last to be picked, finishing on October 15, in the northern vineyards around Seixal and Santana. Results were fine, with age-worthy wines.

1994 ★★★★★

A highly successful year, producing good to excellent quality but reduced quantities. Growers had also improved their treatment of the vines, for example less spraying. These two factors resulted in grapes ripening with exceptional levels of sweetness. The north side of the island produced some exceptional wines as less than usual rain fell during the growing season. The south side of the island saw more variable climatic conditions, with some crops, particularly Bual, reduced by as much as seventy to eighty per cent because of mist and light rain during flowering, but Tinta Negra Mole and Malmsey were excellent.

1993 ★▷★★★

A difficult year as various adverse conditions struck when the vines were at their most vulnerable. Rain and hail fell during both flowering and *pintar* (when grapes begin to change colour).

1992 ★★★★

A successful year for madeira, with particularly advantageous climatic conditions. Rainfall was below average and when it did occur, it was at times least harmful to the vines. These kind conditions allowed for minimal use of fungicides and pesticides. Picking began on the southern side of the island in the Campanario on August 28, with the final wave beginning in the Jardim da Serra on October 6. A little rain fell during the harvest and the crop was slightly smaller than average.

1991 ★★

A good quality vintage, with the grapes being free of any disease. The resulting wines had plenty of fruit and promised well for their future development.

1990 ★★★★

A generally excellent vintage, particularly for the noble varieties. The picking commenced on August 16 in the classic lower-lying districts of the south, particularly famous for their Bual and Malmsey. The Sercial and Verdelho harvest on the north side of Madeira started during the first week of September. The weather was cool during picking, with some rain, though accompanying winds quickly dried the grapes which were generally in perfect condition. Crop slightly smaller than 1989.

1989 ★★

June and July very cold with haze affecting the higher vineyards, all of which delayed development and reduced the crop potential – by as much as fifty per cent in the southerly districts. Heat returned at the end of July and continued throughout August. Overall, however, the quality of grapes was good.

1988★★★

One of the best vintages of the decade following near perfect climatic conditions. All the major grape varieties were suitable for high quality blends, with true vintage potential.

The year saw a notable increase of *Vitis vinifera* on the island, thanks to the Regional Government's programme to switch from hybrid and ungrafted varieties to the classic madeira grape types.

1987★★★★

A satisfactory growing season. Rain, even snow on the higher ground during January and February. Beneficial spring rains and, despite strong winds in April and May, satisfactory flowering. The harvest was three weeks early, commencing the second week in August and continuing in the higher vineyards until the end of September. Towards the middle of September an easterly Sahara wind raised temperatures to 38°C (100°F), necessitating cooling of the must. A substantial crop of good quality.

1986★★

An abundant crop of moderate quality and richness.

1985

One of the worst vintages in living memory. The production was one of the lowest on record since *oidium* and phylloxera swept the island in the mid-nineteenth century.

Winter was cool, but torrential rain throughout the island washed away terracing and soil. Spring was cool and abnormally wet; high humidity during leaf break and flowering resulted in viral diseases and mildews, affecting the development of early shoots. Flowering was late, uneven, and often incomplete. June, July, and August were hot but also relatively humid, causing the spread of mildew and rot. Harvesting was spasmodic, from the first week in September through to early October. Some farmers did not pick at all.

1984

Atrocious weather conditions, with a harvest to match. This was the result of extremely heavy rainfall from late February, and continuing through March. This then caused landslides and much damage to the crops. The pruning was also interrupted by the rain and by the need to replace soil and repair terracing. The flowering was delayed by four to five weeks and when it did begin (late April early May) there was a further period of high winds and torrential rain; also, in the north, severe hail damage. Damp and humid conditions persisted through to early July causing large areas of powdery mildew. And July, August, and September were hot though often cloudy.

The late and uneven ripening delayed the start of picking until September 15: this was one of the latest vintage starts on record. Indeed, in the higher vineyards planted with Sercial and Verdelho the harvest did not begin until the second week in October. Overall, the grapes had a low sugar content and production was well below average, causing severe stock problems.

1983★★★★

This was an outstanding year for vintage quality wine and for top-class blends. A fairly cold and prolonged winter rested the dormant vines and discouraged premature growth, which can be a problem on the island. Spring was cool and damp, bringing problems of mildew but flowering, though late, was generally satisfactory. July and August were both very hot, with scorching winds from the Sahara necessitating picking as early as August 10 in the lower southern vineyards of Camara de Lobos.

The Bual and Verdelho had exceptionally high sugar readings. However, the Sercial crop was reduced by mildew, wind damage, and late ripening. The small crop of Terrantez was of the highest quality and nurtured thereafter by the Madeira Wine Company to produce an outstanding vintage of this rare wine, which after twenty years in wood is now ready for bottling.

1982★★

An exceptionally mild winter did not provide an adequate vegetative rest period, and the low temperatures of mid-April and May resulted in uneven and late flowering. The higher than normal rainfall in the early summer hampered development, causing some mildew damage.

However, despite the cooler temperatures than normal, the weather during the harvest was dry and though it was late, it progressed well. Crop fifteen to eighteen per cent down on previous vintages. Moderate quality.

1981★★★

An average-sized harvest of good quality.

1980★★★★

An unusually mild spring and warm summer, free of damaging winds. Picking began on August 25 in south-coast vineyards and from September 8 in the north, yielding an above-average crop of good quality grapes with higher than usual sugar content. What was particularly noticeable, and welcome, was the larger crop of European grafted vines following the Government-assisted conversion scheme – which was started in 1975 – from hybrids; wine from the latter used only for island consumption. However inflation, running at very high levels since the revolution of 1974, and very high interest rates made the necessary stock-holding a great burden for the major shippers.

THE DECADE OF THE 1970S

Detailed weather statistics and quality ratings for this period are either unavailable or unreliable.

MATURE MADEIRA VINTAGES

1968★★★★ 1967★★★★ 1964★★★ 1960★★★ 1958★★★ 1957★★★★ 1954★★★★

OLDER MADEIRA VINTAGES

1952★★★ (particularly Verdelho and Malmsey), 1950★★ 1944★★★ 1941★★★★ (particularly Bual and Malmsey), 1940★★★★ (especially Sercial), 1939★★★★ 1936★★★★ (Cossart's Sercial the best of the century), 1934★★★★ (all grape varieties and districts excellent), 1933★★★ 1932★★ 1931★

1927★★★★ 1920★★★★ (Cossart's Malmsey★★★★★), 1916★★★ (particularly
Malmsey), 1915★★★ 1914★★★ (small crop, noted for its Bual), 1913★★★
1910★★★★★ (the best all-round vintage of the period), 1907★★★ 1906★★
(small crop, Malmsey especially good), 1905★★★ (small but good),
1900★★★★ (great vintage).

PRE-1900

1899★★★★ 1898★★★★ (the best since the phylloxera scourge), 1895★★★
1893★★★★ 1892★★★ (small crop), 1891★★★ 1890★★ (small crop),
1883★★★★ 1880★★★ 1879★★★★ 1878★★ 1877★★★ 1875★★★★
(minuscule crop), 1883★★★★ 1880★★★ 1879★★★★ 1878★★ 1877★★★
1875★★★★ (a tiny crop), 1874★★ 1872★★★ (the year the phylloxera struck),
1870★★★★ (the last of the good post-*oidium* vintages).

   1869★★★ (Bual excellent), 1867★★★ 1866★★★, and 1865★★★ (all small
crops), 1864★★★ (small but particularly good for Bual and Malmsey),
1863★★★★ (Malmsey excellent), 1862★★★★★ (the Terrantez still magnificent,
one of the best-ever old madeiras), 1860★★★★ 1856★★★

If these pre-1900 years seem to the reader unrealistic, bottles still exist; they
appear from time to time at auction, either from private cellars in England and
America, or from the cellars of the old Madeira families – they are one of life's
glorious experiences.